Investing in Europe

PETER LANG
Bruxelles · Bern · Berlin · New York · Oxford · Wien

Olimpia Fontana

Investing in Europe

Old Problems and New Opportunities

Federalism
Vol. 14

This book was made possible by the Centro Studi sul Federalismo (www.csfederalismo.it)

This publication has been peer reviewed.

International Academic Publishers
Brussels, 2022
1 avenue Maurice, B-1050 Brussels, Belgium
brussels@peterlang.com; www.peterlang.com

ISSN 2294-6969
ISBN 978-2-87574-420-3
ePDF 978-2-87574-421-0
ePUB 978-2-87574-422-7
DOI 10.3726/b19250
D/2021/5678/86

Bibliographic information published by "Die Deutsche Nationalbibliothek".

"Die Deutsche National Bibliothek" lists this publication in the "Deutsche Nationalbibliografie"; detailed bibliographic data is available on the Internet at <http://dnb.de>.

Table of contents

List of acronyms

ACP Group	Africa, Caribbean and Pacific Group of States
AfCFTA	African Continental Free Trade Agreement
AfIF	Africa Investment Facility
AIP	Africa Investment Platform
AMR	Alert Mechanism Report
ATF	Africa Trust Fund
BEPS	Base erosion and profit shifting
BICC	Budgetary Instrument for Convergence and Competitiveness
CAP	Common Agricultural Policy
CBA	Carbon Border Adjustment
CEF	Connecting Europe Facility
COP	Conference of the Parties
COSME	Competitiveness of enterprises and Small and Medium-sized Enterprises
DSSI	Debt Service Suspension Initiative
EBID	Bank for Investment and Development
EC	European Commission
ECB	European Central Bank
ECOWAS	Economic Community of West African States
ECSC	European Coal and Steal Community
EDF	European Development Fund
EDP	Excessive Deficit Procedure
EEC	European Economic Community
EFB	European Fiscal Board
EFSD	European Fund for Sustainable Development
EFSF	European Financial Stability Facility

EFSI	European Fund for Strategic Investment
EFTA	European Free Trade Association
EGD	European Green Deal
EIB	European Investment Bank
EIF	European Investment Fund
EIP	External Investment Plan
ELP	Energy Lending Policy
EMU	Economic and Monetary Union
EPA	Economic Partnership Agreement
ERDF	European Regional Development Fund
ERIB	ECOWAS Regional Investment Bank
ESG	Environmental, social and governance
ESIF	European Structural and Investment Fund
ESM	European Stability Mechanism
ETS	Emission Trading Scheme
EU	European Union
EU-AITF	EU-Africa Infrastructure Trust Fund
FDI	Foreign Direct Investment
FOCAC	Forum On China-Africa Cooperation
FTT	Financial Transaction Tax
GDP	Gross Domestic Product
GHG	Greenhouse Gas
GNI	Gross National Income
HLGOR	High Level Group on Own Resources
ICA	Infrastructure Consortium for Africa
ICT	Information and Communication Technology
IEA	International Energy Agency
IPCEI	Important Projects of Common European Interest
ILO	International Labour Organization
IMF	International Monetary Fund
IPCC	Intergovernmental Panel on Climate Change
IT	Information Technology
JAES	Joint Africa-EU Strategy

JTF	Just Transition Fund
JTM	Just Transition Mechanism
MDGs	Millennium Development Goals
MFF	Multiannual Financial Framework
MTO	Medium Term Objective
NECP	National Energy and Climate Plan
NEET	Not in Employment or in Education or Training
NGEU	Next Generation European Union
NPBs	National Promotional Banks
NRPs	National Reform Programmes
NRRP	National Recovery and Resilience Plan
OCA	Optimal Currency Area
ODA	Official Development Assistance
OECD	Organization for Economic Cooperation and Development
ORD	Own Resources Decision
PEPP	Pandemic Emergency Purchase Programme
PPPs	Public-Private Partnerships
QE	Quantitative Easing
R&D	Research & development
RECs	Regional Economic Communities
RRF	Recovery and Resilience Facility
SCPs	Stability and Convergence Programmes
SDGs	Sustainable Development Goals
SDRs	Special Drawing Rights
SURE	Support to mitigate Unemployment Risks in an Emergency
TENs	Trans-European Networks
TFEU	Treaty on the Functioning of the EU
UNCTAD	United Nations Conference on Trade and Development
UNFPA	United Nations Population Fund
WTO	World Trade Organization

Acknowledgement

I am grateful to Professor Alberto Majocchi for the inspiring conversations during my research activities at the Centro Studi sul Federalismo. I am indebted to him for many of the ideas I developed in this book.

I am also grateful to Alfonso Iozzo and Flavio Brugnoli, President and Director of the Centro Studi sul Federalismo, for their knowledge, trust and encouragement.

Finally, the book has benefitted from valuable suggestions by Elisabetta Tarasco, who has shown great patience whilst editing this book.

Introduction

In recent years, much attention has been devoted to the issue of investment. Today, discussions are quite common in respect of collective efforts by European Union (EU) institutions, national governments, and the private sector to preserve investment spending. At all levels, local, national and European, political and academic, the narrative in Europe has gradually shifted; while until recently the prevailing view was that member states had to pursue structural reforms and stable public finances in order to achieve economic growth, more recently an alternative idea has gained ground, that of seeking the right combination of pursuing structural reforms while at the same time fostering investment.

Of course, to achieve this important change we have, in just a few years, had to go through two of the most serious crises since the Second World War: the financial crisis and the Covid-19 pandemic. However, within Europe due attention has not always been given to this component of economic activity, nor has there been agreement among academics on the effect investment can have on the economy and on the relationship between public and private investment. The two crises we have experienced have led to a change in attitudes towards investment, although in very different ways, and with different timing. While during the financial crisis, which later turned into a sovereign debt crisis in the Eurozone, a discourse about the investment gap compared to pre-crisis levels emerged – especially with reference to private investment – conversely the pandemic crisis has led to a more general questioning about the role of the public sector in the economy, and the relationship between the state and the market. In addition, the climate change challenge has raised doubts about the ability of the market alone to allocate resources (i.e. capital) to specific sectors, beyond profit considerations. Part of this reflection has to do with the traditional role of industrial policy in Europe, which has been absent for years.

Industrial policy has changed over time, from mainly being a national policy with governments promoting national champions in the 1960s, to become a European responsibility by the early 1990s. However, in this second period industrial policy was considered in relation to the creation of the European internal market, with priority put on competition policy. As a consequence, this has made it difficult to implement industrial policy measures to support targeted sectors or industries considered strategic for the EU.

As such, in Europe the issue of industrial policy has for years taken the form of various medium-term strategies and agendas that have been pursued in conjunction with the various multiannual budgets that assign (limited) funding to specific European programmes. Since the financial crisis, a new conception of industrial policy has emerged alongside the need to activate European instruments capable of stimulating greater investment, with a view not only to sustain competitiveness and growth, but also to offer better prospects for societal welfare. For example, in this period an understanding of investment needs was set out in the Juncker Plan, although with its limitations.

In addition to this change of pace in industrial policy, the EU has committed to the Sustainable Development Goals (SDG) set out in 2015 as part of the 2030 Agenda for Sustainable Development, providing a shared blueprint for peace and prosperity for people and the planet. These targets have been assimilated within European policies, in particular in the ambitious long-term plan for climate neutrality, the European Green Deal (EGD). In consequence, industrial policy changed once again, with a more specific qualification of green industrial policy, to be pursued at European and national levels.

Achieving this result, which can be considered as a starting point for rethinking the growth model (if we want to continue to think in terms of growth and not, for example, of human development) has not been easy in the European context; several elements throughout the history of the EU and its institutional settings have made it difficult to move towards what can be defined as a new model of sustainable development, both environmental and social. As already mentioned, the kind of industrial policy that the EU has pursued to solve structural weaknesses of low competitiveness and low growth potential, through its various agendas, like the Lisbon Strategies and Europe 2020, has not delivered the expected results, in particular with reference to targets for employment and research investment.

One of the problems with the EU approach is connected to its economic governance, with, on the one hand, the macroeconomic pillar, based on budgetary discipline and, on the other, the microeconomic pillar, consisting of Lisbon-like strategies. The two pillars are deemed to be incompatible, given the tensions between the simultaneous pursuit of an ambitious agenda of structural reforms, and compliance with fiscal consolidation provisions. As a matter of fact, in an incomplete monetary area like the Eurozone fiscal rules are necessary, as they aim at preserving fiscal sustainability, avoiding the transmission of inflation tensions across countries. However, the European fiscal framework has arguably failed to deliver, with mixed results in term of compliance.

Fiscal rules were suspended in spring 2020 through the activation of the general escape clause, to enable a sizable fiscal response to the Covid-19 crisis. However, the clause should be lifted as soon as a sustained normalisation of economic activity has materialised, and different rules must then be anticipated. Just before the pandemic, the European Commission initiated a review of fiscal rules to assess the strengths and weaknesses of the increasingly complex fiscal surveillance framework. The subsequent pandemic increased the need for new rules that, among other things, have a more conducive approach to investment.

Another relevant issue regards a proper understanding of variable investment, from a macroeconomic perspective. What is lacking is a consideration of investment as a component of a more general equilibrium that must apply both at the domestic and external levels, and concerns the level of savings. Without considering the implication that certain fiscal rules may have on the rest of the economy, in particular with regard to external imbalances, the risks associated with the prevailing export-led growth model cannot be fully understood. This was particularly the case after the financial crisis had evolved into a sovereign debt crisis, where the most hard-hit countries were those with high external debt, not public sector debt. However, the solutions provided by the EU were not commensurate with these states' needs, and neither answered demands for a risk sharing mechanism at the central level, nor those for a massive European investment plan. As such, the European integration process did not make any substantial progress towards a federal arrangement, and the economic situation in the EU has remained mired in prolonged stagnation, with low growth and very low interest rate.

Notwithstanding these critiques, the pandemic has, however, brought about tremendous improvements in the EU, in terms of a new momentum in solidarity between countries. Instruments that had been requested for years were put into place, in particular the Eurobonds.

Although we are still a long way from what many have called the *Hamiltonian moment*,[1] seeds of further European integration have been laid, opening up the possibility of further political ambitions, that will be needed to face climate change and its related implications. This book does not aim to analyse every aspect of the European agenda for next decades, the EGD, which by its nature is broad and cross-cutting across sectors, policies, and levels of government. Rather, it focuses on a few elements that could contribute to making a European climate strategy more effective, based on investment plans that look at the social dimension and external cooperation with the African continent. For this to be possible, further steps on the revenue side of the European budget must be taken, in particular by introducing new European own resources. In this way, the EU would be adequately equipped to manage, in a unified way, not only the fight against climate change, but also the provision of other European public goods that are crucial for the security and prosperity of European citizens.

1 The reference is to Alexander Hamilton (1755-1804), the first American Secretary of the Treasury, who engineered a deal to allow the new government of the United States to assume the individual war-time debts of the former colonies, and convert them to joint obligations of the federal union. Historians have seen this as one of the decisive steps towards the creation of the American system of government.

Chapter 1

Investment policy in European strategies: A brief history

1.1 Industrial policy: A brief description

Investment strategy is not only about putting money in the economy in order to obtain a return. It is part of what is called industrial policy, which has a very large scope, which covers a range of measures aimed at enabling a country to achieve its strategic objectives by enhancing domestic productive capabilities and international competitiveness. Starting with a clarification of what industrial policy is, and what it means for Europe, contributes to an understanding of the context of investment and its long-term trend.

Although it is difficult to define industrial policy precisely, a commonly used definition is "any type of selective government intervention or policy that attempts to alter the structure of production in favour of sectors that are expected to offer better prospects for economic growth in a way that would not occur in the absence of such intervention in the market equilibrium" (Pack and Saggi, 2006, pp. 267-268).[1]

After a long debate two different kinds of measures of industrial policy have been identified: on the one hand, horizontal policies seeking to improve operational conditions and capabilities across a number of sectors, and on the other vertical/selective measures, focused on specific industries, firms or sectors. Examples of selective/vertical measures can include: the promotion of *infant* or fledgling industries in the hope that, through government assistance, they will become profitable and internationally competitive; support for the restructuring and modernisation of industries that are regarded as important because of their role

---

1 Pack H. and Saggi K. (2006), "Is There a Case for Industrial Policy? A Critical Survey", *The World Bank Research Observer*, Vol. 21, Issue 2, Fall, pp. 267-297.

as employers or exporters, or because of their links to national defence, or because they produce technology that will be used in other parts of the economy; the creation of national champions through government-induced mergers; and the rescue of failing firms (Owen, 2012).[2]

The distinction between horizontal and vertical measures may, however, not be as clear. For example, a horizontal measure may have a relative impact that is different depending on how this general measure affects a specific sector. Therefore, a more comprehensive view implies going beyond this apparent trade-off, and thinking in term of a system-based approach, no longer focused on a sequence of disjointed and narrow and sectorial intervention, but rather on a combination of horizontal measures and selective complementary measures needed for specific sectors, that are not necessary or relevant in others. Accordingly, a new, more holistic approach should be: more relevant, through the identification of the most appropriate policies for each sector; more widely applicable, through greater coherence and the integration of policies; and more consensual, through the involvement of key stakeholders (Aiginger and Sieber, 2006).[3] This approach should affect the structure of the economy as a whole, not only manufacturing, in a unifying effort with "traditional goals of industrial policy on the one hand, with the objectives of competition policy, as well as with broader goals like social and economic cohesion and environmental standards on the other, narrow definitions of industrial policy and border fights between sub disciplines are less likely"(Aiginger and Sieber, 2006, p. 581). From these preliminary definitions, it is evident that coordination between the private and public sectors is essential, where market forces and private entrepreneurship would be at the centre of the agenda, and where, as Dani Rodrik (2004)[4] writes, governments would also play a role in coordinating and defining the strategic sphere, beyond simply setting the rules, in an effort to present a new agenda for economic policy.

---

2 Owen G. (2012), *Industrial Policy in Europe since the Second World War: What Has Been Learnt?*, ECIPE Occasional Paper, n.1. Bruxelles: ECIPE.

3 Aiginger K. and Siber S. (2006), "The Matrix Approach to Industrial Policy", *International Review of Applied Economics*, Vol. 20, No. 5, pp. 573-601. DOI: 10.1080/02692170601005507.

4 Rodrik D. (2004), *Industrial Policy for the Twenty-First Century*, KSG Faculty Research Working Paper Series RWP04-047.

The instruments used in industrial policy range from direct and indirect support to specific firms and industries – through, for example, grants, subsidies, loans and tax credits – to support for knowledge institutions, infrastructure and skills. The characteristics of the instruments used for industrial policy vary considerably, ranging from the very narrow to the very broad, including all government initiatives to improve the business environment. An attempt to categorise all possible instruments by broad domains contributing to an industrial policy is set out in Tab. 1.1.

Tab. 1.1: Domains and instruments of industrial policy

Domains	**Instruments**
Economic signals and incentives	Intellectual property rights Price regulation Exchange rate policy (e.g. undervaluation) Monetary (interest rate) policy Countercyclical fiscal policy Tax breaks
Scientific and technological innovation	Scientific policies High-tech lead projects Funding university research Establishment of research centres R&D subsidies and/or tax credits
Learning and improving technological capabilities	Education and training policies Foresight exercises (to identify national research priorities) Labour training subsidies and/or tax breaks Skill formation and upgrading schemes International educational and research collaboration Incentives for Foreign Direct Investment (FDI)
Selective industry support	Impose import tariffs and/or quotas Provide export subsidies/credit/support Establish special economic zones Use of state-owned enterprises/privatisation Create public utilities providing inputs (e.g. electricity) Direct finance/subsidies Provide public guaranties Direct state procurement policy

Tab. 1.1: Continued

Domains	**Instruments**
Selection mechanism	Entry and exit regulation for firms 'Live and let die' principle (political will to end support to failing firms) Anti-trust and competition policy Support national trading companies Preferential access to finance Long-term development finance
Distribution of information	Collective action mechanism Promotion of standards Use of consultative forums Use of business chambers Encouraging firms operation/links Marketing of export industries Dissemination of successful experience
Improving productivity and firms and entrepreneurs	Providing or subsidising management training Firm (SME) monitoring and assistance Infrastructure, funding and management of incubators and cluster formation Promotion of public-private partnerships Location marketing and enhancement Upgrading of economic infrastructure Creation of venture capital funds

Source: Warwick (2013). Warwick, K. (2013), *Beyond Industrial Policy: Emerging Issues and New Trends*, OECD Science, Technology and Industry Policy Papers, No. 2, Paris: OECD Publishing. DOI: 10.1787/5k4869clw0xp-en.

However, what is important to define today is the very purpose of an industrial policy, therefore responding to the crucial question "is the goal of industrial policy to promote industrialisation, to boost productivity growth, to promote the development of a particular sub-sector, to create or preserve employment, to address societal challenges such as combating climate change, to improve the distribution of income, or to address regional imbalances?" (Warwick, 2013, p. 17). Put in these terms, it is clear that beyond the competitiveness and economic growth arguments "governments have other policy goals that contribute to societal welfare, and the pursuit of these goals may have important industrial policy-type effects – examples might include regional policy, energy and climate change policy, health policy and defence/security policy. Often industrial policy is closely integrated with other policies as part of a broader government social and economic strategy with wide ranging goals" (Warwick, 2013, p. 16). A broad and strategic perspective must therefore be adopted, with different fields and instruments interlinked, but only after having defined the societal challenges that are at stake. For the EU, the issue is not only defined in terms of competitiveness, arising from a worrying trend characterising the evolution of its manufacturing base. In fact, although industry is the backbone of the European economy, the decline in manufacturing's share of Gross Domestic Product (GDP) is particularly apparent in some European countries, since the 2008 financial crisis, with marked differences between countries and regions in terms of overall levels of competitiveness, and share of manufacturing in GDP terms. However, European industrial policy today is not only about supporting manufacturing, but also the need to respond to broader societal goals posed by climate change and other pressures on natural resources and the environment. Furthermore, the pandemic and its economic consequences on broader society puts even more pressure on social welfare issues, such as health, poverty prevention, the creation of good quality jobs and the reduction of inequality.

1.2 Industrial policy in Europe

The history of industrial policy in Europe is normally divided into three phases. The first attempt to implement some sort of industrial policy at the European level coincided with the beginning of the European project itself in 1951, with the Treaty establishing the European Coal and Steel Community (ECSC). In this first phase, support for industrial growth took the form of the creation of the customs union. Further, it changed the nature of the spirit that, at the time, shaped European institutions, with a shift towards an intergovernmental approach far removed from the initial communitarian attitude, which has proved difficult to restore ever since.

The second phase began soon after with the Treaty of Rome establishing the European Economic Community (EEC) in 1957, even though the treaty itself did not mention industrial policy. The main economic purpose of European integration at the time was the creation of the internal market. To increase competition and allow the free movement of goods the EEC provided for the reduction of tariffs and trade barriers, whereas assistance to specific sectors was abandoned. In this phase industrial policy was mainly national and particularly interventionist, where governments intervened by picking winners, by selecting and promoting national champions in strategic, and promising, sectors for future development, like steel, chemicals, mechanics, information communication technology and nuclear power. There was an increasing concern about the technology gap between Europe and the US, as European firms were losing ground to their American rivals in high-technology industries and government support was justified if such a gap were to be corrected. In particular, the UK and France were the most active interventionist states in the first thirty years after the war, while West Germany adopted a different approach, with a limited role for government (Owen, 2012).

Although there was some industrial cooperation between countries, as in the cases of Concorde and Airbus, these were intergovernmental agreements that excluded the involvement of the European Commission. The difficulties in developing common industrial initiatives mainly refer to a period when national governments were reluctant "to subordinate their national interest to those of Europe as a whole" (Owen, 2012, p. 20).

The third phase began in early 1990s in concomitance with the Maastricht Treaty, which explicitly established industrial policy as an area of the EU's responsibility and called for the Union and Member States to "ensure that the conditions necessary for the competitiveness of the Union's industry exist" (Art. 173.1 of the Maastricht Treaty). Industrial policy was therefore defined with a horizontal approach, while sectorial measures were deemed to distort competition. In this phase the centre of action was mainly on new technologies, acknowledging in particular the importance of Information Technology (IT). However, at the turn of the century the narrative started to turn towards a new approach where some role for more targeted action could help European economies to face new challenges, like globalisation and competition from low-income countries, fear of de-industrialisation and slow economic growth. It was finally recognised that "the effects of broad horizontal measures can vary significant from industry to industry, that competitiveness needs specific policy mixes for specific sectors, and that some sectors may require complementary measures that are not necessary or relevant in other sectors" (Aiginger and Sieber, 2006, p. 579).

With the financial crisis a further impetus emerged in respect of the public action role in revitalising European industry, as the economic crisis had put manufacturing production and employment under pressure. In this period industrial policies encompassed different policies at the

EU level, like trade, innovation and energy policies. In short, the EU started to use all the instruments at its disposal, and the debate shifted away from whether governments should do industrial policy at all to how they can do it well. In this period, the issue of the long declining trend of investment had become a mantra in the narrative, as well as the search for ways to put investment recovery, particularly public investment, back at the heart of the economy as the key variable for driving economic growth. At the heart of these efforts, industrial policy is the general framework that contributes not only to spur investment, but also to define the direction they have to take.

1.3 European investment policy

In the first phase of European industrial policy an investment strategy appeared in the form of the Jean Monnet investment Plan, from the President of the High Authority of the ECSC. This was a substantial initiative through which the Community intervened in the power generation sector, to finance installations which contributed to an increase in production, leading to an increase in consumption of both coal and steel, and also to promote the introduction of new technologies.

The "investment and financial aid", title three of the Treaty establishing the ECSC, set out that the High Authority could grant loans to undertakings or guarantee loans used for investment, in order to finance installations which would contribute to an increase in production, and to the lowering of production costs (Piodi, 2010).[5] As regards the eligible projects, there was no rigid allocation plan, as it was up to the various enterprises to select which projects required investment in a competitive process where the Community had to provide conditions ensuring the highest possible level of productivity.

It is interesting to note that in addition to these objectives, there was another issue of a more social nature; building housing for workers employed in the coal and steel sectors, some of whom lived in poor conditions, was a key part of the plan. This implies that at that time Jean Monnet was concerned about what he called the 'social question', meaning the impact of the modernisation process on the economy, since

---

[5] Piodi F. (2010), *From the Schuman Declaration to the Birth of the ECSC: The Role of Jean Monnet*, *Cardoc Journals*, n. 6, May. DOI: 10.2861/16402.

gradually replacing the least efficient plants with more advanced installations would have meant job losses on a vast scale.

When it comes to the financing of investment, the Monnet plan was partly funded through self-financings and bonds issuance, with an important role played by the US, which for the first time granted a long-term loan at favourable interest rates, instead of traditional donations.[6] In this early stage of the European integration process, the High Authority could finance its activity through both own resources, in the form of a levy on steel production – that could reach the rate of 1 % of the value by majority voting – and the issuing of debt. From the financing point of view, such provisions indicated a supranational approach that was not replicated in the subsequent development of the European project, at least until the pandemic outbreak.

Between the 1960s and the 1980s the integration process came to a standstill, because of the political tensions that emerged in the institutional setting, with the Council of the European Union and the European Parliament arguing over decisions about the EU's budget. The negotiations on budgets were, and still remain, one of the most critical aspects in the EU's functioning, as member states assess their benefit of EU membership through the lens of net balances, that is the difference between how much they contribute to the EU budget and how much they receive through European programmes in their country. These tensions hinder the possibility of reinforcing the budget in order to perform more tasks.

With the economic crisis of the 1970s, the need for a strategy became more urgent. Moreover, developments in the EU's institutional framework, with the growing role of the European Parliament elected by universal suffrage, had paved the way for a more orderly procedure in the setting of the EU's budget, and the introduction of multiannual programming. In the 1980s the process of integration deepened further with the Single Act and its priority to complete the common market, underlined by the *White Paper on the completion of the internal market* of 1985, launched by the then president of the European Commission Jacque Delors. The

---

6 As Piodi F. (2010, p. 43) reports, the High Authority of ECSC stated that the American loan was a "*turning point in the financial policy of the United States towards Europe. The loan has replaced donations, which was raised from taxes [...] but it is impossible for the US Government to levy taxes to develop the economic power of Europe, which would then become a major competitor of the United States*" (his italics).

report stated that "it is a fact that in order to facilitate the key role which the internal market can play in the policy for the recovery of industrial structures, the suspension of internal borders must be accompanied by actions which strengthen research and the technological base of the Community's industry. Such actions will allow firms to benefit from the size of the single market" (European Commission, 1985, p. 7).[7] According to the Commission's ideas, therefore, the realisation of the internal market corresponded to the implementation of an industrial policy, and that technological innovation manifested its potential for the manufacturing sector in a market without barriers. The paper classified barriers as three kinds of measures, that had to be taken by 1992: the removal of physical barriers, like customs posts at frontiers which perpetuate the costs and disadvantages of a divided market; technical barriers, like different standards for individual products adopted in different Member States for health or safety reasons, or for environmental or consumer protection; and last fiscal barriers, like different indirect taxes commonly raise by EU states such as Value Added Tax, or excise duties, that could distort competition.A better understanding of European investment policy can be gained if seen through the lens of the comprehensive measures of reforms at the European level that have taken place since the 1980s. With the introduction of multiannual programming in 1988, the Multiannual Financial Framework (MFF) the EU started to organise its action across countries following defined priorities, and to design its budget accordingly. From that moment on, the European initiative followed long-term plans that defined main sectors of intervention, which were translated into the financial programming within the budget. It is no coincidence that since the mid-1980s, the EU has made great progress in its integration process, first of all with the establishment of the Single Market in 1993, then with the introduction of the single currency, the euro, in 1999.

1.4 Jacques Delors' *White papers* (1985-1993)

The transition to a broader, more holistic approach in programming came with the first sets of reforms carried out by Jacques Delors, then president of the European Commission. The two *White Papers* J23

[7] European Commission (1985), *White Paper from the Commission to the European Council. Completing the Internal Market*, Bruxelles: European Commission.

by Delors are important because they included proposals in specific policy areas, and provided the instruments for their implementation.

At the beginning of the 1990s, in addition to the priority given to the completion of the Single market, underlined by the *White Paper* of 1985, another problem that called for innovation was the re-emergence of unemployment.[8] From the Commission's perspective, the problem was important for two reasons: first, the inability of the demand side of the labour market to absorb an increasing supply of labour, created by the demographic boom at the beginning of the 1970s; second, this inadequacy was even more evident when compared to the performance of other industrialised countries. In 2004, the Sapir report highlights these points. In the EU there had been a steady decline of the average growth rate over the decades, and per-capita GDP has stagnated at about 70 % of US levels since the early 1980s (Sapir et al., 2004).[9] The twin ambitious projects of the single market, and the single currency, were seen as prerequisites to compete on the international market, but not sufficient to restore the EU to a path of economic growth and increased employment. Additional measures of economic policy at the European and national levels were deemed necessary to counter negative economic and social development.

---

8 The second Delors *White paper* opened by stating that "The one and only reason is unemployment." (European Commission (1994), White paper on Growth, competitiveness, employment. The challenges and ways forward into the 21st century, p. 9). However, rising unemployment was part of a worrying macroeconomic situation. Between the 1970s and 1980s, the European economy's potential rate of growth had shrunk (from around 4 % to around 2,5 % a year); unemployment had been steadily rising from cycle to cycle; the investment ratio had fallen by five percentage points; Europe's competitive position in relation to the US and Japan had worsened as regards employment, our share of export markets, R&D and innovation and its incorporation into goods brought to the market, the development of new products.

9 Sapir A. et al. (2004). *An Agenda for a Growing Europe*. Oxford: Oxford University Press. The main issue is the lag in productivity of the EU with respect to its main competitor, the USA. The disappointing performance of productivity in Europe was linked to the inadequate results of certain high-tech sectors. In particular, the EU did not suffer from the absence of large world-class companies, but rather from the absence of emerging companies in new high technology industries. In practice, this meant that the EU economy did not have a high added value in the high-tech industry, but rather in medium tech sectors, like transport, chemical and electronics.

The *White paper* on *Growth, competitiveness and employment* indicated a European strategy directed not only at tackling the problem of unemployment, but also on drawing the lines of a new economic model at the beginning of the 1990s. Reading the paper, divided in three parts, is surprising today, because it touched on topics that still recur in public debate after almost thirty years. One way to tackle the problem of unemployment was thought to be by improving competitiveness in the age of globalisation; between the 1980s and 1990s the industrial sector in European member countries had been challenged by an increased penetration of imports, and falling European exports. One of the measures suggested by Delors was an investment in tangible and intangible infrastructures to allow a better positioning of domestic industries within the international market, and them to reap the benefits of the nascent IT revolution. A substantial amount of investment was required in the trans-European networks (TENs), that is the transport infrastructure, the energy transport infrastructure of electricity and natural gas, and the telecommunication networks. As the Commission argued, "Networks are the arteries of the single market. They are the lifeblood of competitiveness, and their malfunction is reflected in lost opportunities to create new markets and hence in a level of job creation that falls short of our potential" (European Commission, 1994, p. 89). Other key elements identified to improve competitiveness were: investment in research and technological development, which would contribute to the creation of a new *information society*, in which management, quality and speed of information would be key factors for competitiveness of economies at all stage; as well as investment in human capital, deemed necessary to make it easier to assimilate and spread new technologies. When considered in this manner, the Delors programme should not only be understood as a Keynesian public sector plan (from the father of macroeconomics, John Maynard Keynes, main proponent of a proactive public sector) to sustain aggregate demand, but more widely as a strategy for a structural change of the productive side of the economy (Paramithiotti, 1995).[10] Furthermore, based on the consideration that existing European development would lead to a sub-optimal combination of nature and labour (namely too little labour, too much use of environmental resources), the *White paper* proposed a new model built on the idea of environmental

10 Paramithiotti G. (1995), "Il libro Bianco di Delors per la crescita economica, la competitività e l'occupazione in Europa", *Il Politico*, Vol. 60, No. 2 (173), pp. 293-311.

sustainability, aimed at decoupling future economic prosperity from environmental pollution, and even to making the economic-ecological relationship a positive instead of a negative one.

With the entry into force of the Maastricht Treaty, public finance constraints had a significant impact on the ability of individual Member States to sustain domestic demand in a period of moderate recession such as the one that characterised the economy in the early 2000s. This made member states even more difficult to push ahead with the reforms that Europe needed, including the required investment in infrastructure and human capital. With this in mind, the *White Paper* proposed the creation of the best possible conditions for financing by the market in the framework of a public and private sector partnership (Public-Private Partnerships – PPPs), on the basis of three principles: financial equilibrium must be ensured to the greatest possible extent by the contribution of private investors; the financial interventions of Member States must be compatible with public finance constraints; and the European level must intervene to support the efforts of the Member States and encourage the mobilisation of private capital. In order to face the financing need for infrastructure investments, beyond budgetary contributions, a significant role would be played by loans from the European Investment Bank (EIB) and by European Investment Fund (EIF) guarantees. Further, a new option was proposed by the Commission, *Union Bonds*, which have since been re-proposed on several occasions in the policy debate, but have not been implemented, not least because of a misunderstanding of their nature, particularly during the period of the financial crisis.

In the intentions of the Delors Commission,

> 'Union Bonds' for growth would be issued on tap by the Union for long maturities to promote major infrastructure projects of strategic interest covering the TENs plus cross-border projects with the European Free Trade Association (EFTA), Central and Eastern Europe and North Africa. The beneficiaries would be project promoters (public sector agencies, private companies) directly involved in TENs. The EIB would be invited to appraise and advise the Commission on the overall structure of the financial arrangement and act as agent for individual loan contracts. (European Commission, 1994, p. 34).

The use of Union Bonds would allow significant financial resources, beyond the limit of 1 % of the budget, raised through bonds backed by the guarantee of the European budget. Thanks to the reputation of the

Union and its credit rating, these bonds could be issued at a low interest rate and would make it possible to finance the European development plan by absorbing the excess liquidity, i.e. savings, that characterised the financial markets at both the European and global levels. A macroeconomic framework that allows debt at low cost, and the need for a safe asset, are conditions that we are experiencing today and reinforce the need to resort to Union Bonds.

1.5 The Lisbon Strategy (2000-2010)

The basic assumption of the need for a structural change of the EU economic model was based on a critical understanding of the EU's development trajectory since the 1970s; European problems in productivity and innovation were largely interpreted by the dominant view in the literature to be the result of economic and social rigidities (Alesina and Giavazzi, 2006).[11] The inability to pursue both full employment and productivity growth, as was the case in the US, was understood to be the result of fragmented labour and financial markets, resulting from a lack of political will by the governments of the euro area Member States to liberalise their goods and labour markets. Structural reforms had to be introduced to boost productivity and employment rates. More investment in IT, fewer obstacles to the freedom of services provision, and the liberalisation of transport and energy markets were some of the innovations that had to be introduced (Daveri, 2002).[12] However, the role played by economic policy should also be emphasised, that may contribute to explaining the relative decline of Europe (Majocchi, 2007).[13] Macroeconomic policy would support growth not only indirectly, through the stability of prices and exchange rates, as the dominant view holds, but also once the goods and labour market had been liberalized, through an

---

[11] Alesina A. and Giavazzi F. (2006), *The Future of Europe: Reform or Decline*, Cambridge: MIT Press.

[12] Daveri F. (2002), "The New Economy in Europe 1992-2001", *Oxford Review of Economic Policy*, Vol. 18, No. 3, pp. 345-362.

[13] Majocchi A. (2007), *Un'agenda per promuovere la crescita europea*, Working Paper No. 509, Pavia: Società italiana di Economia Pubblica.

expansive fiscal policy, based in particular on investment.[14] In Europe, on the other hand, the approach of fiscal policy had been consistent with the priority to consolidate public finances in order to comply with the Maastricht Treaty and the Stability and Growth Pact (SGP) constraints.

The 2000 Lisbon Strategy was the long-term European initiative to make the EU, by 2010, "the most competitive and dynamic knowledge-based economy in the world capable of sustainable economic growth with more and better jobs and greater social cohesion" (Lisbon European Council, 2000).[15] It was the response adopted by the EU to face the challenges of globalisation, demographic changes, and knowledge society, and aimed at making Europe more dynamic and competitive. The Strategy pursued six measures at the European level, where the Commission assumed the role to monitor:

- the creation of an information society for all, where businesses and citizens have access to infrastructure and are equipped with the skills needed to live and work in this new reality;
- the establishing of a European area of research and innovation;
- the creation of a friendly environment for starting up and developing innovative businesses, especially small medium enterprises;
- the completion of a fully operational internal market;
- the promotion of efficient and integrated financial market;
- and the coordination of macro-economic policies, such as fiscal consolidation and sound public finances.

The role of the EU was to define the direction of the path of industrial progress and economic growth by steering the policies of Member States, through a new mode of governance, the Open method of coordination, as the means of spreading best practice and achieving greater convergence towards the main EU goals. In practice, common European challenges were translated into national reform policies, thus maintaining the respect for national diversity and sovereignty.

---

14 As reported by Majocchi (2007), in cases of an investment policy inspired by the Lisbon Strategy and in general of an expansionary fiscal policy, the growth rate would have increased by half a point, to 1,5 %, instead of the observed real growth rate of 1 % in the euro area.

15 Lisbon European Council (2000), Presidency Conclusions, 23-24 March, https://www.consilium.europa.eu/uedocs/cms_data/docs/pressdata/en/ec/00100-r1.en0.htm

One of the key targets of the Strategy was the European social model, and its role in contributing to a revamping of economic growth. Social protection was defined as a productive factor and part of the *Lisbon triangle* (based on social, economic and employment policies) or *quadrilateral*, depending on whether or not the fourth leg, environmental policy, was included in this geometric metaphor (Armstrong et al., 2008).[16] All this was consistent with a more evident commitment to a social Europe.

However, according to a mid-term evaluation of the Lisbon Strategy, the 2004 Kok Report, the outcome of the strategy proved deceiving, mainly because of a poor implementation of structural reforms. Limits were evident in its ability to adjust social cohesion and economic competitiveness; environmental policy and productive growth; fiscal stability and structural reforms (Kok, 2004).[17] In 2005 the Commission recognised that although modern infrastructure (transport and energy) was an important competitiveness factor in many enterprise decisions, affecting the economic and social attractiveness of locations, in this sector progress had been disappointingly slow.

From a quantitative point of view, the Strategy turned out to be disappointing. As the European Parliament observed, the employment targets of the Lisbon Strategy were not met by 2010 (Rodriguez et al., 2010).[18] In several Member States high long-term unemployment, high levels of poverty risk, high rates of early school leavers, and low rates of lifelong learning were recorded. To this must be added limited, and in several cases decreasing, national research and development (R&D) expenditure, which in 2007 barely reached 2 % investment in the EU-27 as a whole, with no progress towards the target of 3 %.

Conversely, at the EU budget level, expenditure devoted to internal issues (research and innovation, trans European network employment,

---

16 Armstrong K., Begg I. and Zeitlin J. (2008), "JCMS Symposium: EU Governance After Lisbon", *Journal of Common Market Studies*, Vol. 46, No. 2, pp. 413-50.

17 Kok W. (2004), *Facing the Challenge: The Lisbon Strategy for Growth and Employment*, Report from the High-Level Group. Bruxelles: European Commission.

18 Rodriguez R., Warmerdam J. and Triomphe, C.-E. (2010), *The Lisbon Strategy 2000-2010. An Analysis and Evaluation of Methods Used and Results Achieved. Study for the European Parliament, Directorate General for Internal Policies*, Bruxelles: European Parliament, https://www.researchgate.net/publication/305606346_The_Lisbon_Strategy_2000-2010_An_analysis_and_evaluation_of_methods_used_and_results_achieved_Study_for_the_European_Parliament

and sustainable development) was increased. Between the 2000-2006 MFF and 2007-2013 MMF, policies related to the Strategy were assigned more resources, with an increase of 41 %. This was, nevertheless, lower than the initial proposal made by the Commission in 2004 to allocate €121,7 bn. to growth and employment (Paramithiotti and Zatti, 2015, p. 35).[19]

1.6 The Europe 2020 Strategy (2010-2020)

In 2010 the Lisbon Strategy was substituted by a new cycle for the next decade, the Europe 2020 Strategy. In line with the past, the *new* Strategy tried to address the unresolved concern of international competitiveness, and the promotion of productivity, growth, and sustainability (Bongardt and Torres, 2010).[20] Indeed, it aimed to transform the EU into a smart, sustainable, and inclusive economy with high levels of employment, productivity, and social cohesion. To raise EU investment levels a focus on innovation, education, and the digital society was still favoured, to promote smart growth by improving general conditions, as well access to financing of research and innovation.

In order to implement the Strategy, the EU adopted eight targets, belonging to five thematic areas: employment, education, poverty and social exclusion, climate change and energy, and R&D and innovation. Related to these, eight headline targets were set at the EU level, although for each Member State targets were translated into national targets according to specific circumstances, and reflected the levels of ambition they hoped to reach as part of a EU-wide effort to implement European strategy.

The headline targets related to the Europe 2020 Strategy's key objectives cover:

- employment: 75 % of the population aged 20 to 64 years to be in employment by 2020;
- R&D: 3 % of GDP to be invested in the R&D sector;

[19] Paramithiotti G. and Zatti A. (2015), *Il bilancio dell'Unione europea. Origini, principi ed elementi costitutivi*, Pavia: Pavia University Press.

[20] Bongardt A. and Torres F. (2010), "The Competitiveness Rationale, Sustainable Growth and the Need for Enhanced Economic Coordination, in Europe 2020 – A Promising Strategy?", *Intereconomics*, Vol. 45, No. 3, pp. 136-170.

- climate change & energy:
  - o greenhouse gas (GHG) emissions to be reduced by 20 % compared to 1990;
  - o share of renewable energy sources in final energy consumption to be increased to 20 %;
  - o energy efficiency to be improved by 20 %;
- education:
  - o share of early school leavers (aged 18 to 24) to be reduced under 10 %;
  - o at least 40 % of 30 to 34 years old to have completed tertiary or equivalent education;
- poverty and social exclusion: at least 20 million fewer people at risk of poverty or social exclusion.

The coordination of efforts between countries and within each country was brought within the European Semester, which provided a framework of discussion between the Commission and Member States to achieve the EU's targets, set out in the terms of the two pillars – Lisbon and Maastricht – of EU economic governance. The European Semester came into force in 2011, at the same time as the financial crisis, as a tool for EU institution to intervene *ex-ante* in the formulation of national fiscal policies, and not only *ex-post* as before. It also introduced greater constraints on each individual government to recognise and explain the fiscal consequences of each structural reform through the joint presentation of the National Reform Programmes (NRPs), and the Stability and Convergence Programmes (SCPs) (Fantacci and Papetti, 2013),[21] with the intention of reinforcing the achievement of national 2020 targets.

1.7 A smarter, greener and more inclusive EU?

As we reach the end date of the Europe 2020 Strategy, expected results are still far from being achieved. Although progress has been made in the area of education, where the EU as a whole has reached the objective for tertiary education attainment – important for its links to

---

21 Fantacci L. and Papetti A. (2013), *Il debito dell'Europa con sé stessa. Analisi e riforma della governance europea difronte alla crisi*, Costituzionalismo.it, 2/2013. (Accessed October 12, 2021).

research and innovation as it provides highly skilled human capital – targets have not been met, with of course different performance across countries, mainly in three sectors: innovation, poverty risk and climate change.[22] Ultimately, the EU is:

- not so smarter: the EU R&D expenditure surpassed 2 % of GDP in 2013 and has more or less stagnated close to this level since then, without moving towards the 3 % target for 2020. This stagnation is even more evident when compared to trends recorded in other advanced economies such as the United States, Japan and South Korea. While in 2000 the EU accounted for 25 % of global R&D expenditure, this share had fallen to 20 % by 2015. In contrast, in China R&D expenditure has risen particularly strongly, increasing from 5 % of global R&D expenditure in 2000 to 21 % in 2015;[23]
- not so inclusive: Although the share of people at risk of poverty or social exclusion has decreased in the majority of Member States, the strategy has not been successful in lifting at least twenty million people out of this condition, leaving 22,4 % of the EU's population at risk of experiencing one or more forms of poverty, like monetary poverty (16,9 % of the EU's population), material deprivation (6,6 %) and very low work intensity (9,5 %). The most affected by the threat of poverty are women, children, young people, people with disabilities, single parents, people with lower educational attainment, people born in a different country than the one they reside in, people out of work and those living in rural areas.
- not so greener: of the three sub-targets of the climate and energy strategy: a 20 % reduction in GHG emissions compared with 1990 levels; a 20 % share of renewable energy in gross final energy consumption; and a 20 % cut in energy consumption compared to a 2020 business-as-usual projection – only the first one has been met: in 2017 GHG emissions in the EU decreased by almost 22 %, putting the continent on a pathway to becoming a low-carbon economy. In 2019 the EU set the long-term target of net zero emission by 2050. However, further efforts need to be made in order

---

22 See Eurostat (2019), *Smarter, Greener, More Inclusive? Indicators to Support the Europe 2020 Strategy*, Luxembourg: Publications Office of the European Union. DOI:10.2785/379691.

23 European Commission (2020), *Science, Research and Innovation Performance of the EU 2020. A Fair, Green and Digital Europe*, Luxembourg: Publications Office of the European Union. DOI:10.2777/534046.

to meet the revised target of 32 % share of gross final energy consumption by 2030, as well as the target to increase energy efficiency by 20 %.

1.8 Internal inconsistency between the Maastricht and Lisbon pillars

Unfortunately, some of the progress made through the Lisbon Strategy, and many of the expected results for Europe vanished as a result of the financial crisis that hit in 2008, and its persistent economic consequences, dragging the EU back in terms of growth potential and revealing its structural weaknesses – the poor competitiveness of its national economies, and low growth potentials. With the 2008 crisis, much criticism of the philosophy of both the Lisbon and the subsequent Europe 2020 strategies has emerged, in particular on the coherency between the two pillars of the EU economic governance, the Maastricht pillar for macroeconomic policy, based on budgetary discipline, and the Lisbon pillar for microeconomic policy (Mabbet and Schelkle, 2007).[24]

The fiscal philosophy of Maastricht was based on arbitrary rules on public deficit, while macroeconomic stabilisation was promoted through the EU reform agenda based on structural reforms.[25] In general, structural reforms have been associated with the notion of increasing the role of market forces, including competition and price flexibility, and the term is often used interchangeably with deregulation (Helbling et al., 2004).[26] The reform strategies in the Lisbon Agenda were particularly focused on the labour market, and aimed to increase employment through measures such as reduced labour protection, which would provide an incentive for companies to hire without fear of reducing their workforce later on; a reduction in labour costs, either through taxation or wage levels; increased labour mobility, which would allow competitive pressure on

---

24 Mabbet D. and Schelkle W. (2007), "Bringing Macroeconomics Back into the Political Economy of Reform: The Lisbon Agenda and the 'Fiscal Philosophy' of EMU", *Journal of Common Market Studies*, Vol. 45, No. 1, pp. 81-103.

25 Rules based approach is opposed to discretionary automatic stabilisers, which vary counter-cyclically with household income or expenditure and thus add to their disposable income in the event of a recession and reduce it in booms.

26 Helbing T., Hakura D.S. and Debrun X. (2004), "Fostering Structural Reforms in Industrial Countries", in *World Economic Outlook 2004,* Washington, D.C.: IMF.

wages; investment in education and training, which would have positive effects not only on employment but also on productivity growth.

However, with the economic crisis the internal consistency of European governance has been questioned. In the political economy literature, the idea that fiscal constraints would create a political environment which facilitates reforms is challenged by those who see tensions between an ambitious agenda of structural reforms and fiscal consolidations, therefore a sequential timing is necessary: a rise in the budgetary deficit at the beginning of the reform process may be necessary to bear the upfront costs of reform. Even the Lisbon Strategy itself is affected by a lack of consistency, in terms both of conflicting objectives, and of objectives and instruments designed to achieve them. Accordingly, the implementation of the structural reforms of the kind needed by the EU in 2005 without coherent growth-friendly macroeconomic governance is considered almost an impossible task (Creel et al., 2005).[27] For example, the objective to reduce simultaneously unemployment and increase productivity, as implied in the Lisbon Strategy *motto* “to become the most competitive and dynamic knowledge-based economy in the world, capable of sustainable economic growth with more and better jobs and greater social cohesion”, may result in a trade-off where labour market reforms may promote the inclusion of the inactive in productive activities implying more labour-intensive production techniques, with a negative effect on labour productivity.

More generally, the Lisbon objective to modernise the European social model in the sense of implementing national reforms, like welfare system or labour market reforms, has to deal with the lack of a proper active macroeconomic policy, that could be particularly important in supporting demand in hard economic times. The risk of time inconsistency of reforms materializes whenever the economy is not robust enough and fiscal policies are not committed to a full-employment oriented macroeconomic policy.

In a critical assessment of the results of the Lisbon Strategy and its unfulfilled targets, the contradictions are not only about the inconsistency of the Maastricht–Lisbon economic governance, but also about

---

27 Creel J., Laurent É. and Le Cacheux J. (2005), *Delegation in Inconsistency: The Lisbon Strategy Record as an Institutional Failure*, Documents de Travail de l’OFCE 2005-07, Paris: Observatoire Francais des Conjonctures Economiques (OFCE).

another urgent challenge, climate change. If all these aspects are taken into account, the result is a trilemma where the reduction of public debt, the preservation of the welfare state, and the investment in green infrastructure cannot be achieved simultaneously (Pochet, 2010).[28] Faced with the trilemma, in 2010 the Commission clearly indicated that fiscal consolidation and long-term financial sustainability will need to go hand in hand with important structural reforms, in particular of pension, health care, social protection and education systems implying that to solve the trilemma posed by Pochet the cost of education and health would be transferred to the private sector. However, the choice between social justice and environmental justice is misleading. In recent years a growing consensus has developed; the two dimensions are not mutually exclusive, but in fact are complementary, moving towards the same objective of sustainable equality, since the transition towards a carbon free economy must be designed with due consideration for the social effect it may have. The 2020 Strategy has the merit of having better explained that social and environmental sustainability are elements that will characterise future EU growth model. On the other hand, the extent to which Member States will be able to direct expenditure towards sectors oriented towards sustainable growth beyond national fiscal rules is still an open question, given the internal inconsistency between the structural reform of the Lisbon Pillar and the fiscal policy of the Maastricht Pillar.

At the end of its life cycle an evaluation of the Europe 2020 Strategy is controversial. On one hand, the Commission recognises the important contribution to the EU's socio-economic development since its launch in 2010. Before the Covid-19 crisis Europe's employment was at a record high, the GHG emissions objective and the higher education targets had been met, and Europe was on track with renewable energy and energy efficiency targets. On the other hand, considerable progress is still needed to stimulate more investment in research and innovation and for fighting poverty and social exclusion.

---

[28] Pochet P. (2010), *What's Wrong with EU2020?*. Bruxelles: The European Trade Union Institute, https://www.etui.org/publications/policy-briefs/european-economic-employment-and-social-policy/what-s-wrong-with-eu2020 (Accessed October 12, 2021).

Chapter 2

Investment: Some definitions and macroeconomic dynamics

Firstly, there is sometimes confusion about what investment is. In the common parlance, investment often refers to the purchasing of a financial assets, like government bonds or firms' shares. However, in the political economy debate, the term has a more specific meaning. Only the flow of expenditure that increases the physical stock of capital and generates rewards over time is defined as investment; it therefore assumes a long-term dimension.[1]

In order to understand the role and impact of investment on the economy, clarification is needed on different types of investment that exist. For example, public investment and infrastructure are sometimes used interchangeably, as if synonymous. The two concepts may indeed overlap to some extent; although a large part of public investment is in infrastructure, not all infrastructure investment is of a public nature, nor is all public investment dedicated to traditional infrastructure (Kappeler and Valila, 2007).[2]

Moreover, the public debate usually lacks a macroeconomic perspective on investment, which is not normally seen as a component of a more general equilibrium that must apply both at the domestic and external levels. The inherent risk is to have too strict a focus on the public sector fiscal balance, without considering the implications that certain rules on debt and deficit may have for the rest of the economy. This perspective has been particularly relevant in the aftermath of the financial crisis, when external imbalances between Eurozone countries played a crucial role in amplifying the crisis. Furthermore, without a broader macroeconomic

---

1 The flow of investment is the yearly increase in the stock of capital, where the former is just a small part of the letter.

2 Kappeler A. and Valila T. (2007), *Composition of Public Investment and Fiscal Federalism: Panel Data Evidence from Europe*, Luxembourg: European Investment Bank, Economics Department.

understanding of investment, the role of fiscal policy, as well as of the public sector in the economy, is underestimated. With the Covid-19 crisis a massive intervention of the State was swiftly legitimated, at least in practical terms, as it was deemed necessary to counter a more dramatic and pervasive emergency than the previous crisis. However, a macroeconomic and external dimension perspective on investment is even more pressing, given its implication on European domestic fiscal rules, which are fundamental in determining trends of investment. This chapter tries to shed some light on this less debated aspect of investment in Europe.

2.1 Private investment

A first distinction to bear in mind is that between private and public sector investment, which differs from the point of view of motivation, and from the factors driving investments. Private sector investment (generally machinery and equipment) is mainly determined by the firm sector, whose decisions are not only driven by current and expected future economic developments, but also on the particular business environment, in particular the institutional context in which they operate (European Central Bank – ECB, 2016).[3]

In the decision to undertake a new investment project, a firm considers two aspects. First, it has to compare gains with costs arising from the project, the former being the marginal product of the capital, on the one hand, and the cost of capital (i.e. the real interest rate a firm has to pay on loans, to support the project) on the other. It is only when the marginal product of capital is higher than the cost of capital that it is expedient for a firm to increase its stock of capital, at least until the two are equal. This relation is rational from a neoclassical theory point of view, where monetary policy can affect the investment rate in the economy through variations of the nominal interest rate.

Second, private sector investment decisions also depend on the expected output in the economy. This explanation has to do more with Keynesian theory, where the interest rate is not a variable that monetary policy can use in order to stimulate investments. According to this

---

3 Rodriguez-Palenzuela D., Dées S., Andersson M. et al. (2016), *Savings and Investment Behaviour in the Euro Area*, Occasional Paper Series 167, Frankfurt am Main: European Central Bank.

perspective, in situations of uncertainty, investment behaviour is independent of interest rate levels, and reacts to other factors, like expectations of future growth, or of rising consumption.

The household sector also invests, mainly in the private housing sector. Factors influencing their investment behaviour therefore relate to developments in the residential real estate market, while demographic trends also have an impact. Households finance investment by using their current income, which is considered to be the most important determinant of household investment, or by borrowing from the credit market or using their accumulated savings.

The traditional dichotomy between public and private investment has largely been challenged in recent years, as it is rather artificial. In fact, a combination of the private and public is increasingly becoming a prominent method for delivering key public services. The Organisation for Economic Co-operation and Development (OECD) defines PPPs in a broad manner: "long term contractual arrangements between the government and a private partner whereby the latter delivers and funds public services using a capital asset, sharing the associated risks".[4] This definition shows that a wide array of financing objectives, in various sectors such as transport, social housing and healthcare, can be structured under PPPs. The main difference with respect to traditionally procurement projects regards the risk-sharing between the public and private partner; the private partner is often responsible for risks associated with the design, construction, financing, operation and maintenance of infrastructure, while the public partner usually takes on regulatory and political risks. Other benefits from PPPs include earlier delivery of a planned capital investment programme, as PPPs can provide an important additional funding to complement traditional budgetary envelopes, and the possibility of better maintenance and service levels than traditional projects through a whole-life approach.[5] Furthermore, the possibility of combining public and private expertise in the most effective manner facilitates in-depth

---

4 For PPPs definition see OECD website at the page https://www.oecd.org/gov/budgeting/oecd-principles-for-public-governance-of-public-private-partnerships.htm (Accessed October 8, 2021).

5 Another financial benefit from PPPs relates to EU accounting framework (ESA 2010) which allows public involvement in PPPs, under certain conditions, to be registered as off-balance sheet items. Accordingly, this incentivises their use for compliance with the EMU fiscal rules.

project assessment, and an optimisation of projects' scope. With respect to the public sector, good governance and a strong administrative capacity are considered to be necessary preconditions to achieving investments with long-lasting effects on growth. The economic and social impact of public investment on growth critically depends on its efficiency. According to the International Monetary Fund (IMF), most efficient public investors get twice the growth for their investment capital as the least efficient ones (IMF, 2015).[6]

Therefore, strengthening the planning, allocation and implementation of investment is a relevant factor that could reduce up to two-thirds of the public investment efficiency gap. Before the financial and economic crisis, the PPPs market in the EU had experienced a sharp increase in volume, but since 2008 the number of new PPPs projects has decreased considerably. In 2016, most projects were in the transport sector, which accounted for one-third of all PPPs investment, followed by the healthcare and education sectors (European Court of Auditors, 2018).[7]

2.2 Public investment: Not only infrastructure

In the literature public investment is differentiated according to its productivity. Accordingly, some types of expenditure are more productive than others, meaning that they support growth by improving the economy's resources of production factors (labour and capital) or their productivity. The items which are frequently mentioned in this context are infrastructure investments, education and training (which, together with other spending categories such as active labour market policies, are associated with improved human capital and skills), R&D (which is associated with technological development and innovation), and health care (which increases both the quantity and the productivity of labour, via an increased length of years of healthy life) (European Commission, 2012a).[8]

---

6 IMF (2015), *Making Public Investment More Efficient*, Staff report, Washington, D.C.: International Monetary Fund.

7 European Court of Auditors (2018), *Public Private Partnerships in the EU: Widespread Shortcomings and Limited Benefits*, Special Report N. 9, Luxembourg: Publications Office of the European Union. DOI:10.2865/154598.

8 European Commission (2012a), *The Quality of Public Expenditure in the EU*, Occasional Paper, n. 125, Bruxelles: European Commission. DOI: 10.2765/25458.

According to the functional classification, we can distinguish four categories of public investment:

(1) the traditional infrastructure sector, which mainly comprises transport. It has the most direct economic impact by reducing firms' production and transaction cost;
(2) the social infrastructure, that is health and education, with a more long-term and less direct effect, as it facilitates the increase in, and maintenance of, the stock of human capital;
(3) public goods, like defence, general public services, environment protection, law & order and safety. They indirectly affect the economy's allocation efficiency through framework conditions for productive activity;
(4) investment defined as redistribution: a small part of investment in housing, recreation and social protection. They affect the economy's income distribution rather than the allocative or productive efficiency *per se*.

Much of the economic research and literature supports the growth-conducive role of public investment, in particular in times of crisis. The results on the fiscal multiplier, the impact of a public deficit on economic activity, are mixed; the majority of studies seem to concur on the positive impact of public investment on growth, although with heterogeneous results. The debate has gained momentum since the publication of a famous article by Blanchard and Leighs (2013),[9] in which the authors acknowledged that fiscal multipliers were substantially higher than earlier estimates by economists, while a strong fiscal consolidation programme was associated with lower levels of growth than expected. In other words, the impact of public expenditure was positive and higher with respect to the effect that an austerity programme would have in the medium term.[10] The IMF suggests that for advanced economies in

[9] Blanchard O. J. and Leigh D. (2013), "Growth Forecast Errors and Fiscal Multipliers", *American Economic Review*, vol. 103, n. 3, pp. 117-20.

[10] The *expansive austerity* view considers that a fiscal contraction will determine an increase in private sector expenditure, thanks to a restoration of confidence among firms and households. This would more than compensate the contraction in the public sector. This approach was strongly favoured within European institutions. A case in point was the then President of the ECB, claiming that "we have the experiences of fiscal consolidation episodes in less exceptional times, which make clear the long-term benefits of reducing sizeable fiscal imbalances. These experiences also suggest that, provided consolidation is pursued as part of a comprehensive reform

a period of low growth, a public-investment spending shock increases the level of output by about 1,5 % in the same year and by 3 % in the medium term (IMF, 2014, p. 82).[11]

The positive effect of public spending on economic activity means that fears of a *crowding-out* effect on private investment are overstated.[12] On the contrary, public investment can create favourable conditions that *crowd-in* private investment. In particular, by providing relevant infrastructure, like highways, railways and ports, public intervention may increase the productivity of private investment, which takes advantage of better infrastructures and potentially improved business conditions. However, beyond traditional infrastructure, other categories of public investment are considered crucial for growth. Although projects need to be examined on a case-by-case basis to determine their return and effect on growth, it is generally assumed that social infrastructures and intangible investments are also positively correlated with long-term growth. Even if returns on different public investment categories are not directly comparable, estimates suggest that returns on investment are in the range of 17 % to 35 % for traditional infrastructure and education, while returns on research and development investment is slightly less (10 % to 30 %) (Szczepański, 2016).[13]

---

strategy, the short-term costs for economic growth tend to be contained or very limited" (Trichet J. C. (2010), "Stimulate No More – It Is Now Time for All to Tighten", *The Financial times*, 22 July).

11 IMF (2014), "Is It Time for and Infrastructure Push? The Macroeconomic Effects of Public Investment", in *World Economic Outlook*, Washington, D.C.: International Monetary Fund. DOI: 10.5089/9781498331555.081.

12 In economics, the crowding-out effect is explained by the reaction of private investment after an increase in public expenditure, through an increase in the interest rate. Technically, the increase of public investment needs to be financed, which may imply more taxes or impose a higher demand for funds from the government in the capital markets, causes interest rates to rise. This would reduce the amount of savings available for private investors and decrease the expected rate of return of private capital, leading to a crowding-out effect on private investment, (Afonso A. and St. Aubyn M. (2008), *Macroeconomic Rates of Return of Public and Private Investment, Crowding-in and Crowding-out Effects*, ECB Working Paper Series No. 864, Frankfurt am Main: European Central Bank).

13 Szczepański M. (2016), *Public Investment to Support Long Term Economic Growth*, EPSF Briefing, Bruxelles: European Parliamentary Research Service.

2.3 Intangible investments

In advanced economies the capacity to be competitive is mainly driven by intangible investment, that is knowledge-based capital (OECD, 2013). [14] Investment in intangible assets (such as R&D, software and databases, training of employees or organisational and business processes) is recognised as the main driver of productivity, long-term prosperity and economic growth. In addition, new products, services and processes may also address pressing policy and societal challenges – including an ageing population, climate change, and many environmental and health issues. As explained by endogenous growth theory, returns on intangible investments do not exhibit diminishing returns, as is the case with tangible investments, therefore in principle they can drive long-term growth as long as human capital accumulates, without boundaries. They can also explain growth differences between countries (Aiginger and Janger, 2015).[15]

While remaining at the frontier of innovation, the EU is investing less in R&D, as a percentage of GDP, than other major economies, like the US, which is the economy that invests most in R&D (Fig. 2.1). However, the relative weights of the US and the EU in global R&D expenditures have been falling over time, while that of China, which is becoming a leader for innovation at the technological frontier, is rapidly increasing.

---

14 One widely accepted classification groups intangible assets into three types: computerised information (software and databases); innovative property (patents, copyrights, designs, trademarks); and economic competencies (including brand equity, firm-specific human capital, networks of people and institutions, and organisational know-how that increases enterprise efficiency) (OECD (2013), *Supporting Investment in Knowledge Capital, Growth and Innovation*, Paris: OECD Publishing. DOI:10.1787/9789264193307). Firms' purchases of software programs and licenses and expenditures in research and development (R&D) are recorded as *fixed capital investment* in EU national accounts since 2014.

15 Aiginger A. and Janger J. (2015), "Intangibles and Green Investments for Restarting Growth", in Austrian Federal Ministry of Science, Research and Economy (ed.), *Investing in Europe's Future Restarting the Growth Engine* (pp. 116-146), Wien: Federal Ministry of Science, Research and Economy.

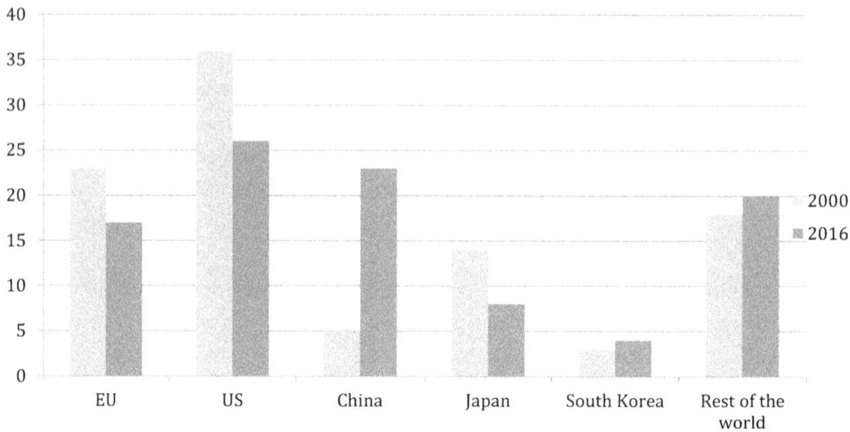

Fig. 2.1: Share of global R&D expenditures in 2000 and 2016 (%)
Source: EIB (2019, p.110). EIB (2019), *Investment Report 2019/2020. Accelerating Europe's transformation*, Luxembourg: European Investment Bank. DOI: 10.2867/68943

Over the past decade, the global R&D landscape has changed rapidly, due to the rising importance of the digital economy. The top ten of the R&D global ranking is dominated by digital technologies, with US and Asian companies producing electronic and hardware technology equipment or software and computer services (EIB, 2019). On the other hand, the EU specialises less in the new technology sectors, while it is a global leader in R&D investment in the automotive industry, one of its historically strongest sectors. However, the automotive sector is experiencing a transformation, due to digitalisation and new trends – such as electrical vehicles, autonomous driving and car sharing.

Obstacles for firms using innovation as a competitive strategy are mainly due to difficulties in finding appropriately skilled employees, given the scarcity of high-skilled employees. This means that if workers are under-educated firms are not operating at their productive limits, as they employ less productive workers than they should (International Labour Organization – ILO, 2014).[16] Investing in skills matters for

16 ILO (2014), *Skills Mismatch in Europe. Statistics Brief*, Geneva: International Labour Office, https://www.ilo.org/wcmsp5/groups/public/---dgreports/---stat/documents/publication/wcms_315623.pdf (Accessed October 14, 2021). The skill mismatching question refers also to the opposite situation when workers are overeducated for the jobs they perform. This means, for example, that firms are not fully utilising the productive capacity of their workers.

structural reasons, including demographic and technological change. Persistent skill shortages and mismatches can negatively affect the adoption of new technology, while ageing population dynamics will make skills a more pressing structural issue at a time when global competition will require a more skilled workforce.

2.4 The EU budget

The EU has placed a large share of its regulatory and financial instruments at the disposal of Member States, their regions, and their industries, to foster investments, in particular in the innovation sector and to increase competitiveness. The MFF is the public finance programming tool, in which the allocation of resources for expenditure items is established over a medium-term perspective. With the exception of agricultural policy, it is mainly used for capital investments in specific areas and cannot cover operational costs.

The EU budget performs its functions of public finance in combination with lower layers of government, both national and subnational. Based on fiscal federalism theory about the functional decomposition of the economic role of the State (Musgrave, 1959),[17] the three functions of public finance should correspond to different levels of government. First, the stabilisation function, intended as a response to the need to sustain demand following shocks that can lead to a slowdown in the economic cycle, should be carried out centrally. Second, the income redistribution function, aimed at modifying the redistribution of resources generated by the market in order to make it more in line with equity criteria, should be conducted centrally, because of the risk that a decentralised redistribution could encourage the migration of tax bases and attract more disadvantaged groups. Third, the allocation function of all those goods and services (public goods) that the market may not produce or produce inadequately, should be distributed between levels of government, so that the central level is responsible for providing goods and services consumed by the entire population, while local governments provide those goods and services that affect their own populations.

The EU is a particular case of fiscal federalism, differing from the theory. When comparing the central (EU) and local (States) levels, both stabilisation and redistribution functions are carried out mainly at the

---

[17] Musgrave, R. A. (1959), *The Theory of Public Finance*, New York: McGraw-Hill.

national level, and therefore are decentralised, while a small part of investment in public goods is centralised. However, looking at the internal composition of the budget, which is very limited in size (just about 1 % of EU GDP), reveals that: it is mainly devoted to redistribution at the territorial level, through the policy of cohesion and the Common Agricultural Policy (CAP); macroeconomic stabilisation exists only as an indirect effect, to the extent that the budget has long-term stability; the provision of public goods still remains relatively limited.

The breakdown of the 2014-2020 MFF shows that around 73 % of the budget is used to support territorial redistribution (under the headings *Economic, social and territorial cohesion* and *Sustainable growth, natural resources*) which comprises most of the funds (approximately 80 %) managed by national administrations, with locally determined plans and priorities, while 21 % finances the provision of European public goods (*Competitiveness for growth and jobs, Global Europe*, and *Security and citizenship*) that are centrally managed (Fig. 2.2).

Fig. 2.2: EU budget by headings financed, 2014-2020 MFF (billion euro and %, current prices)

Source: European Commission. European Commission (2017b), *Reflection paper on the future of EU finances, Bruxelles: European Commission https://ec.europa.eu/commission/sites/beta-political/files/reflection-paper-eu-finances_en.pdf (Accessed October 14 2021)*

In practice, however, the distinction between the three functions is not so clear-cut, as they intersect with each other. For example, cohesion policy in recent years has helped to support the decline in public investment as a result of the financial crisis by increasing the co-financing rate from the EU budget, while the second pillar of the CAP (*Rural development*) promotes environmental protection and climate change mitigation through agriculture. Or, in the stabilisation function debate that proliferated after the Eurozone crisis, the European Commission proposed the creation of a budget stabilisation function, in the form of a protection scheme for European investments within the budget, as a complementary measure to national budgets in the event of major asymmetric shocks.

As reported by Pellegrin et al. (2015),[18] for the 2014-2020 MFF the EU has invested 87 % of its budget (€820 bn. over seven years) to address the EU 2020 strategy through the objectives of smart, inclusive, and sustainable growth. There is a range of initiatives, beyond regulatory tools, with which the European budget contributes to improving European competitiveness, therefore, as such, they are part of the EU industrial policy.

Under the heading *Economic, social and territorial cohesion* the European Structural and Investment Funds (ESIF) allocated to European regions €322 bn. within the framework of the Cohesion Policy.[19] These investments are guided by the strategic approach of *smart specialization*, which establishes a link between regional and innovation policies, based on competitive advantages at the national and regional levels. The programmes of Horizon 2020 (innovation investment, in particular in *key enabling technologies*, like micro- and nano-electronics, nanotechnologies, advanced materials, biotechnology and advanced manufacturing and processing), Connecting Europe Facility (CEF - investment to infrastructures in the energy, broadband and transport sector) and COSME (devoted to small and medium-sized enterprises) are more devoted to the

---

18 Pellegrin J., Giorgetti M. L., Jensen C. and Bolognini A. (2015), *EU Industrial Policy: Assessment of Recent Developments and Recommendations for Future Policy*, Bruxelles: European Parliament Policy Department A: Economic and Scientific Policy.

19 Through the European Regional Development Fund (ERDF), European Social Fund (ESF) and Cohesion Fund. The other structural funds are European Agricultural Fund for Rural Development (EAFRD), European Maritime and Fisheries Fund (EMFF), European Agricultural Guarantee Fund (EAGF).

industry sector and to improving framework conditions for the competitiveness of enterprises. All in all, these financial instruments are relevant for the European economy. Although limited in size, the role played by the EU budget is significant. As Núñez Ferrer and Katarivas (2014) [20] observe, almost half of the EU budget (representing 15 % of total EU public investment) is "direct investment" which is aimed at gross fixed-capital formation (i.e. mainly infrastructures). They also remind us that much of the EU budget is either co-financed, or supporting financial instruments (like guarantees or blending) that attract a range of funds from financial institutions and other investors. Therefore, the funding mobilised by the MFF is very substantial, leading to a EU mobilised size of funds of €2 tr., or 2 % points of GDP.

One aspect of the EU budget that has been criticised, beyond its dimension, concerns the quality of spending. As the Sapir report already asserted in 2004:

> as it stands today, the EU budget is a historical relic. Expenditures, revenues and procedures are all inconsistent with the present and future state of EU integration. Half its spending goes on supporting a sector whose economic significance is declining, little is used to provide economic or non-economic public goods typically featuring large economies of scale, while convergence policy is very dispersed across EU countries and is not focused regarding the activities it should support (Sapir et al., 2004, p. 162).

Analysts have raised growing concerns about the gap between commitments and promises, for example, grand strategies such as Europe 2020, but also the 2030 Agenda for Sustainable Development and the Paris Climate Agreement of 2015, on the one hand, and what the budget can really deliver over its programming cycle, on the other. It is a common opinion that the EU Budget should be reformed, both on the spending and the revenue sides, adopting a sustainability approach for both. From an expenditure point of view, the current structure shows various sustainability gaps (Schratzenstaller-Altzinger, 2017),[21] which

---

[20] Núñez Ferrer J. and Katarivas M. (2014), *What Are the Effects of the EU Budget: Driving Force or Drop in the Ocean?*, CEPS Special Report n. 86, Bruxelles: CEPS.

[21] Schratzenstaller-Altzinger M. (2017), *The Next Multiannual Financial Framework (MFF), Its Structure and the Own Resources, European Parliament In-depth Analysis*. Bruxellles: European Union, https://www.europarl.europa.eu/RegData/etudes/IDAN/2017/603800/IPOL_IDA%282017%29603800_EN.pdf (Accessed October 14, 2021).

refer to various sectors. For example, expenditure in the first pillar of the CAP mainly serves to preserve existing, conventional production structures, that are large agricultural units, with conventional methods, while the budget devoted to the more sustainability oriented second pillar, which could actively support organic farming and rural employment in smaller units, is actually quite limited in size. In addition, expenditure for research, which has a particularly large impact on growth and productivity, and infrastructure, still accounts for a comparatively low fraction of overall expenditure, while only a relatively small share of R&D expenditure actively supports a socio-ecological transition in the EU (20 % of Horizon 2020 is dedicated to climate related R&D, still below the target of 35 % envisaged by the European Commission). On the revenue side, the current structure of the EU system of own resources can be seen as an obstacle to further integration, as well as an obstacle to policies necessary for a sustainable economy. The main problems are the increasing dominance of direct contributions from Member States national budgets to the European budget, which undermines the EU's financial autonomy, or the fact that the current system neither reflects nor directly supports central EU policies such as sustainable growth and development (see Chapter 8 for a discussion on own resources). The High-level group on own resources (HLGOR – known as the Monti Report),[22] established in 2013 at the specific request of the European Parliament in order to re-examine the EU financing system and see how to reform it, recommended that: "In times of scarce public resources but growing financial needs, the EU budget needs to focus on areas bringing the highest 'European added value', or on European public goods for which action at EU level is not only relevant, but indispensable, or where national financing possibilities are insufficient for achieving our European goals" (HLGOR, 2016, p. 11).

As such, the introduction of new own resources is legitimated to the extent that these are oriented towards the production of European public goods that can lead to economies of scale, efficiency gains and better address external issues.

---

[22] HLGOR (2016), *Future Financing of the EU: Final Report and Recommendations*, Bruxelles: European Union, https://ec.europa.eu/info/sites/default/files/about_the_european_commission/eu_budget/future-financing-hlgor-final-report_2016_en.pdf (Accessed October 14, 2021).

2.5 Investment and savings: Two sides of the same coin

To understand the multidimensional nature of investment it is important to adopt a macroeconomic perspective, looking at the character of the national account, which describes the way in which GDP is measured. This perspective strictly relates the level of investment to that of savings, since, by definition, in an economy the level of investment and of savings must always be equal (see Box 1; Blanchard et al., 2010).[23]

Although savings and investment must by definition be equal, one of the most controversial issues in the macroeconomic debate is precisely about this equivalence, and the mechanism through which investment and savings are able to reach equilibrium (Saraceno, 2018).[24]

According to Neoclassical theory, the decision of firms to invest always adjusts to the decisions of households and government to save. In the literature this is known as the Say's law, basically implying that supply creates its own demand. This simply means that when production is sold, a corresponding amount of income is generated to compensate production factors (labour and capital), which in turn demands an equal quantity of goods. Accordingly, the economic system is, by itself, able to generate sufficient demand to absorb all its production through variations in prices (in particular the interest rate). However, it may be the case that not all income earned is spent, and not all production is realised in the same period. The decisions of the business sector to invest, and those of households to save, may differ with respect to the required level. Nevertheless, at the end of the process the economic system will reach equilibrium, where the level of the two variables is equal. This is possible thanks to variations of the interest rate, and to the fact that both savings and investment react to these changes. In fact, an increase in the interest rate is followed by a reduction of investment, whereas savings will increase, since it is expedient to invest (in a financial sense) and earn at an increased interest rate. Whenever the required level of investment does not equal the level of saving, then a decrease in the interest rate will stimulate an increase in investment alongside a commensurate reduction in savings.

---

23 Blanchard O., Amighini A. and Giavazzi F. (2010), *Macroeconomics. A European Perspective*, Harlow: Pearson Education Limited.

24 Saraceno F. (2018), *La scienza inutile*, Roma: LUISS University Press.

Box 1. Macroeconomic equilibrium: savings and investment equivalence

There are two equivalent ways to describe the equilibrium on the goods market: production (Y) is equal to demand, where C, I and G stand for consumption, investment, and public expenditure respectively

$$(Y=C+I+G) \quad [1]$$

or, alternatively, investment is equal to saving

$$(I=S) \quad [2]$$

In order to derive the second identity, we consider national savings in the economy, which is formed from private savings from households (Sp) and public savings from the government (Sg). Private savings is all that is not consumed, after having paid taxes, while public savings is the difference between taxes T (a revenue for the government) and the public spending G (an outflow). In formula, we have

$$Sp=Y-T-C \quad [3]$$

$$Sg=T-G \quad [4]$$

and the total saving is thus

$$S=Sp+Sg=Y-T-C+T-G \quad [5]$$

after simplification

$$S=Y-C-G \quad [6]$$

Now, we recall the other equation for the equilibrium in the goods market where production is equal to demand and put it equal to Savings

$$S=C+I+G-C-G \quad [7]$$

which, after simplification, gives

$$S=I \quad [8]$$

Put simply, equation [8] gives another way of thinking about equilibrium in the goods market, other that eq. [1]. It says that equilibrium in the goods market requires that the sums firms want to invest must be equal to that which people and the government want to save.

From a different perspective, Keynesian theory does not recognise this price adjustment process. In his works, Keynes rejected Say's law, since variations of prices and interest rates may not be able to stimulate a sufficient level of investment to absorb total savings. In real life, economic agents face a *radical uncertainty*, which influences their behaviour in terms of consumption and investment. For Keynes, investment is not mainly influenced by levels of interest rates, but rather by the *animal spirits* of entrepreneurs, that are subject to expectations about future levels of income. On the other hand, uncertainty may also have an effect on savings behaviour. Money has not only the function of a means for transaction, but is also a liquid, and risk-free, reserve of value. Therefore, savings may be kept in form of hard cash, and not lent through the banking system to then flow to the business sector. Therefore, this part of money that is hoarded exits the production-income-expenditure-production circuit – predicted by Say's law – and as a result effective demand becomes lower than that required. If the effective investment is an autonomous variable not depending on decreasing interest rates and is lower than savings, then only a reduction in the quantity, not in prices, will bring the production to equate the effective demand at a lower level.

2.6 The paradox of savings and possible ways out

The savings-investment picture can be extended by including the role of the public sector in the macroeconomic equilibrium, and this gives some insights related to the European context. If the public sector is included in the analysis, the national accounting identity eq. [1] also implies that, in a closed economy, the public (G-T) and private sector (S-I) must be in balance. In other words, whenever the private sector is in surplus (meaning that it is saving more than it is investing, S>I) the public sector must be, by definition, in deficit (i.e. public expenditure is higher than fiscal revenues, G>T).[25]

From this macroeconomic perspective, it is clear that the public sector fiscal position can have an effect on the rest of the economy, and this is particularly relevant in Eurozone governance. The narrative in macroeconomics considers savings as a virtue: "Those who spend all their income

---

[25] If you add T (taxes) to the equilibrium in the goods market eq. [1], then pose S= Y-C, you obtain: S-I=G-T, which is a macroeconomic identity in a closed economy.

are condemned to end up poor. Those who save are promised a happy life. Similarly, governments tell us, an economy that saves is an economy that will grow strong and prosper" (Blanchard, et al., 2010, p. 53). However, if for example consumers decide to save more of their income, equilibrium output decreases; as people save more, without any increase in income, they must decrease consumption, but this decreased consumption decreases demand, which decreases production. The public sector can have a counterbalancing role through an increase in its expenditure.

However, as Kregel (2018)[26] observes, the measures adopted to support stability in the Eurozone – the Maastricht criteria and the SGP provisions – lead on the one hand to national financial stability, as they imply that governments should always be in fiscal balance or in surplus, without recourse to external financing;[27] but, on the other, these public sector rules eventually lead to the paradox of surplus, as Kregel explains:

> for countries that currently have debt and deficit ratios above the SGP limits, as this requires not only budget balance, but a rising fiscal surplus that can only be achieved through a combination of higher growth and taxation. Since governments cannot produce this growth through appropriate demand management policies, it must come from *either domestic consumption and investment or from net foreign demand*. But increased domestic expenditures cannot be generated by reducing government expenditures or rising taxes to generate the required fiscal surplus, since this only reduces domestic demand. Improving the external account can no longer be achieved by exchange rate adjustment but must involve [downward] domestic wage and price adjustment, which also exerts a negative impact on domestic income and investment incentives. Further, these adjustments must be relative to major trading partners who may also be engaged in domestic price adjustments, making the required adjustments even greater (Kregel, 2018, pp. 42-43; emphasis added).

---

26 Kregel J. (2018), "Growth and the Single Currency: The Fiscal Policy Paradox", in Savona P. (ed.), *Una politeia per un'Europa diversa, più forte e più equa*, Presidenza del Consiglio Dipartimento per le Politiche Europee, http://www.eurojus.it/wp-content/uploads/2018/09/per-uneuropa-piu-forte-e-piu-equa-2-versione-finale-impaginato-1.pdf (Accessed October 14, 2021).

27 Maastricht criteria are based on Art. 140 of the Treaty on the Functioning of the European Union (TFEU). Member States are required to meet these criteria to enter the third stage of the EMU and adopt the euro as their currency. The fiscal criteria are that the ratio of the annual general government deficit must not exceed 3 % of GDP at market prices and that the government debt-to-GDP ratio must not exceed 60 % at the end of the fiscal year.

All this means that if a country has to pursue (following fiscal rules) a public sector surplus in order to lower the level of its public debt, then a deficit position in the private sector must necessarily occur, through an investment level that is higher than savings.[28] Nevertheless, the private sector invests only if expectations of future growth and profits are met, which is not the case with depressed consumption and internal devaluation that constrains wages, as it was the case particularly after the Eurozone crisis. In the end, for this to happen, an exogenous boost from the public sector in the form of higher government expenditure (and investment) would be necessary; without the intervention of the State, the economic system would remain mired in a deflationary spiral of falling prices, persistent unemployment, negative expectations, and insufficient private spending, which would feed off each other.

If an expansionary fiscal policy were not possible because of European fiscal rules – temporarily suspended since the outbreak of the pandemic – the solution to the paradox of thrift would be found in the external sector. Further expanding the picture, in an open economy a macroeconomic equilibrium implies that if both the public and the private sectors were in surplus, then the current account (i.e. payments for goods and services between an economy and the rest of the world) might compensate through a surplus. In practice, domestic production that is not absorbed, through domestic consumption, investment or government, must be exported.[29] These macroeconomic rules, that are correct within national accounting definitions, imply that in the EU economic framework the fiscal rules that the EU itself has given to its Member States can only be met by a country if it has an external surplus large enough to compensate for an excess of savings generated by both the government and the private sector domestically. All this is needed to

---

28 In other terms, it must be that if $T>G$, then $I>S$. The private and public sectors cannot be both in surplus, otherwise Y would decrease. The two sectors cannot be both in surplus or both in deficit: one sector must be in surplus while the other in deficit.

29 The sum of the excess saving in the three sectors (private, public, and external) must be zero: $(X-M) = (T-G) + (S-I)$, where $(X-M)$ is the current account surplus (X is exports and M is imports). In other words, a volume of production higher than the domestic demand (implying a domestic excess of savings) must be absorbed by the demand of the rest of the world, through exports higher than imports. Vice versa, an excess of domestic demand requires a current account deficits, with imports higher than exports.

generate growth; otherwise, the economy becomes mired in a deflationary spiral.

In the Eurozone two different growth models have emerged since the inception of the single currency.

While after the Second World War most developed European economies had a wage-led growth pattern, meaning that wage growth was the most important determinant of growth, from the 1980s onwards a number of factors changed this trend; the institutionalisation of a tight monetary policy, economic globalisation and capital market liberalisation, the advent of shareholder value orientation and the declining strength of trade unions organising power (Gräbner et al., 2020).[30] Decreases in domestic consumption, associated with increasing levels of inequalities observed in most Western countries over the last decades, have been compensated for through various strategies. On the one hand, a group of countries (Austria, Belgium, Finland, Luxemburg, Germany, and the Netherlands), that are labelled as the *core* of the Eurozone, have pursued export-led growth. This dynamic has been made possible by the ability of companies in these countries to accumulate specific skills and knowledge, enabling them to compete on the international market in terms of the quality of their traded products. Since this countries typically run substantially current account surpluses, they are also called *surplus* countries, as they are creditor for countries that are in an opposite situation of current account deficit. On the other, *periphery* states (Greece, Ireland, Italy, Portugal, and Spain)[31] have followed debt-led private sector expansion in order to stabilise their demand. Since the introduction of the euro, firms in these countries have displayed a low level of technological capabilities, that only makes it possible for them to compete at a lower level of technological sophistication, where wage dynamics are more relevant in determining export performance. However, this race to the bottom in prices, exacerbated by competition from China, where the level of wages is even lower than in the European periphery countries, only leads to wage cuts that reduce domestic demand. As a result, these countries are embarking on a debt-driven growth path, in large parts based on

30 Gräbner C., Heimberger P., Kapeller J. and Schütz B. (2020), "Is the Eurozone Disintegrating? Macroeconomic Divergence, Structural Polarisation, Trade and Fragility", *Cambridge Journal of Economics*, Vol. 44, Issue 3, pp. 647-669. DOI: 10.1093/cje/bez059.

31 Also referred to as the PIIGS.

increasing private sector indebtedness, that foreign capital inflows made possible. For this reason, they are called *deficit* countries due to current account deficit reflecting an external debt position.

According to Gräbner et al. (2020) the contrast between *core export-led surplus* countries and *periphery debt-led deficit* countries lies in a structural polarisation in terms of technological capacity. This will continue, thus exacerbating macroeconomic divergences, unless a set of active policy interventions are made to change this pattern, like investment in knowledge policy, public investment, and redistribution policies to counteract income inequality, the underlying reason for such polarisation.

Countries with a current account surplus, headed by Germany, can continue to support fiscal discipline as a key principle of economic policy as long as they can grow with their export-led model, leaving domestic private sector demand for consumption and investment weak. As Martin Wolf (2019)[32] observed, Germany shares socio-economic similarities with Japan, as they both are relatively large and rapidly ageing high-income countries and dynamic exporters of manufactured goods. This leads to huge surpluses of private savings over investments; between 2010 and 2017 private surpluses were 7 % of GDP in Germany and 8 % in Japan. However, while in Japan the current account surplus absorbed just a third of the private surplus, with the rest ending up in fiscal deficits, in Germany, the external surplus absorbed all the private surplus, since the government too runs with a fiscal surplus. As the world economy slows and foreign demand lags, the case for shifting the balance towards investment grows.

2.7 The Eurozone's flaws

The creation of the single European currency raised expectations of positive socio-economic developments in terms of per-capita incomes and further integration. The belief that the single currency would have been the first step towards the creation of a political union was based on the idea that the European integration process had a self-sustaining dynamic. Proponents of functionalism theory believed that "limited

---

32 Wolf M. (2019), "How the Euro Helped Germany Avoid Becoming Japan", *The Financial Times*, 29 October.

integration will lead to more integration" (Spalaore, 2013);[33] integration in one or more functional areas, in this case economic and monetary fields, would tend to spill over into other areas, namely the political one.[34] The achievement of political unification would result from two dynamics.

The first was related to expectations of income convergence between countries joining the Economic and Monetary Union (EMU, i.e. the Eurozone). This presupposition was based on the idea that, following the elimination of barriers such as exchange rates, capital would move from one country to another in search of higher yields made possible by higher marginal productivity of capital associated with its initial relative scarcity. As a consequence, the reallocation of investment would rebalance capital endowments across countries. In fact, in the period between 2000 and 2018, aggregate nominal per-capita GDP grew more in the EU (23,5 %), than in the Eurozone (17,2 %), although the lower performance of the euro area is mainly explained by the negative performance trends of Italy and Greece. Once they are excluded, the real per capita GDP in the rest of the euro area increased by an average of 22 %, quite similar to the EU growth rate.

However, although income increased almost everywhere, the expected convergence process has not taken place. The richer and more advanced countries generally improved their per-capita real income. Similarly, some of the countries that started from more backward positions gained strong relative positions after adopting the euro, (an increase of 154 % in Lithuania in 2000-2018, 137 % in Latvia, 101 % in Estonia and Slovakia) (Fig. 2.3). The general increase in per-capita income, and the lack of divergence – if not an actual convergence – across EU countries, as well as the great enthusiasm among economists, overshadowed the

---

33 Spalaore E. (2013), "What Is European Integration Really About? A Political Guide for Economists", *Journal of Economic Perspectives*, Vol. 27, No. 3, Summer 2013, pp. 125-44. DOI: 10.1257/jep. 27.3.125.

34 Padoa-Schioppa's famous description of the functionalist view applied to the EMU is the "inconsistent quartet": the mutual incompatibility of free trade, mobility of capital, fixed exchange rates, and independence of national monetary policies. Therefore, assuming a gradual approach, first fixed exchange rates were established for Europe's single market, then the transition from commercial integration to liberalisation of capital movements through the loss of national monetary autonomy and the creation of the ECB (Padoa-Schioppa T. (2004), *The Euro and Its Central Bank: Getting United After the Union*, Cambridge: MIT Press).

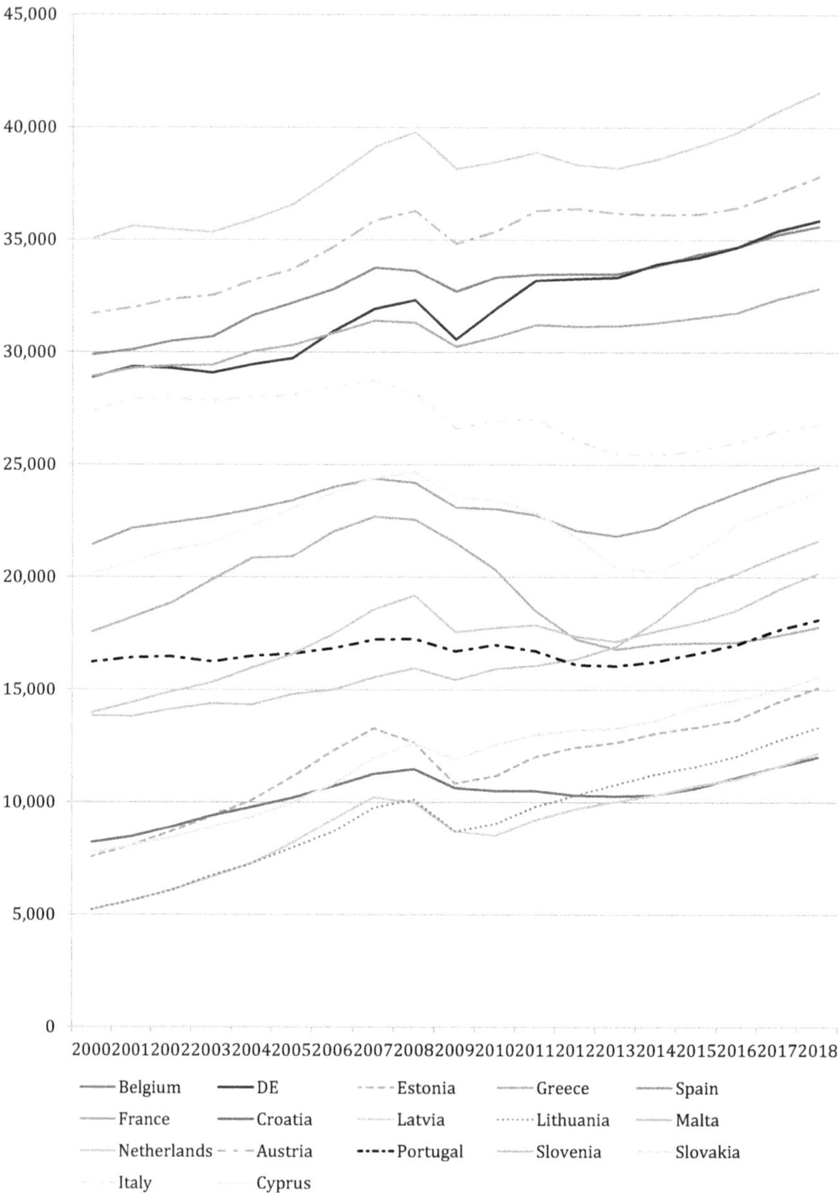

Fig. 2.3: Real per-capita GDP in EMU countries (euro, 2000-2018)
Source: Eurostat

emerging problem of growing structural divergences between countries, in particular in terms of differences in production structures. As Celi et al. (2018)[35] point out, in the process of European integration, the countries of the periphery have undergone a push towards de-industrialisation, but without embarking on restructuring policies of their productive structures as Germany did.[36] Therefore, inflows of capital from the core have not eliminated production bottlenecks. Without restructuring their productive activity, these countries were unable to compete in the open economy created by capital liberalisation and the euro, and with stronger countries. Germany had embarked on a modernisation process that based its development model on export demand, restructuring its production base with a view to competing not on price but on product. It is usual to think of competitiveness only in terms of price, and not of product competitiveness. The latter requires a plurality of factors, linked to the ability to innovate production processes, the furniture of production factors, and the organisation of production. The economies of the periphery suffered from a lack of conditions that met the requirements to compete in the European single market, and ended up in having to resort to downward pricing to achieve competitiveness.

The second aspect examines industrial restructuring processes through the lens of the theory adopted to evaluate the cost/benefit of joining the euro, in particular in the case of shocks. Following the theoretical model of the Optimum Currency Area (OCA) proposed by Robert Mundell, the only way through which the EMU can respond to an asymmetric shock, affecting one or several Member States, is through downward price flexibility, in such cases where product competitiveness is not an available tool. Other mechanisms are proposed by OCA theory in order to absorb a shock, but these are not fully operationalised in the European context. First, mobility of labour has traditionally played a minor role in Europe; through this readjustment process, labour moves from one country to another to escape high unemployment. The low level of labour mobility in Europe can be explained by cultural factors

---

35 Celi G., Ginzburg A., Guarascio D. and Simonazzi A. (2018), *Crisis in the European Monetary Union. A Core-Periphery Perspective*, Abingdon: Routledge.

36 Since 1970 the restructuring process in Germany was aimed at diverting domestic investment from the manufacturing sector to services, in particular the finance sector, and at the same time to increase the presence of Germany in the international market through higher FDI.

and different fiscal regimes, which can be a crucial aspect for a European citizen living in a Member State with a more generous welfare regime. Second, a central budget with a stabilisation function. The idea of a centralised budget, provided with a well-funded stabilisation function for countries in needs of transfer (in the form of unemployment benefits, for example), has for a long time not been a political option due to the scarcity of solidarity among countries, although Covid-19 crisis management has demonstrated some openness in this regards with the creation of a European Recovery Plan.

After the financial crisis, the question of a centralised budget with a stabilisation function has been lengthily debated. This is related to the fiscal policy response that the EU could implement to support their Member States, which may suffer from a decline in public investment. However, it is well-known that the EMU, since its inception, has been characterised by an asymmetry between the monetary policy dimension, on the one hand, and fiscal policy, on the other. Monetary policy has been completely federalised, to become the exclusive competence of the ECB, whereas fiscal policy has remained decentralised and subject to a series of fiscal rules and intergovernmental coordination mechanisms. This type of structure has made it difficult to cope optimally with a crisis affecting only one, or a sub-set of member States. On the one hand the ECB only responds on the basis of aggregated data for the euro area as a whole, so it cannot take into account national specificities, and in any case the scope of its intervention is limited to monetary stimulus; on the other hand, the strict budgetary constraints set by the fiscal rules do not allow changes to individual Member State's fiscal policy to make budget stabilisers work fully through increasing social spending. The economic and financial crisis has highlighted the weaknesses inherent in this structure; however, the various response measures have not called into question the economic governance of the EMU, the completion of which therefore remains at the centre of the debate.

2.8 Macroeconomic dynamics before the financial crisis

The 1990s were marked by large differences in the cost of borrowing in EU member countries. Faced with high and varied inflation rates, markets demanded very large risk premiums for lending. With the creation of the EMU and the introduction of the euro, things changed, as interest rates in the countries that adopted the single currency started to converge. The risk premium disappeared thanks to the elimination of exchange rate risk.

In the EMU the mobility of capital has had important implications on external relations through the current accounts of countries. In fact, increased financial integration in the euro area brought about a lower nominal interest rate, i.e. the cost of borrowing, clearly making it more attractive to borrow, inducing periphery countries to borrow more from the core. At the same time, increased integration in the goods market should have made it easier for the periphery to repay foreign debt in the future by exporting to the core states (Blanchard and Giavazzi, 2002).[37] The drop in interest rates, and the disappearance of interest rates spreads between EMU countries, encouraged some states to access cheaper credit through borrowing within the monetary union. There is a wide consensus that in the Eurozone this lending/borrowing dynamic was particular important in contributing to the euro debt crisis, at least at the beginning (Baldwin et al., 2015).[38]

According to a study by the ECB (Rodriguez-Palenzuela et al., 2016),[39] the correlation between the lending/borrowing position of a country and its saving/investment balance is empirically observed within the Eurozone.[40] A number of euro countries saw large net foreign capital inflows, well above euro area levels, into their private and public consumption sectors, as reflected in relatively low saving rates. Conversely, the net lending position that was registered in other countries mainly reflected high savings rates. More precisely, these flows of capital took a geographical pathway within the Eurozone from its core (Germany, Netherlands, Austria, Luxemburg, Finland, Belgium) to the periphery (Greece, Cyprus, Portugal, Latvia, Spain, Estonia, Slovakia, Italy).

---

[37] Blanchard O. and Giavazzi F. (2002), "Current Account Deficits in the Euro Area", *Brookings Papers on Economic Activity*, Vol. 2002, No. 2, pp. 147-186.

[38] Baldwin R. et al. (2015), *Reeboting the Eurozone: Step I – Agreeing a Crisis Narrative*, CEPR Policy Insight n. 85, https://cepr.org/sites/default/files/policy_insights/PolicyInsight85.pdf (Accessed October 14, 2021).

[39] Rodriguez-Palenzuela D., Dées S., Andersson M. et al. (2016), *Savings and Investment Behaviour in the Euro Area*, Occasional Paper Series 167, Frankfurt am Main: European Central Bank.

[40] Developments in savings and investment are closely related to the interactions an economy has with the foreign sector. Whenever the macroeconomic equilibrium between savings and investment is not guaranteed domestically, the foreign sector plays a role in filling the domestic gap. In fact, the difference between domestic

It is interesting to note the sectorial direction that the flows followed. The crucial aspect of the lending to the periphery was the misallocation of resources towards the least productive sectors. The funds were channelled into the construction sector, thus fuelling an unsustainable boom in housing, and government consumption sectors.

A macroeconomic imbalance between investment and savings is understood by some analysts to be determined not by the behaviour of agents, but by policy or institutional decisions that affect savings rates in one country as well as, through trade relations, the macroeconomic equilibrium of others (Pettis, 2013).[41] In this perspective, European problems after the financial crisis are seen as related to relative competitiveness within Europe, and are simply a consequence of domestic trade imbalances. For Pettis, "abnormal savings rate over long period of time are largely consequences of trade and industrial policies at home and abroad that have distorted the relationship between domestic production and sustainable domestic production." (Pettis, 2013, p. 127). In particular, he refers to Germany, which after reunification in the early 1990s, pursued policies aimed at generating rapid employment growth by restraining consumption in order to subsidise German manufacturing, resulting in large trade surpluses. As a rule, in an open system an increase in the gap between German savings and investment in one country must be matched by an opposite shift in the gap elsewhere. Furthermore, high and sustained net lending positions in Eurozone core countries were linked to internal dynamics, partly associated with demographic trends in the form of aging populations and structurally weak demand. In the case of peripheral countries, one explanation underpinning this issue of the quality of investment prior to the crisis is given by Celi et al. (2018, p. 69): "in the absence of a policy aimed at strengthening the industrial base of the receiving countries, capital finances mainly real estate business that provides the financial system with a collateral that is considered safer than the more uncertain alternative uses".

---

savings and investment is equal to the net borrowing/lending position with respect to the rest of the world. Accordingly, in cases where domestic investment is higher than domestic savings the economy has to rely on net borrowing to finance its growth, while the opposite holds for economies acting as net lender, since they have an excess of savings.

41 Pettis M. (2013), *The Great Rebalancing: Trade, Conflict, and the Perilous Road Ahead for the World Economy*, Princeton University Press.

2.9 The adjustment process after the crisis

With the onset of the financial crisis these savings-investment and current account patterns proved unsustainable, with a sudden reversal of private capital flows away from stressed countries. When the financial crisis started, there was a *sudden stop* in lending, with investors becoming reluctant to invest abroad. An analysis of the aggregate adjustment process after the crisis clearly shows the way the macroeconomic equilibrium in the Eurozone responded to the financial crisis. Initially, the private sector went through a reduction of consumption and an increase of savings, rising from 1,7 % of GDP in 2008 to 6,7 % in 2009; this was almost entirely offset by an increase in government deficits, while the foreign sector played a limited role (Saraceno 2018, p. 57). However, in the second phase of the crisis, private savings began to decrease, while at the same time public spending reduced due to fiscal consolidation measures imposed by austerity measures. As a result, a modest growth recovery was made possible by exports, with an aggregate current account surplus at 3 % in 2017.

In conclusion, the rebalancing process in the most affected countries worked by means of a deflationary adjustment, caused by a reduction of unit labour cost, a process called internal devaluation, making economies more competitive. In other words, the decrease in demand led to an increase in unemployment, which reduced wages and thus price inflation. In turn, this had an effect on the current account since the reduction of prices stimulated an increase of exports whereas the reduction of demand spurred a decrease of imports. It has been estimated that in order to eliminate the current account deficits accumulated in periphery countries a reduction of GDP by 47 % would be necessary, due to a decrease of internal demand (Stockhammer and Sotiropoulos, 2014).[42] Therefore, any faith placed in the self-stabilising properties of market price adjustment as a source of rebalancing must take into consideration the considerable costs these entail; these must be seriously weighed-up in the way the EU policy package faces asymmetric shocks.

These adjustments were also driven by a severe decline in investment, not only in stressed countries, but also in other euro countries, although of a smaller magnitude. The fiscal consolidation process that

---

42 Stockhammer E. and Sotiropoulos D. (2014), "Rebalancing the Euro Area: The Costs of Internal Devaluation", *Review of Political Economy*, Vol. 26, No. 2, pp. 210-233. DOI: 10.1080/09538259.2014.881011.

over-indebted countries went through was the other channel that served the macroeconomic adjustment process, with public investment particularly penalised by consolidation efforts. The decline has been higher in the Eurozone countries then elsewhere (Rubio et al., 2016).[43] If at the beginning of the crisis large cuts in public investment were generally observed (according to the OECD, about 25 % of fiscal consolidation affected investment), since 2012 public investment has improved in developed countries, regaining 2015 levels, while a marked drop was still recorded in the Eurozone's periphery.

43 Rubio E., Rinaldi D. and Pellerin-Carlin T. (2016), *Investment on Europe: Making the Best of the Juncker Plan*, Studies & Reports No. 109, Paris: Notre Europe Jacques Delors Institute.

Chapter 3
Investment and the financial crisis

3.1 Growth and investment trends before and after the financial crisis

Investment is a good indicator for assessing macroeconomic conditions. It is also the most volatile variable in reflecting economic fluctuations; developments that took place before and after the financial crisis were particularly reflected by investment activities (Koll, 2015).[1] A look at the long-term trend in the EU shows that investment developments were coherent with the overall economic background, and generally over-reacted to output variations. Specifically, investment fell strongly during recession, more than overall output, and recovered when the cycle became more mature.

Some characteristic markers can be seen before and after the financial crisis. In the decade before the creation of the EMU, those countries that eventually took part in the euro area recorded investment growth rates that were higher than those experienced for example in the UK (a non-euro country), but significantly lower than those in the US. After 2000, growth rates saw a dramatic deceleration, in part due to the financial crisis. Between 2011 and 2014 investment recovered well in in the US and UK, while in the EU they slowly improved, whereas they continued to decline in the Eurozone. This is explained by the fact that although the global financial crisis drew policy stances around the world based on massive responses, the measures adopted by the US and other advanced economies were bolder and more reactive in comparison to the EU. European countries all followed a similar pattern by adopting

---

1 Koll W. (2015), "Investment in the European Union – Beyond the Juncker Plan", in Austrian Federal Ministry of Science, Research and Economy (ed.), *Investing in Europe's Future˙ Restarting the Growth Engine*, Wien: Federal Ministry of Science, Research and Economy.

a standard *Keynesian sequence* – an initial monetary response, followed by fiscal expansion when the former lost its impact – but later and on a smaller scale, pursuing what is known as the *too little too late* approach (Saraceno, 2016).[2]

The period from the mid-1980s until the end of 1990s, known as the Great Moderation, was characterised by the relative stability of significant macroeconomic aggregates, due to a reduction in the volatility of business cycle fluctuations in developed nations as compared with the previous decades.

In contrast, the years after the introduction of the euro were characterised by massive fluctuations, due to a range of upheavals, like the collapse of the New Economy bubble and, even more significantly, the financial and euro area crisis, which have had a deeply decelerating impact on growth. After these crises, but before the outbreak of the Covid-19 crisis, the European economy went through a phase of recovery from the financial crisis, with consecutive years of growth, declining unemployment rates and improvements in public finances.

However, since 2018, economic as well as investment growth rates have weakened, and have been affected by a much less supportive economic and geopolitical environment. In particular, trade tensions and the uncertainty defined by the rivalries between the US and China affected the European manufacturing sector (European Commission, 2019e).[3] As a result, after a period of recovery from 2014, by 2018 the EU, and the EMU in particular, were in a phase of more subdued growth, which was followed by a sharp fall caused by the sudden outbreak of the Covid-19 crisis (Tabs. 3.1 and 3.2).

Even despite a favourable macroeconomic context, due to an expansionary monetary policy carried out by the ECB through its Quantitative Easing (QE) programmes, historically low interest rates and weak euro exchange rates, investment in Europe has been a concern in recent years,

---

[2] Saraceno F. (2016), *When Keynes Goes to Brussels: A New Fiscal Rule for the EMU*, SciencesPo publications n. 32, https://ideas.repec.org/p/spo/wpmain/infohdl2441-19jos6046o8m6qe8fce98t1bmp.html (Accessed October 14, 2021).

[3] European Commission (2019e), *Annual Sustainable Growth Strategy 2020*, Bruxelles: European Commission, https://ec.europa.eu/info/sites/default/files/2020-european-semester-annual-sustainable-growth-strategy_en.pdf (Accessed October 14, 2021).

Tab. 3.1: Real GDP growth rates (% change), selected countries

	Five years average						Autumn forecast			
	2001–05	2006–10	2011–15	2016	2017	2018	2019	2020	2021	2022
EU27	1,7	1	1	2	2,8	2,1	1,5	-7,4	4,1	3
EMU	1,5	0,8	0,8	1,9	2,6	1,9	1,3	-7,8	4,2	3
Germany	0,5	1,2	1,7	2,2	2,6	1,3	0,6	-5,6	3,5	2,6
France	1,7	0,8	1	1,1	2,3	1,8	1,3	-9,4	5,8	3,1
Italy	0,9	-0,3	-0,7	1,3	1,7	0,9	0,3	-9,9	4,1	2,8
Spain	3,3	1	0	3	3	2,4	2	-12,4	5,4	4,8
Portugal	0,9	0,6	-0,8	2	3,5	2,8	2,2	-9,3	5,4	3,5
Ireland	5,3	0,4	6,8	2,7	9,1	8,5	5,6	-2,3	2,9	2,6
Greece	3,9	-0,3	-4	-0,5	1,3	1,6	1,9	-9	5	3,5
US	2,6	0,9	2,2	1,6	2,4	2,9	2,3	-4,6	3,7	2,5
Japan	1,2	0,1	1	0,5	2,2	0,3	0,7	-5,5	2,7	0,9

Source: Statistical Annex, European Economic Forecast, Autumn 2020.

Tab. 3.2: Investment growth rate (% change), selected countries

	Five years average						Autumn forecast			
	2001–05	2006–10	2011– 15	2016	2017	2018	2019	2020	2021	2022
EU27	1,4	-0,2	0,8	3,3	4,1	3,5	5,7	-10,3	5,6	4,2
EMU	1,2	-0,6	0,4	4	3,8	3,2	5,8	-11,2	6,1	4,2
Germany	-2	1,5	2,1	3,8	2,5	3,5	2,5	-3,8	2,8	2,7
France	1,9	0,5	0,5	2,7	4,7	3,2	4,2	-10,9	10,8	1,7
Italy	1,8	-1,9	-3,7	4	3,2	3,1	1,6	-13,6	7,2	5,6
Spain	5,4	-3,5	-2,1	2,4	6,8	6,1	2,7	-17,3	3,8	8,5
Portugal	-1,9	-1,2	-5,6	2,5	11,5	6,2	5,4	-10,2	6,3	5,2
Ireland	9,1	-7,7	14,6	50,6	0	-6,3	74,9	41,3	15,3	13,5
Greece	1,9	-2,3	-11,9	2,3	8,1	-6,6	-4,6	-8	5,5	4
US	2,8	-2,7	4,7	1,9	3,7	4,1	1,8	-3,6	1,6	2,7
Japan	-0,9	-3,4	3	-0,3	3	0,6	1,3	-1,3	2,4	0,8

Source: Statistical Annex, European Economic Forecast, Autumn 2020.

and still remains a critical issue for recovery, and for shaping economic growth in the direction of environmental and social sustainability.

The need for more investment in Europe (both private and public) has become a recurrent issue since the outbreak of the financial and economic crisis, as it caused a strong contraction in investment, a decline of growth, and a rise in unemployment. Put simply: the Great Recession.

Immediately after the outbreak of the financial crisis, economic recovery in Europe was slow and falls in investment were pinpointed as one of the causes of lacklustre growth. While real GDP had grown by 2,5 % on average between 1998 and 2008, after the financial crisis growth briefly resumed in 2010, but entered a new recession in 2012/13. At the same time, investment as a share of GDP declined.

In 2019 total investment was still below pre-crisis period levels, but was slowly recovering, in particular in the Eurozone countries, where investment as a share of GDP has always been a bit higher than in the EU (Fig. 3.1).

Between 2002 and 2008, the average level of total investment in EU Member States was 22 % of GDP, with a peak in 2007 of almost 23 %, followed by a sharp decline to its lowest level in 2013 (19,6 %). This was not the first time that Europe had seen rises and falls in investment; between 2000 and 2002, after the dotcom bubble of 1999-2000, the level of investment decreased from 22,7 % to 21,5 %, without however matching the scale of the fall that the Eurozone experienced during the last decade.

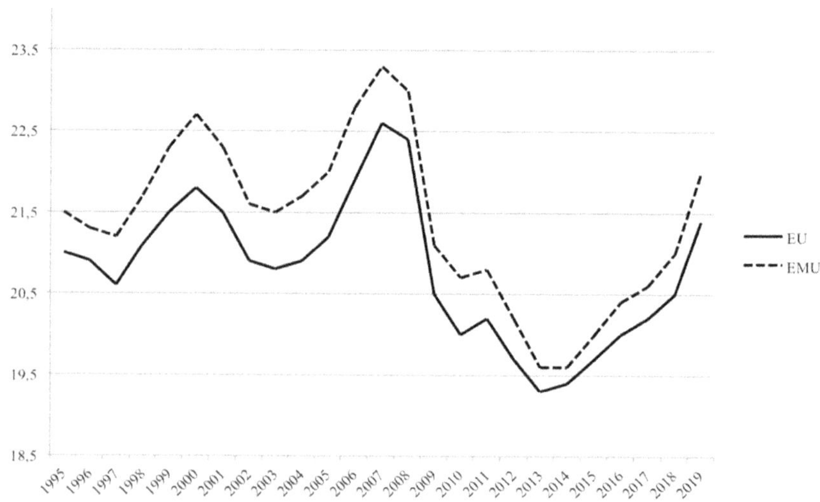

Fig. 3.1: Total investment in EU and Eurozone (% of GDP) (1995-2019)
Source: Eurostat

3.2 Investment: The missing part of the narrative

In response to this situation, the European institutions agreed to build a common framework to identify and stimulate investments commonly qualified as able to contribute to a sustainable growth path in the future. The renewed interest in a European initiative, in particular for private investment, was illustrated by the words of the former President of the European Commission, Jean Claude Juncker: "Investment was in the past the missing part of our economic narrative: yes, we need to step up structural reforms, to enrich the job and productivity potential of the economy; yes, we need to pursue fiscal responsibility, and keep public finances sustainable; but we also need to restore investment levels, to overcome the crisis, kick-start growth and sustain it" (Juncker, 2015).[4]

From this time onwards, we have seen the emergence of a vast economic policy debate on investment covering a range of different aspects. The first one relates to the existence, and the measurement, of an *investment gap* in Europe. This gap can be defined in historical terms, as the difference between pre-crisis and current investment levels. Although it is difficult to estimate the precise extent of the gap, some authors look at the long-term rate of investment as an approximation of the issue. Different estimations show that the gap with respect to the long-term investment is between 240 and €380 bn.[5] The European Commission expected that EU investment levels should be about 21 % of GDP to be sustainable in the long run, therefore estimating a gap between €270-330 bn. per year.[6] This estimate is consistent with those related to the global

---

4 Juncker J. C. (2015), "Preface", in Austrian Federal Ministry of Science, Research and Economy (ed.), *Investing in Europe's Future. Restarting the Growth Engine*, Wien: Federal Ministry of Science, Research and Economy.

5 For example, Dauderstädt M. (2015), *How to Close the European Investment Gap*, Bruxellles: Friedrich Ebert Shiftung, https://brussels.fes.de/fileadmin/public/editorfiles/publications/562_European_investment-june_adpt.pdf – Accessed October 14, 2021) calculates that the gap with respect to the pre-crisis period is around 300 billions euro annually, but it raises to 450 billions if one consider the peak level of 2007. Even when the investment in construction, a large share of the total, is excluded, the gap still amounted at 160 billions euro (Wolff G. (2015), "The Juncker Plan – No Risk, No Return", in Austrian Federal Ministry of Science, Research and Economy (ed.), *Investing in Europe's Future. Restarting the Growth Engine*, Wien: Federal Ministry of Science, Research and Economy).

6 European Commission and EIB (2015), *Why Does the EU Need an Investment Plan?, Factsheet 1*, https://ec.europa.eu/info/sites/default/files/factsheet1-why_en.pdf (Accessed October 14, 2021).

investment to GDP ratio that was 22 % in 2013.[7] However, efforts to measure the investment gap rely on an implicit assumption that more investment is always better, meaning that the pre-crisis levels must be restored. This argument neglects the fact that in some countries the high level of investment was in those sectors that do little to create conditions to sustainable growth, so the comparison with the peak level reached just before the crisis is inappropriate (Gros, 2015).[8]

In fact, the 2007 investment boom (22,6 % of GDP in the EU and 23,3 % in the Eurozone) coincided with a peak in the credit and housing boom in some countries, with negative consequences on current account imbalances that the introduction of the euro had helped to create. This suggests that it is important to go beyond a simple analysis of a narrow measurement of the investment gap with respect to pre-crisis levels, and to consider, for example, long-term demographic projections. With an ageing population, the growth rate of the working age population falls and so does the potential growth rate of the economy, meaning that the equilibrium investment to GDP ratio is lower.

In relation to the second aspect of the investment discussion, it is also important to look at the qualitative dimension of investment. While immediately after the financial crisis the priority was to close the gap with both past European dynamics, and trends observed in other countries – notably the US – in more recent years the focus has been about allocation, which sectors investment should focus on to pursue sustainable growth. Part of the discussion looked at investment as a driver for the EU's international competitiveness, particularly in comparison to the US where companies have performed better in reducing the investment gap. In addition, there has been an emphasis on public investment, which has a broader scope, as "public intervention targeting social challenges such as education and climate change has the potential to create economic growth as a super dividend on an already desirable investment

---

7 This global estimate comprehends both cases like US, Japan and Russia with ratios similar to the global value, and cases like those of India and China, with very high rates (around 30 and 45 % respectively), that are to a large extent driven by FDI.

8 Gros D. (2015), "Investment as the Key to Recovery in the Euro Area?", in Austrian Federal Ministry of Science, Research and Economy (ed.), *Investing in Europe's Future. Restarting the Growth Engine*, Wien: Federal Ministry of Science, Research and Economy.

in itself." (Losch, 2015, p. 8).[9] To achieve this outcome, additional effort is needed, beyond reducing investment gaps as compared with past levels. As already mentioned, empirical evidence suggests there are types of investment that are more likely to produce high returns and sustainable growth. The gap could be re-evaluated in terms of what would be needed to cover, for example, potential infrastructure needs (tangible or intangible) or to achieve a zero-carbon economy.

3.3 The reasons for low investment

Understanding the reasons for low investment allows us to tackle the issue with a multidimensional approach, explaining why in presence of large excessive savings, as is the case today, the required productive investment continues to be insufficiently available. There are various explanations behind the weak EU investment trend, which concern both short and long term dynamics (Rubio et al., 2016).

One of the main drivers is sluggish growth, observed during crises, which is considered at the same time a cause and a consequence of weak investment. From a Keynesian perspective, the fall in investment could be part of a vicious circle where weak market performance in the short term induces the business sector to postpone or delete scheduled investment, thus in turn driving down economic growth. In addition to weak market prospects, the de-leveraging process put in place by households, firms and government, which cut investment and other forms of spending to fund the repair of their balance sheets after years of unsustainable accumulation of debt, has negatively affected investment rates (see Section 4.2).

When we look at the Eurozone, a public sector de-leveraging process is a necessary consequence of the requirement for fiscal consolidation. As a response to the crisis, in particular the sovereign debt crisis, fiscal consolidation was implemented. Budgetary pressures have led to myopic policymaking in which governments cut public investment in

---

9 Losch M. (2015), "Introduction: The economic policy debate on investment", in Austrian Federal Ministry of Science, Research and Economy (ed.), *Investing in Europe's Future. Restarting the Growth Engine*, Wien: Federal Ministry of Science, Research and Economy.

order to achieve savings. As Buti and Mohl (2014)[10] have observed, the decline in public investment is mainly the result of the sovereign debt crisis, but to some extent also reflects a process that began before the crisis, namely the shifting of parts of public investment, like sections of health, education, and transport infrastructure, to the private sector. Finally, high political uncertainties, as was the case after the sovereign debt crisis of 2010-2011, have also played a role in hampering a higher level of investment.

3.4 Investment developments at sectorial and country level

In the EU, investments in the economy are mainly made by the firm sector, accounting for almost 13 % of GDP in 2018, followed by households (5 %) and public investment (2,89 %) As Fig. 3.2 shows, private investment rose before the financial crisis, collapsed in 2007 and recovered substantially in the following years, almost reaching the pre-crisis level. However, despite these trends of increasing investment, a survey by the EIB revealed that the need for further investment perceived by EU firms remains unchanged, with perceived shortfalls driven by firms' fears that they could fall behind in terms of technology and competitiveness (EIB, 2018).[11] The quality of their machinery and equipment is not perceived to be state-of-the-art; improvements would entail more investment in digital technologies, but, as the survey reports, one of the main obstacles is limited availability of staff with appropriate skills.

---

10 Buti M. and Mohl P. (2014), *Lacklustre Investment in the Eurozone: Is There a Puzzle?,* VOXeu.org CEPR, https://voxeu.org/article/raising-investment-eurozone (Accessed October 14, 2021).

11 EIB (2018), *Investment Report 2018/2019: Retooling Europe's Economy – Key Findings,* Luxembourg: European Investment Bank. DOI: 10.2867/592592.

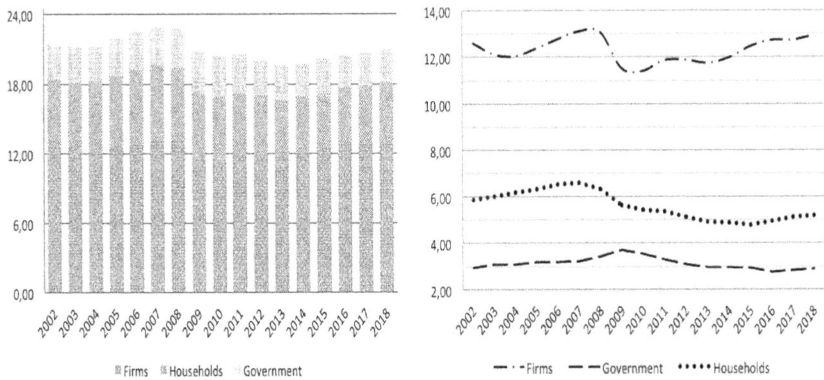

Fig. 3.2: EU total investment (by sector, % on GDP, 2002-2018)

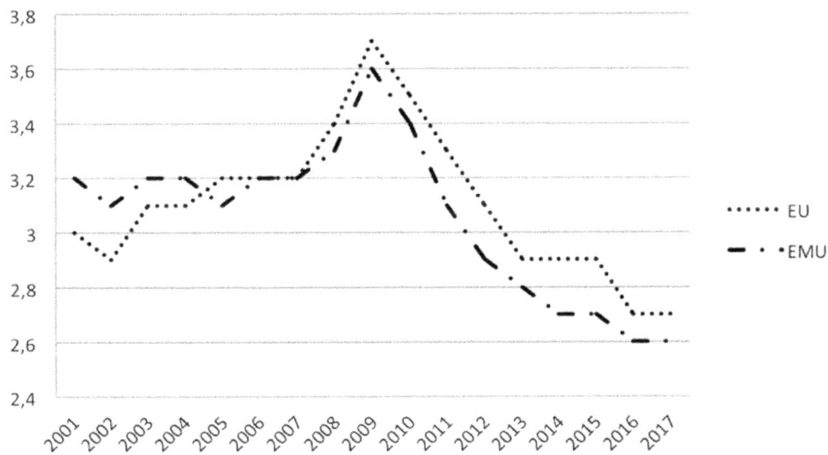

Fig. 3.3: Public investment trends in the EU and the EMU (% of GDP, 2001-2017)

On the other hand, public investment has shown similar high and low trends, closely aligned to the financial crisis, it never returned to its pre-crisis level, reaching its lowest level in 2018 both in the EU (2,8 % of GDP), and in the EMU (2,6 %), where the collapse was more evident (Fig. 3.3), especially in the periphery states.

As regards public investment, and in terms of functions, infrastructure accounts for half of EU public investment (1,4 % of GDP in 2017), with traditional infrastructure accounting for nearly one third and social infrastructure for less than a fifth of the total. The allocation for public goods accounts for one third (0,90 %), while redistribution function covers the smallest part (0,40 %) (Fig. 3.4).

At the level of the Member States, aggregate investment trends hide some differences; total investment as a percentage of GDP falls everywhere (the only exception is Malta), with rate of fall below the EU average in the majority of countries (Fig. 3.5).

In absolute terms, however, EU countries performed quite differently (Fig. 3.6). Although the majority of them showed negative changes after the crisis, in a few cases large increases were recorded. The pattern of investment trends is in some sense coherent with the traditional classification of EU Member States, notably southern, eastern and northern countries. The first group, states which have been most affected by the crisis, and are part of the EMU, are those where investment has declined dramatically, while for the second and third group the picture is more varied. Only northern countries can be considered on average more resilient in terms of investment.

At the sectorial level, a distinction between private and public investment reveals some common features within each group of countries.

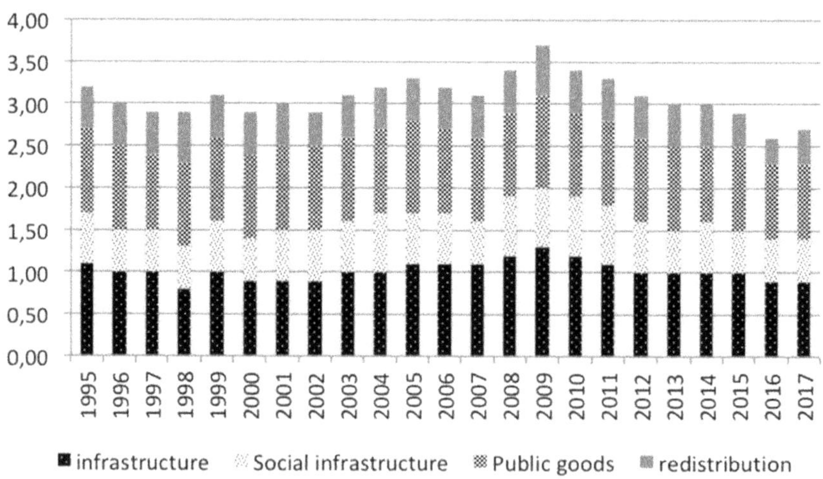

Fig. 3.4: Public investment by function (% of GDP, 1995-2017)

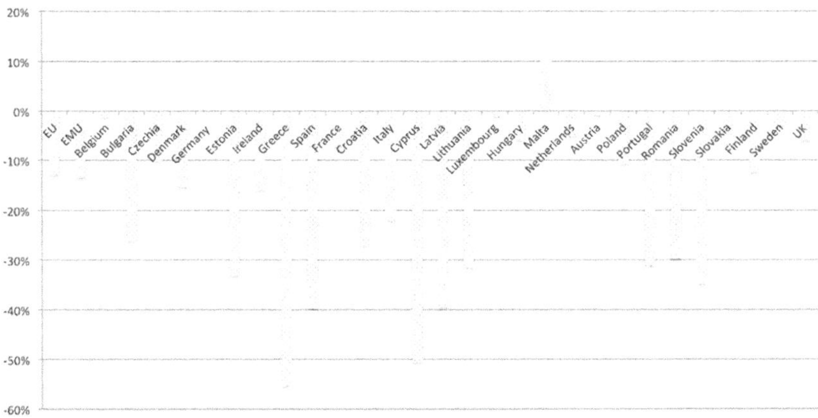

Fig. 3.5: Gross fixed capital formation % of GDP (% change 2007-2015)
Source: AMECO

For the group of euro area countries heavily hit by the crisis,[12] both private and public investments have fallen significantly after the crisis (see Fig. 3.7). This was particularly striking for private investment, reflecting a rapid adjustment of capital stock following an investment boom before the crisis, notably in construction and to a lesser extent in equipment, in particular in the wake of competitiveness losses before the crisis associated with rising unit labour costs, with the exception of Ireland. Public investment also declined with the crisis and the ensuing fiscal consolidation process required by fiscal rules;

In east European countries investment has performed slightly better than in the south, although most of these *catching-up* countries also saw a decrease in private investment, while public investment has been more resilient and increased in almost all cases (Fig. 3.8). The better performance is partly explained by the role played by European funds, as these countries are large beneficiaries of EU budget payments.

Core EMU countries and other north EU countries[13] were affected by the investment gap at a lower magnitude with respect to the other two groups (Fig. 3.9). However, there are different patterns across countries

[12] Cyprus, Greece, Spain, Ireland, Italy, Portugal.

[13] Austria, Belgium, Denmark, Germany, Finland, France, Luxembourg, the Netherlands, Sweden and the United Kingdom.

Fig. 3.6: Gross fixed capital formation (% change 2007-2015, constant prices 2015)
Source: AMECO

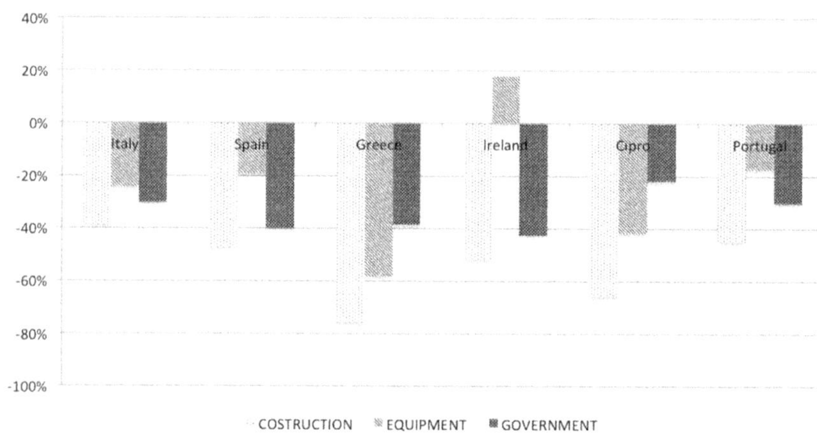

Fig. 3.7: Investment by sector (% change 2007-2018, South countries, constant prices 2015)
Source: AMECO

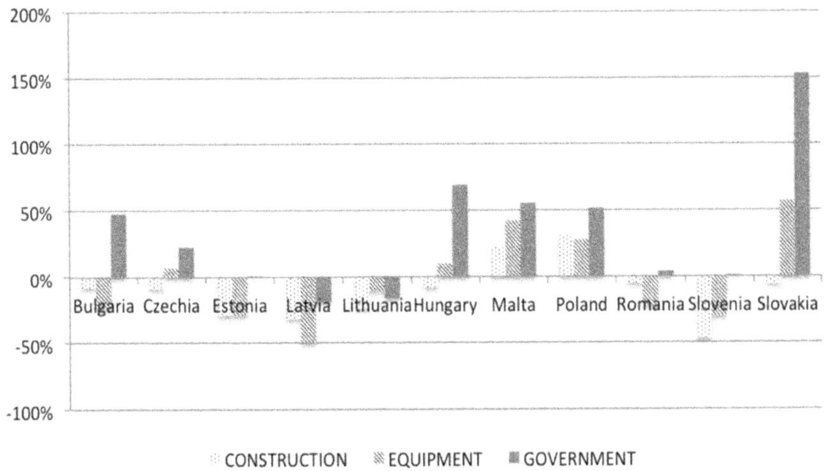

Fig. 3.8: Investment by sectors (% change 2007-2018, catching-up countries, constant prices 2015)

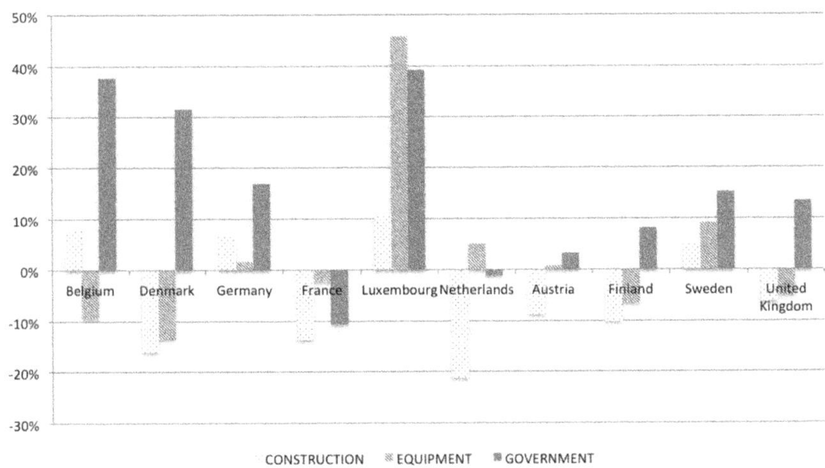

Fig. 3.9: Investment by sector (% change 2007-2018, core countries, constant prices 2015)
Source: AMECO

in this group in terms of the level and composition of investment. In particular, public investment was relatively low, even before the crisis in countries like Germany and Belgium, well under the EMU level.

3.5 Long terms causes: Secular stagnation and financialization

The low level of investment can also be considered against the backdrop of a more secular trend, and a broader macroeconomic framework, when two sides of the same coin – investment and savings – are considered. The financial crisis, with its protracted period of stagnation, has stimulated a debate among economists on the possibility that advanced economies may not be able to return to the growth performance experienced in the period of the Great Moderation, which started in the mid-1980s with stable growth, low inflation and low volatility of business cycle fluctuations. Some scholars have tried to explain the situation of low growth, low inflation and low interest rates by reviving the *secular stagnation* hypothesis. This seeks to explain economic developments, not only in the euro area but in advanced economies in general, as a long-term dynamic, beyond the *hysteresis* argument, which emphasises the persistence of the recession as a consequence of the crisis (Teulings and Baldwin, 2014).[14]

According to secular stagnation theory, advanced economies suffer from an imbalance resulting from an increasing propensity to save and a decreasing propensity to invest. The result is excess savings which tends to drive the natural interest rates (i.e. the interest rate level where savings are equal to investment) down, possibly even into negative territory, inducing a low growth and low inflation environment. Given the zero lower bound that binds nominal interest rates, it is difficult for central banks to sufficiently lower real interest rates to raise investment to a level compatible with full employment.

From a demand side perspective, the drivers of secular stagnation are factors that are structural, and difficult to reverse, which exert downward

---

[14] Teulings C. and Baldwin R. (2014), *Secular Stagnation: Facts, Causes, and Cures*, London: CEPR; VoxEU.org Book.

pressure on the natural interest rate. According to Summers (2014),[15] various elements have increased the propensity of population in developed countries to save: an ageing population, which increases the need to save for retirement; increases in inequality with a higher concentration of income to the richest, which typically show a higher propensity to save; greater uncertainty about the age of retirement and the availability of pensions, which increases the need to save for retirement; reductions in the ability to borrow, and a greater accumulation of assets by foreign central banks and sovereign wealth funds; persistent de-leveraging efforts by households, that reduce aggregate demand and by that the natural rate of interest.

The decline of investment in advanced economies has also been linked with an increase in the share of total output represented by sectors that have lower investment rates over time, namely business and real estate services, or public administration. One consequence of such sectorial reallocation of resources, called *servicification*, would be, in principle, a lower need for investment. However, in Europe, such trend has not been clearly observed (European Commission, 2017a).[16] Here what has been found is that the change in aggregate investment rates is mainly due to a *within effect*, instead of a reallocation effect; this means that the main driver of investment evolution in the EU was the intrinsic performance of the investment itself, and not the shift of economic activity towards less capital-intensive sectors.

Other explaining factors, from the supply side perspective, concern technological progress. Here worries have emerged about the ability of the digital and Information and Communication Technologies (ICT) revolution to parallel the exceptionally high productivity gains reaped in the period between the 1920s and 1970s (Gordon, 2012).[17] A structural reduction of investment has been driven by reduced dynamic

---

15 Summers, L. H. (2014), *Reflections on the 'New Secular Stagnation Hypothesis'*, VoxEU CEPR, https://voxeu.org/article/larry-summers-secular-stagnation (Accessed October 14, 2021).

16 European Commission (2017a), *Investment in the EU Member States. An Analysis of Drivers and Barriers*, Institutional Paper No. 062, Luxembourg: Publications Office of the European Union, https://ec.europa.eu/info/sites/default/files/ip062_en.pdf (Accessed October 15, 2021).

17 Gordon R. (2012), *Is U.S. Economic Growth Over? Faltering Innovation Confronts The Six Headwinds*, NBER Working Paper 18315, Cambridge: National Bureau Of Economic Research, https://www.nber.org/system/files/working_papers/w18315/w18315.pdf (Accessed October 15, 2021).

technological progress, that generates fewer attractive investment opportunities. Furthermore, we have seen lower growth in the labour force, with a reduction of the share of working people in the total population; this is an inverse shift in what Gordon (2012) called the *demographic dividend*, which is no longer observable.[18] Lastly, the availability of cheaper capital goods is a factor, as any given level of investment can be reached by means of fewer resources, and tighter credit, as lending has become more highly regulated than before, again contributing to lower investment.

All these factors are long-term trends to which are added short- and medium-term elements, arising from the persistence of the recession, thus contributing to the decline in productivity growth and interest rates in the aftermath of the crisis. In this *hysteresis* perspective, the total effect of these factors on productivity results not only from long-term developments, but also fluctuates pro-cyclically as the key drivers of technological progress, like R&D expenditure, increase during upswings and fall during downturns. Therefore, the use of *hysteresis* can explain the acceleration of both a slowdown in productivity growth, and a decline in the natural rate of interest within a framework of persistent sluggishness.

From this perspective, expansion can occur even in an environment of secular stagnation, as the case was for the Eurozone in the last years before the pandemic outbreak, even if the basic conditions for secular stagnation, like an ageing population or technological pessimism, have not been removed (Schmöller, 2018).[19] As soon as these key structural factors change, the natural interest rate will increase, bringing the economy closer to normal territory.

---

18 The demographic dividend is defined as "the economic growth potential that can result from shifts in a population's age structure, mainly when the share of the working-age population (15-64) is larger than the non-working-age share of the population (14 and younger, and 65 and older)." (see United Nation Population Fund (UNFPA) website, https://www.unfpa.org/demographic-dividend – Accessed October 15, 2021). Recent developments show an inverse shifting, as the share of working people in the total population is decreasing with respect to the young and the retired, resulting in a declining worked hours per capita. The reduction in human capital accumulation reduces the potential growth.

19 Schmöller M. (2018), *Secular Stagnation: A False Alarm in the Euro Area?*, Bank of Finland Bulletin No. 4, https://www.bofbulletin.fi/en/2018/4/secular-stagnation-a-false-alarm-in-the-euro-area/ (Accessed October 15, 2021).

In addition to these structural aspects, the long-term process of financialization has also had negative implications on investment. The diffusion of financialization that started in early 1980s in the US, with a combination of high interest rates and strong fiscal expansion, created punishing conditions for productive investment. There are two possible interpretations of the relation between financialization and investment in the real sector (Celi et al., 2018). First, in the US profit margins in the non-financial sector started to fall from the 1970s, a tendency associated with economic stagnation, due to income inequality and underconsumption, or the exhaustion of profitable market opportunities. In this environment of falling profits, decisions on investment increasingly favoured finance, facilitated by financial concessions and deregulation. Second, in the era of the introduction of new business models based on information and communication technology, the aim of firms became shareholder value maximisation, which produced widespread *short termism*. The consequence was a higher propensity to shift resources from long-term real investment towards short-term financial transactions, with the sole intention of supporting the value of shares for fund managers. Although the two interpretations assume opposing causal links – either financialization derives from unresolved problems of real economy, or is what causes them – in both cases they recognise that long-term periods of stagnation are associated with a declining process of capital accumulation.

In the EU, and in the Eurozone in particular, the secular stagnation hypothesis has been more visible than elsewhere, when comparing the real GDP growth of the US, of the non-euro EU countries and the Eurozone; both prior to and post the global crisis of 2008, the Eurozone shows a slower growth rate.

The Eurozone has suffered a double-dip recession, where the second dip, a sovereign debt crisis, was only present in Europe. The first recession took the form of a subprime crisis, and originated in the financial sector in US, but also had heavy consequences in Europe. The Eurozone countries saw a cumulative drop of 3,7 % of GDP in the years 2007-2008, caused mainly by a reduction of European exports due to the effects of the fall of the GDP in the US, where the crisis in the real sector was caused by the credit restriction implemented by the Federal Reserve after the turmoil in the financial sector with the failure of Lehman Brothers. In 2010 another recession began in the Eurozone countries, especially in southern European states. Here the problem was restricted to the dimension of public sector financial sustainability, indicating a case of sovereign debt crisis, whose origins were linked to the first recession caused by the financial crisis. In fact, the risks of systemic effects originating from the banking crisis required a robust intervention from the public sector that caused increases in public debt.

The second dip was caused by the sovereign debt crisis. Although early explanations of that crisis were based on the rhetoric of profligate behaviour of governments of southern periphery states, later on a group of prominent economists interpreted the double-dip recession as an external imbalances crisis, which bring to the discussion the external relation between countries and the role of the private sector:

> the EZ Crisis should not be thought of as a government debt crisis in its origin – even though it evolved into one. Apart from Greece, the nations that ended up with bailouts were not those with the highest debt-to-GDP ratios. Belgium and Italy sailed into the Crisis with public debts of about 100% of GDP and yet did not end up with Troika programmes, while Ireland and Spain, with ratios under 40%, needed bailouts. The real culprits were the large intra-EZ capital flows that emerged in the decade before the Crisis. These imbalances baked problems into the EZ 'cake' that would explode in the 2010s. All the nations stricken by the Crisis were running current account deficits (Baldwin et al. 2015, p. 2).

One of the main root causes that explains why Europe failed to recover after the financial crisis concerns the growth model followed by the Eurozone since the introduction of the single currency. As Celi et al. (2018) observe, in the Eurozone two different patterns prevail:

> the core countries growth driven by exports of manufactured products and investments (in the Eastern periphery (EP)) aiming at consolidating the German production network; the Southern Periphery (SP) relying mainly on debt-led consumption sustained by financial and housing bubbles. In the South capital inflows finance real estate and consumption, leading to the accumulation of private debt, increasing current account deficit and greater fragility of the production structure. In the EP, FDI (foreign direct investment) contributes to expand and modernize the productive base, strengthening the economy (Celi et al., 2018, p. 96).

In the coming years the dominant model, based on export-led growth, seems less plausible since it will become more difficult to transfer excess production to the rest of the world. Firstly, because of the war on tariffs between the US and China, which threatens to involve Europe as well, with damage to international trade. Secondly, because of the effect of Covid-19, that is pushing towards a re-organisation of global value chains towards local value chains, hence diverting the production of intermediate and capital goods to the internal market. Thirdly, because compensating for a lack of private and public investment now seems to be the only way to counter the secular stagnation we will continue to be subject to in the coming years, especially if we consider the demographic trend that characterises the old continent and which is unlikely to change in the coming decades. Although growth projections give us a picture of buoyant growth, this should not be confused with a phase of a rebound in the economy after a period of severe recession, as was the case after the Eurozone crisis, for expansions can occur even in an environment of secular stagnation, unless the underlying structural conditions change.

3.6 Post Covid-19: Searching for strategic autonomy and trade diversification

The 2008 financial crisis has left Europe in a situation of persistent polarisation between the core and periphery. The core has preserved its industrial base and increased its exports to the periphery and emerging states, while current accounts of periphery countries have only avoided major imbalances because of import reductions, due to lower domestic demand. Since then, economic growth has remained anaemic, and within a framework of secular stagnation, divergences between industrial structures of states continue, with weak countries, regions, industries and firms becoming progressively weaker. Given the high level of interconnections that characterises the European economy, a lower level of demand in those countries also negatively affects richer countries, with the result that all countries will end up with a reduced ability to develop new economic activity. Covid-19, although a symmetric shock affecting the EU equally, has produced different consequences at economic and fiscal levels, fostering concerns of an intensification of divergences.

Europe faces multiple challenges at the internal level that can be summarised as follows: upgrading its economic structure with the creation of new employment activities; extending public action and public goods provision after decades of privatisations and oppressive fiscal rules; reducing the polarisation between core and periphery states emerging from the crisis, moving towards an ecological transformation of the economy and society. However, all these realities could be addressed through a new European industrial policy. This tool could also be an answer to a more fundamental issue, the neoliberalism approach adopted by the EU from the 1980s, when beliefs were strongly held in the market's ability to operate efficiently both in the short- and long-run, to develop new activities and markets. The result was a general departure from industrial policy as a means to steer industrial change and development.

As Mario Pianta has observed (2014),[20] there are manifold reasons to support a role for industrial policy at the European level. A first main issue for industrial policy regards the need to respond to the urgent ecological transformation of Europe's economy and society. The decarbonisation target – to reduce CO_2 emission to net zero – requires a comprehensive approach based on a coherent framework that integrates different policy tools needed for making Europe sustainable, from increasing the use of renewable resources to reducing waste and generalising recycling practices.

Other motives that would justify a common industrial policy are linked to a need to counter the trend, over past decades, of massive liberalisation and privatisations, which has resulted in a lack of long-term vision by businesses, and the dominance of financialization over real sustained investment, employment and sustainable growth. In order to pursue activities in specific sectors, like those related to environment protection and the production of knowledge, as well as services in the health and welfare sectors, substantial action will be required by the public sector at all levels, the EU, national and local. Public action could provide direction to innovation, and synergies between the private and public sectors could increase efficiency over the life of investment projects. Finally, the need to counter divergences between countries, not only in term of industrial structure but also of GDP per-capita, is strong, and even greater as a result of the pandemic crisis.

In March 2020 the Commission presented a communication on the *New Industrial Strategy for Europe*. After the Covid-19 crisis, this strategy was updated, with a strong emphasis on terms like *strategic dependency* and *strategic autonomy*. The pandemic required governments to impose lockdowns on social and economic activity that impacted negatively on global supply chains and led to shortages in Europe. In particular,

---

20 Pianta M. (2014), *An industrial policy for Europe*, Working Paper Series in Economics, Mathematics and Statistics, No. 2014/1, Milan: Università degli Studi "Carlo Bo", http://www.econ.uniurb.it/RePEc/urb/wpaper/WP_14_01.pdf (Accessed October 15, 2021).

disruptions along the supply chain of the health ecosystem, resulting from a combination of surging demand as well as supply and workforce shortages, were particularly challenging for Member States. The pandemic accelerated an awareness of Europe's strategic dependency on the rest of the world with reference to goods and services, notably relating to areas like security, safety and the health of European citizens. Therefore, the assessment of strategic dependency involves not only the identification of dependencies, but also an assessment of whether they are of a strategic nature that leads to a vulnerability for the EU, given the EU's core strategic interests.

Accordingly, the identification of such strategic dependencies give rise to an approach to industrial policy based on the concept of open strategic autonomy, which has been defined in several ways. For example, Anghel et al. (2020, p. 1)[21] describe it as "the ability to act autonomously, to rely on one's own resources in key strategic areas and to cooperate with partners whenever needed". In practice, strategic autonomy does not mean autarchy or sovereignty. Rather, it is about being able to set objectives, make decisions and "mobilise the necessary resources in ways that do not primarily depend on the decisions and assets of others" (Grevi, 2019, p. 10).[22]

From this perspective, the first step for a new European industrial policy would therefore consist of identifying where these precise dependences lie in order to design measures to reduce them. These could mean diversifying production and supply chains, ensuring strategic stockpiling, as well as fostering production and investment in Europe.

According to the Commission, out of 5.200 products imported into the EU, 137 products (representing 6 % of the EU's total import value of goods) are in sensitive ecosystems on which the EU is highly dependent. These are mainly related to energy intensive industries (such as raw materials) and health ecosystems (such as active pharmaceutical ingredients), as well as other products relevant to supporting the green and digital

---

21 Anghel S., Immenkamp B., Lazarou E., Saulnier J. L. and Wilson A. B. (2020), *On the Path to "strategic autonomy": The EU in an Evolving Geopolitical Environment*, Bruxelles: European Parliamentary Research Service. DOI:10.2861/60568.

22 Grevi G. (2019), *Strategic Autonomy for European Choices: The Key to Europe's Shaping Power*, Discussion Paper Europe in the World Programme, Bruxelles: European Policy Centre, https://www.epc.eu/content/PDF/2019/190719_Strategicautonomy_GG.pdf (Accessed October 15, 2021).

transformation. About half of the imports of these dependent products originate in China, followed by Vietnam and Brazil (European Commission, 2021, pp. 22-23).[23]

One solution to managing strategic dependence is to strengthen the Internal Market in such a way as to enhance supply solidarity during crises. Another option is to invest in critical technology areas. In both cases, as one field of strategic interest for Europe is in green and digital transitions, the EU's ability to access inputs, technologies and services that are key to these crucial challenges must be prioritised. Unfortunately, the process of de-industrialisation in Europe has led to manufacturing and skills gaps in key sectors, that need to be countered through important European initiatives under the label Important Projects of Common European Interest (IPCEIs) in areas such as batteries and micro-electronics. As regards the diversification of resource supplies, European strategic autonomy recognises the importance of open trade and trade relations with strategic partners, not only in order to guarantee raw material supplies, but also in terms of other related fields of security, like migration management and geopolitical equilibrium.

Africa is a strategic partner for Europe; the High Representative of the Union for Foreign Affairs and Security Policy, Josep Borrell, underlined the importance of diversification and pointed to a reduction of dependence on China by enhancing trade relations with Africa (Caslin, 2020).[24] However, this change would firstly imply the consideration of the African continent as a partner, and no longer in terms of a beneficiary of development aid. Secondly, the EU would need to evaluate all the risks and benefits that could be associated with such a diversification of supply strategy. According to Fiott and Theodosopoulos (2020),[25] there are three sources of risk to take into consideration, and all of them may have implications for EU-African relations. The first is state fragility, which could undermine EU trade relations with countries embroiled

---

23 European Commission (2021), *Strategic Dependencies and Capacities*, Staff Working Document, SWD (2021) 352 final, Bruxelles: European Commission.

24 Caslin O. (2020), Josep Borrell, chef de la diplomatie européenne: "L'Afrique n'a pas besoin d'un concours de bonté", *JeuneAfrique*, May 6.

25 Fiott D. and Theodosopoulos V. (2020), Sovereignty Over Supply? The EU's Ability to Manage Critical Dependences While Engaging with the World, *EU Institute for Security Studio* (ISS), Brief No. 21, https://www.iss.europa.eu/content/sovereignty-over-supply (Accessed October 15, 2021).

in breakdowns of governance, *coups d'état*, civil war, conflict or disease; this risk is higher for least developed countries, most of them located in Africa. However, the second risk, i.e. economic coercion, seems to be lower in the case of trade relations with African economies, because it is less likely that their governments have the actual capacity to manipulate supply flows and therefore coerce the EU through trade. The third relevant factor to consider is climate vulnerability to shocks like droughts and flooding. These events hit industrial and agricultural production and may aggravate already fragile states. However, the decision of the EU to enhance trade relations with these vulnerable Africa countries could have a positive effect in term of boosting environmental standards and norms as well as climate-related investment, which in turn could lower a country's overall vulnerability.

Chapter 4

Proposals to boost investment in the post-financial crisis

Since the Maastricht Treaty of 1992, the EMU has been built on an asymmetric institutional setting where monetary and fiscal policies are managed in very different ways. On the one hand, for Member States that adopted the euro as their currency, monetary policy has been fully federalised through the creation of a supranational monetary organisation, the ECB. In 2004, a book issued by the ECB rightly observed that there was no other policy area of the EU that had reached the same depth of integration as the single monetary policy; they also argued, in words which seem less valid today, that "Nowhere else has the Community developed its own identity more convincingly than in the euro and the ECB" (Scheller, 2004, p. 12).[1] On the other hand, fiscal policy has remained a national competence, where decisions on public spending and taxes are ultimately taken by governments. In order to keep this incomplete union together, the EU has given Member States fiscal rules, through an intergovernmental means of governance, the open method of coordination, to keep national budgets under control and avoid the risk of inflationary pressure within the Union. In this framework, therefore, Member States have lost control over their currency, meaning that devaluation to stimulate demand in exports is no longer an option, and they are also subject to strict budgetary constraints – the 3 % and 60 % thresholds for budget deficit to GDP and debt to GDP, respectively. They basically have a limited capacity to take counter-cyclical responses to economic busts, while at the EU level a central mechanism to cushion asymmetric shocks (a stabilisation function) is still lacking, although countering the Covid-19 crisis has introduced some tools in this sense.

1 Scheller H. K. (2004), *The European Central Bank. History, Role and Functions*, Frankfurt am Main: European Central Bank.

4.1 Economic surveillance during the financial crisis

The incomplete institutional architecture of the Eurozone has always been a source of concern for scholars, and the financial and sovereign crises have validated these worries. When the sovereign debt crisis hit part of the Eurozone, there was no mechanism at the central level that would allow affected countries to pursue both a process of budgetary consolidation in line with fiscal rules, while having the necessary support from the EU through fiscal measures. The second objective, i.e. stabilisation, would have had an impact on public finances in the opposite direction to fiscal rules. European fiscal constraints have led policy makers to sacrifice public spending, in particular on investment. Fiscal policy has been dominated by consolidation efforts after the sovereign debt, through rescue programmes and/or by the strengthening of the SGP framework. In terms of effort, the overall extent of fiscal consolidation until 2015 was more than 5 % of GDP for the Eurozone on average, with some countries like Greece (23,2 %), and other periphery countries (9,4-11,9 %) particularly affected (Truger, 2015).[2] Of these austerity measures, net investment reductions constituted 20 % of the total for the Euro area, and even more for Spain and Portugal. This was possible as that public investment is not tied to any reference value – unless a rule preserving it is foreseen at the level of the State – and it is politically relatively easy to cut.

The measures that have been undertaken in Europe to respond to the financial crisis brought some changes in the institutional framework of the EU, although innovations introduced since 2010 did not point towards any correction of the asymmetry between monetary and fiscal policy. In the field of crisis prevention measures, there has been a strengthening of macroeconomic surveillance of national fiscal budgets – first through a tightening of the SGP, and then through its constitutionalisation at Member State level – and second with the creation of the European Semester (Fantacci and Papetti, 2013). In particular, the Six and Two-pack regulations issued within the community framework have had a double effect. On the one hand, they introduce more flexibility than the SGP, which was considered too rigid and too binding,

---

2 Truger A. (2015), "Austerity, Cyclical Adjustment and the Remaining Leeway for Expansionary Fiscal Policies within the Current European Fiscal Framework", *Journal for a Progressive Economy*, 6 July, pp. 32-37.

as countries may temporarily deviate from medium-term objectives in the event of a severe recession or extraordinary circumstances. But, on the other hand, these give the Commission a greater role in monitoring public finances, in particular for Eurozone countries. For these Member States, a further intergovernmental agreement, known as the Fiscal Compact, requires the introduction of budget balance into national law, preferably at constitutional level. The European Semester, then, lays the foundations for the governance of the Eurozone against future financial crises, through a cycle of procedures that take place every year to allow the European institutions to directly influence economic policy decisions of EU Member States *ex ante*, i.e., when drafting national budgets for the following year.

As far as crisis management is concerned, there has been a progressive shift away from the community method in favour of the intergovernmental method with the creation of bail-out institutions. A new international organisation, the European Stability Mechanism (ESM), which replaced the European Financial Stability Facility (EFSF), was meant to provide financial assistance to the most affected countries; however, it has shown limits in terms of democratic legitimacy, in particular with regard to its mode of voting and its constitutional basis (Padoa-Schioppa, 2012).[3]

During the crisis, priority was given to keeping public finances under control in the belief that extensive austerity measures would lead to renewed confidence and economic recovery thanks to cutting government spending. In 2012 Paul Krugman mocked the idea of the *confidence fairy*; although this proved to be a failed economic solution during the financial crisis, it now seems difficult to abandon, especially in Europe where "leaders spent years in denial, insisting that their policies would start working any day now, and celebrating supposed triumphs on the flimsiest of evidence" (Krugman, 2012).[4]

On the monetary policy side, the role of the ECB has been increasingly strengthened, through a series of effective measures targeted first at protecting the euro from speculative attack, and second at stimulating

3 Padoa-Schioppa A. (2012), *Il trattato ESM. Osservazioni critiche*, CSF Discussion paper 06, http://www.csfederalismo.it/images/policy_paper/06_a_p_schioppa_it.pdf (Accessed October 15, 2021).

4 Krugman P. (2012), "Death of a Fairy Tale", *The New York Times*, 26 April.

investment in the real sector. In 2012, the famous *whatever it takes* statement by Mario Draghi proved to be truly enough in calming the financial markets and lowering spreads.[5] In practice, the ECB was ready to purchase any amount of public debt securities of countries in difficulties on the market, thus playing the role of lender of last resort for national governments and overcoming Art. 125 of the TFEU, which is colloquially called the *no bailout clause* by the ECB itself.[6] Indeed, after the *whatever it takes* statement monetary policy has played a key role in creating the necessary conditions to prevent the Eurozone from imploding, and subsequently ensured that the cost of public debt remain low, allowing more room for manoeuvre for fiscal policy.

4.2 Not all imbalances are equal

Within this evolving economic governance, however, some progress has been made in recognising, albeit late, the importance of macroeconomic imbalances (see the saving investment relation) in both the public and private sectors, and in particular their impact on the external account of a country. In this way, the Commission should be able to monitor and correct other variables beyond those related to public finances, that are also important in evaluating the general condition of a country.

The Macroeconomic Imbalance Procedure (MIP) aims at identify, prevent and address the emergence of potentially harmful macroeconomic imbalances that could adversely affect economic stability in a particular EU country. It starts with the Alert Mechanism Report (AMR) where the Commission looks at a scoreboard of indicators to gauge whether imbalances might exist in EU countries.[7] Each of the fourteen

---

5 In his speech Mario Draghi said: "Within our mandate, the ECB is ready to do whatever it takes to preserve the euro. And believe me, it will be enough".

6 The *no bail out* clause was introduced in the Treaty to avoid morally hazardous behaviour by Member States, which could not rely on the ECB buying sovereign bonds and prevent speculative attacks, as is normally the case for other central banks around the world.

7 The external and competitiveness dimension of the scoreboard captures the current account, the net international investment position, the export market share, the real effective exchange rate, the harmonised index of consumer prices deflated and the unit labour costs; the internal imbalances perspective is covered by house prices and private sector credit flow as well as private sector debt, public debt, the unemployment rate and total sector financial liabilities. Later in 2016, the Commission added three employment indicators (youth and long-term unemployment and the

indicators (complemented by twenty-five auxiliary indicators) has a threshold attached which should indicate when a country-specific value becomes too high, judged by historical standards. It is interesting to note that within the external dimension, where the current account position and the net international investment position are captured, these thresholds suffer an asymmetry according to the surplus or deficit position of a country. More precisely, a country can have a surplus current account balance (3-year backward moving average) no higher than 6 % of GDP, while it cannot have a deficit higher that 4 %. This provision seems to promote the idea that deficits are more detrimental to an economy than surpluses. However, as we have seen in Chapter 2, a surplus for a country means on the other side a deficit for another country, that could encounter difficulties in terms of growth and excessive foreign debt.

In general, this extension of the scope of monitoring by the Commission – although not necessarily followed up with a stronger sanctioning procedure – is positive practice. However, a very defensive attitude by European institutions is maintained, as unlike fiscal surveillance, they consider it very challenging to evaluate which part of observed adjustments has been achieved by explicit policy measures, as variables such as the unemployment rate, private debt, credit growth or house price growth are only to some extent under the control of policy-makers. And whenever policy action is deemed necessary to correct macroeconomic imbalances, structural reforms to achieve greater competitiveness are mentioned as the preferred strategic approach to pursue macroeconomic corrections (Pierluigi and Sondermann, 2018).[8]

4.3 How to manage a balance sheet recession?

In 2015 the situation in Europe was rather complex. There were some positive aspects: on the one hand, the developing monetary policy stance, and the stabilising fiscal situation in most of the Eurozone countries.

---

activity rate) to the scoreboard, although they do not have the same weight as the other variables as high values *per se* are not seen as an aggravation of macro-financial risks, and consequently are not used to trigger any steps in the MIP.

8 Pierluigi B. and Sondermann D. (2018), *Macroeconomic Imbalances in the Euro Area: Where Do We Stand?*, ECB Occasional paper series No. 211, Frankfurt am Main: European Central Bank, https://www.ecb.europa.eu/pub/pdf/scpops/ecb.op211.en.pdf (Accessed October 15, 2021).

As we have seen, the ECB's intervention in the financial markets was decisive in stifling the risk of the disintegration of the Eurozone, and created the conditions for countries to issue public debt without fear of speculative attacks. However, the fact that on the fiscal side governments had their hands tied in stimulating their economies led to a generalised handicap on economic recovery. On the other hand, negative trends in aggregate demand continued, with weak household and government spending depressing investment outlooks. One of the reasons that reductions in investment were seen in almost all Eurozone countries was the process of de-leveraging, caused by a balance-sheet recession.

Since 2008, both the private sector and governments had accumulated high levels of gross debt. As Koo (2014) [9] explained, when a debt-financed bubble bursts, a large number of businesses and households find themselves with liabilities that are still current in their balance sheets, while on the other side the assets they bought with borrowed funds have collapsed in value. In order to restore their financial situation, they have no choice but to pay off debt using their cash flow. In other words, recovery depends mainly on the resolution of the debt problem.

Once again, in order to support aggregate demand, the ECB intervened massively on the secondary markets with the purchase of long-term public, but also private, securities, decreasing long-term (real) interest rates – the QE programme. The intended effects of such an expansionary measure would be manifold. First, it would stimulate the creation of credit available to banks. Second, the purchasing of private sector securities would reduce the cost of investment, making these more profitable, through a reduction of interest rate costs.[10] Third, QE would have a positive effect on consumption, stimulated by an increase of the value of households financial wealth. Fourth, it would lead to a boost in exports, thanks to a currency depreciation; excess liquidity would also turn towards foreign securities denominated in foreign currency, resulting in a depreciation of the euro.

---

9 Koo R. (2014), *Balance Sheet Recession Is the Reason for 'secular stagnation'*, VoxEU CEPR, https://voxeu.org/article/balance-sheet-recession-reason-secular-stagnation (Accessed October 15, 2021).

10 An investment to be profitable must yield a rate of profit at least equal (if not higher) to the long-term interest rate, which represents the cost of the capital for entrepreneurs. The purchase of securities increases their value leading to a decrease in their yield, that is the interest rate that is paid.

All in all, these measure proved to be ineffective or problematic, and actually postponed the addressing of the problem at the heart of the matter, the need of coordinated fiscal policy. If the economy were going through a de-leveraging process, the QE programme would have had no chance to be successful, because, as Koo argued,

> after the bursting of a nationwide asset price bubble, those with balance sheets under water are not interested in increasing borrowing at any interest rate. There will not be many lenders either, especially when the lenders themselves have balance sheet problems. The lack of borrowers means a significant portion of the newly saved and deleveraged funds that are entrusted to the financial sector are unable to re-enter the real economy. This in turn means that those unborrowed savings become a leakage in the income stream and a deflationary gap for the economy. If left unattended, this deflationary gap will push the economy ever deeper into balance sheet recession, a highly unusual recession that happens only after the bursting of a nationwide asset price bubble (Koo, 2014).

In the post-crisis period all private sectors (households, firms and financial institutions) were committed to saving, while at the same time states' current accounts in the Eurozone were on average in equilibrium, but with countries like Germany and Netherlands carrying current account surpluses. In this situation, possible solutions to restore growth in the Eurozone would need to be of a different nature. One possibility was that those countries with current account surpluses would start to spend and invest more, and reduce their monetary wealth, therefore allowing a process of rebalancing from the side of excess savings. Another solution (possible from a macroeconomic theory perspective, but impossible in the Eurozone experience) is that the public sector might borrow and spend available savings in the private sector, hence offsetting deflationary forces derived from private sector de-leveraging. In general, a wide consensus built up on the need to stimulate investment (both private and public), through a vast programme of investment, in particular in infrastructure.

4.4 Eurobonds, Union bonds and European taxes

The long-standing debate over the issuing of a common instrument able to finance investment has been going on since 1993, when Jacques Delors proposed the idea of European bonds. Ever since, the proposal has been seriously considered, and in particular after the financial and sovereign crisis that made it clear that the absence of any formal pooling of resources required the designing of additional arrangements for fiscal support to respond to countries in crisis. Nevertheless, after the crisis, the focus on common debt quickly shifted towards the issue of debt sustainability of Eurozone countries, rather than the promotion of pan-European investment.

Quadrio Curzio (2011)[11] has clarified the terms and functions of various proposals; this offers useful paths for further development. Two types of bonds, with very different meanings and implications, have basically been under consideration over time: growth bonds and stability bonds. The growth bond model was originally proposed by Jacques Delors in 1993 during his term of office as President of the European Commission. Delors' Union Bonds were a means to finance investment in large infrastructure projects (in fields such as energy, transport, telecommunications and environment), with the aim of stimulating growth by issuing long-term securities, using the EU budget as a collateral. Conversely, the stability bond model has the objective of restructuring the debt of Eurozone countries. In a pioneering contribution, Juncker and Tremonti (2010)[12] warned that the Union should send a strong signal to markets and citizens about its political commitment to economic and monetary union, and the irreversibility of the euro. Accordingly, they advocated the issuance of *European Sovereign Bonds*, issued by a European Debt Agency, which should have replaced the EFSF, i.e. the temporary financial rescue tool later transformed into the ESM. At that time, since great uncertainties and weaknesses threatened the Eurozone, most attention was diverted onto how to stabilise financial markets in the short time, and to improve in the long-run the euro area economic governance framework through a combination of enhanced fiscal discipline and risk-sharing.[13]

The issue of public bonds issued by a European institution has been more strongly influenced by political factors than by economic analysis.

---

[11] Quadrio Curzio A. (2011), "On the Different Types of Eurobonds", *Economia Politica*, Issue 3, December. DOI: 10.1428/35912.

[12] Juncker J.C. and Tremonti G. (2010), "E-bonds Would End the Crisis", *Financial Times*, 5 December.

[13] A review of eurobonds proposal is in Claessens S., Mody A. and Vallée S. (2012), *Paths to Eurobonds*, IMF Working Paper n. 172, Washington, D.C. : International Monetary Fund.

In particular, in the Eurobond debate, the provision in the Maastricht treaty for a cap on public debt should provide sufficient guarantees for fiscal sustainability, and thus help avoid excessive risks for the most virtuous countries in managing their public debt. Depla and von Weizsäcke (2010)[14] proposed a reference to the 60 % of GDP threshold to draw a dividing line between jointly guaranteed debt and the other national liabilities. EU countries should pool up to 60 % of GDP of their national debt under joint and several liability sovereign debt, called *blue* Eurobonds, thereby reducing borrowing costs for that element of their indebtedness. For the balance, any national debt beyond a country's Blue Bond allocation should be issued as national and junior debt, *red* bonds with sound procedures in place to ensure an orderly default. However, this kind of solution would imply the mutualisation of pre-existing national debts between countries with different fiscal positions and risk premiums and could reduce incentives on governments to put their public finances in order. This position, notably held by Germany, seems rather irrational, since the original idea behind Eurobonds was to create market incentives for highly indebted countries to work on their public spending, given that only a part of debt would be pooled together, while the rest would be subject to the effects of market pressure.

In addition to the stabilisation of Eurozone debt, Eurobonds could serve other function, in a direction suggested by Delors, that is to engage in a large investment-led recovery programme that could boost the Juncker plan capacity. In order to deal with the overall under-investment crisis, Holland and Varoufakis (2012)[15] suggested using institutions such as the EIB to issue bonds to finance infrastructure projects, alongside the EIF providing venture capital. As such, finance required for recovery would be acquired by recycling global surpluses invested in Eurobonds. Their proposal has the merit of relying on existing institutions that can be effective with respect to European treaty conditions. First, the EIB has issued bonds for project financing since 1958, and its mandate has been enlarged to cover investments beyond infrastructure, such as transport and communication networks, to extend to education, health, urban renewal and environmental protection (see Section 6.8 for

---

[14] Depla J. and von Weizsäcke J. (2010), *The Blue Bond proposal*, Bruegel Policy Brief, Issue 2010/03 (Accessed October 15, 2021).

[15] Holland S. and Varoufakis J. (2012), "A Modest Proposal for Resolving the Eurozone Crisis", *Intereconomics*, Vol. 47, No. 4, pp. 240-247.

the transformation of the EIB in the Climate Bank). Second, there was little awareness that the EIB's investment financing need not count as national debt. The idea that new debt could not solve the crisis, due to the fact that the crisis has been caused by piling debt on debt, was a false but ubiquitous presumption in that period. The issuing of debt, however, has to be qualified since

> it depends on which debt, borrowed for what purpose. Piling up national debt at interest rates of up to seven per cent is unsustainable. Funding inflows to the EU through Eurobonds is not, especially when interest rate could be less than two per cent and when this funds investments that generate not only recovery, but also direct and indirect tax revenues through growth and higher levels of employment (Holland and Varoufakis, 2012, p. 244).

The value of bonds issued by the EIB would amount to that required for an ecological transition in Europe, with the ECB standing by ready to purchase as many of them as necessary in the second market.

A different vision has been pursued by a group of French academics and politicians, headed by Thomas Piketty. One of the purposes of the 2018 *Manifesto for the Democratization of Europe* is to support investment projects targeted at effecting a transition towards a sustainable system of growth. However, their approach is more radical, as they call for institutional change in Europe to solve the broader issues of genuine democratic legitimacy and fiscal justice. Accordingly, a new European Assembly would raise new taxes, for example, on the profits of major firms, or on the wealth of the richest European citizens, ensuring that "those who have gained from globalisation contribute to the financing of the public goods".[16]

Although the two perspectives, by Holland/Varoufakis and Piketty, differ in their approach, they are alike in recognising the need for a major investment plan to finance economic recovery in an environmentally and socially sustainable way. They are basically opposite in the way such a plan should be financed; one through debt and the other through taxation. However, they highlight two fundamental issues affecting investment in Europe:

---

[16] *Manifesto for the Democratization of Europe,* http://tdem.eu/wp-content/uploads/2018/12/Manifesto_EN.pdf (Accessed 15 Orcober, 2021)

(1) the savings surplus (both public and private) that has accumulated over time needs to be reinvested in activities that can provide lasting growth prospects in order to create virtuous dynamics for debt sustainability;

(2) the need for future European policies, aimed above all at financing investment in European public goods, to be anchored in an institutional context with greater democratic legitimacy.

A program like the one proposed by Holland and Varoufakis can help finance investments, and urgently needs to be implemented, to contribute to restoring confidence both in the financial markets and in society as a whole through growth prospects and job creation. However, in the longer term, the European institutional architecture needs to be completed with a fiscal capacity, to respond not only to the issue of financing investment, but also to more existential concerns, such as an enhanced democratic legitimacy over EU spending decisions, and the pursuit of greater justice, both in social and environmental terms.

4.5 The European Commission response: The Juncker Plan

Several proposals were made to boost investment after the financial crisis, focusing on incentives (through subsidies, reduced risk and co-financing) designed to mobilise private capital by leveraging funds from the EU, government budgets or the EIB, with a common intention of channelling this capital into projects with long-term benefits for Europe.[17] In most cases, the amounts raised varied, within a range of €100-200 bn. per year, which is clearly less than the sums needed to close the investment gap, estimated at €300 bn.

The solution proposed by the European Commission, in close collaboration with the EIB, was essentially to mobilise investment through a reduction of risk, making investment more profitable, and through structural reforms, that should remove all the bottlenecks that hitherto hampered investment. The Investment Plan – known as the Juncker Plan from the former President of the Commission Jean-Claude Juncker – relies on the private sector as the prime source of capital, ideally by using existing

---

[17] See Dauderstädt (2015), for a review.

financial wealth not yet invested in the real economy. The Plan aimed to close the gap between the abundant liquidity in global capital markets and the pressing need for investment in Europe. With this objective, it was based on three interrelated and mutually reinforcing strands.

The first pillar was the short-term mobilisation of at least €315 bn. in additional investment over three years (2015-2017), through the establishment of a new fund – the European Fund for Strategic Investment (EFSI). This would provide a sufficient guarantee to reduce the risk of projects, thus increasing the capacity to attract investors to projects on the *strategic* side of the EFSI, with relatively low or no returns, like infrastructure. [18] The second pillar includes specific initiatives to make sure that additional investments reflect the needs of the economy. For example, this included the creation of an online platform that provides visibility to projects in search of financing, and an advisory hub providing technical assistance for project structuring. Finally, a third strand concerned the investment environment, and will affect the economy in the long run. The removal of barriers to investment at the national level – resulting in greater regulatory predictability – and the reinforcing of the Single Market, would create optimal framework conditions for investment in Europe.

According to the Court of Auditors (2019),[19] in practice the Juncker Plan has achieved positive results, although some critical aspects need to be considered for the future. In its first three years, the total approved EFSI financing reached the amounts originally expected. In particular, EFSI-supported projects, approved as of June 2019, generated more than 1 million jobs, with a positive contribution to GDP of 0,9 % over the baseline (Christensen et al., 2019).[20] From a quantitative perspective, the problem was not the capacity of the Plan to mobilise the desired amount of €315 bn., that was largely met, but rather the fact of not being

---

[18] The EFSI is a fund backed by a €16bn. guarantee from the EU budget, and €5bn. allocated from the EIB's own capital. Technically speaking, thanks to the EFSI, the EIB will be able to issue additional bonds for an amount of around three times the guarantee, and such amounts will be used by the EIB to invest in high risk projects, taking a first-loss position.

[19] European Court of Auditors (2019), *European Fund for Strategic Investments: Action Needed to Make EFSI a Full Success,* Special Report No. 03, Luxembourg: Publications Office of the European Union. DOI:10.2865/074156.

[20] Christensen M., Weiers G., Conte A., Wolski M. and Salotti S. (2019). *The European Fund for Strategic Investments: The RHOMOLO-EIB 2019 Update*, https://ec.europa.eu/jrc/sites/default/files/jrc118260.pdf (Accessed October 15, 2021).

ambitious enough with respect to real investment needs. Lamoigne et al. (2016)[21] agree that the Plan was "too little and too late", proving to be an ineffective anti-cyclical tool: had the Juncker plan been implemented in a timely manner, it would have helped to contain the recession.

This lack of ambition has been one of the most criticised aspects of the Juncker Plan. In theory, the risk that the Plan would have financed operations that could have otherwise been financed by the private market alone could have been avoid by confining its use to the financing of riskier projects, like those in innovation and trans-European transport. In practice, however, the EFSI's ability to increase the EIB's higher-risk financing fell short of expectations. Further, a perceived risk of a geographical concentration, in the sense of disproportional benefits to some countries or regions, has also been confirmed. Since there are no geographical or sectorial quotas for EFSI – on the contrary, it follows a demand driven approach – the Plan ended up with 82 % of all signed EFSI financing going to the 15 Member States pre-dating the 2004 EU enlargement. Essentially, EFSI financing addressed the investment needs of some of the most crisis-hit countries, like Italy, Spain, Greece and Portugal, but it was not an instrument of cohesion policy.

Nevertheless, after an initial phase, the Juncker Plan was extended in 2018, with a proposal that it become a permanent tool to boost investment in Europe. This took the form of the Commission's proposal of the new InvestEU fund for the 2021-27 MFF, endowed with a guarantee of €26 bn. The adoption of the Juncker Plan was a turning point in policy making, demonstrating the need of public support (albeit limited) to investment. And for the first time it was recognised that markets alone are incapable of properly assessing investment opportunities. On the other hand, however, the Plan maintained a continuity with respect to the logic of sound fiscal budgets and structural reforms, as it aimed at improving conditions for private investment, committing a small amount of public money to lower the risk for the private sector, and promoting a more favourable business climate, through the achievement of its third pillar.

---

21 Le Moigne M., Saraceno F. and Villemot S. (2016), *Probably Too Little, Certainly Too Late. An Assessement of the Juncker Investment Plan*, Document de travail de l'OFCE (10), Paris : Observatoire Francais des Conjonctures Economiques (OFCE).

4.6 From the investment clause to the golden rule

At the same time as the launch of the Juncker Plan, the Commission reminded Member States that they could exploit the flexibility margin available for public investment within the framework of the SGP, without the need to change the existing rules. After all, structural reforms and fiscal rules are all crucial components of the European economic governance strategy, to which the investment dimension was added on top. According to the interpretation provided by the Commission, flexibility would vary depending on whether a Member State was in the preventive or the corrective arm of the SGP. This status would reflect one of two phases of progressive deterioration in the level of compliance (or non-compliance) with the agreed adjustment path towards a country-specific Medium-Term Objective (MTO) for the budgetary position to which each country has to adhere.[22]

The Commission clarified the potential synergies between the EFSI – the financial arm of the Juncker Plan – and the SGP (see Box 2). The EFSI's funds comprise an initial contribution made from the EU budget and from the EIB's own resources, amounting to €21 bn. Beyond this, Member States, directly or through their National Promotional Banks (NPBs) or similar bodies, can contribute to the Fund in the form of capital. In addition, Member States can also co-finance individual projects within the EFSI. The Commission explained that, on the one hand, national contributions to the EFSI would not be taken into account when defining the fiscal adjustment under either the preventive or the

---

22 The preventive arm aims at guaranteeing a sound budgetary position in all Member States, and is the ordinary arm for any country, while the corrective arm of the SGP deals with situations in which the government's deficit and/or debt are above the reference values set in the Treaty. In these cases, Member States are then subject to an Excessive Deficit Procedure (EDP), which entails stricter conditions and monitoring. Compliance with the preventive arm of the Pact should ensure that Member States are kept out of the corrective arm under all except the most unusual of circumstances. Therefore, the EDP ought not to be thought of as being part of the normal budgetary procedure in the Member States, but as being the end of the line where previous budgetary policy errors are rectified. For more details on fiscal rules under SGP see the European Commission (2019d), *Vade Mecum on the Stability & Growth Pact 2019 Edition*, European Economy Institutional Paper 101, April 2019, Luxembourg: Publications Office of the European Union, https://op.europa.eu/en/publication-detail/-/publication/780c3262-a83c-11e9-9d01-01aa75ed71a1 (Accessed October 15, 2021).

corrective arms of the Pact, because these contributions are considered exceptional one-off measures, which have by definition no effect on structural balances. On the other hand, as regards the co-financing of single projects – which may take several forms, such as equity participation, loans, guarantees – only Member States who are in the preventive arm can accommodate public investment, temporarily deviating from their adjustment path (provided that some conditions related to negative economic performance and the expenditure does not breach the deficit limit). Put in these terms, the flexibility foreseen by the existing rules allows for a (kind of) partial golden rule for those countries that respect the fiscal rules. As such, this investment clause does not appear to be an effective means of promoting public investment, since the choice for a country lies between, on one hand, negotiating with the Commission to stay a little longer in "purgatorio" (the corrective arm) where it is asked to reduce its excessive deficit but over a longer period of time or, on the other, making initial efforts to consolidate the deficit in order to be able to enter into "paradiso" (the preventive arm) and take advantage of the golden rule (Fantacci and Papetti, 2013). In both cases, an early boost in public investment for productive use is not possible. Against this normative backdrop, the situation observed in the Eurozone was of falling public investment, and those countries most in need of investment were also those with the worst economic and fiscal conditions, while those with more fiscal space were those less likely to increase their levels of public investment. Most EU countries were under the excessive deficit procedure during the period of fiscal adjustments, and therefore would have not been able to benefit extensively from the investment clause, while in the preventive arm, the treatment of public investment would only have a limited effect (Barbiero and Darvas, 2014).[23]

[23] Barbiero F. and Darvas Z. (2014), *In Sickness and Health: Protecting and Supporting Public Investment in Europe*, Bruegel Policy Contribution, Issue 2014/02, https://www.bruegel.org/wp-content/uploads/imported/publications/pc_2014_02.pdf (Accessed October 15, 2021).

Box 2. Summary for national contributions regarding the European Fund for Strategic Investments

As regards financial contributions from member states to the EFSI the Commission stated:

"In its assessment of the necessary fiscal adjustment *under the preventive and corrective arms*, the Council specifies targets in structural terms. Such targets exclude exceptional one-off measures, which have no bearing on the underlying fiscal position. This would typically be the case for initial cash contributions to the Fund… National contributions to the EFSI will not be taken into account by the Commission when defining the fiscal adjustment under either the preventive or the corrective arm of the Pact."

As regards the co-financing by Member States of investment projects also co-financed by the EFSI it said that:

"*Under the preventive arm* of the Pact, some investments deemed to be equivalent to major structural reforms may, under certain conditions, justify a temporary deviation from the MTO of the concerned Member State or from the adjustment path towards it. The Commission has provided first guidance in the past on how these provisions apply to public investments with positive, direct and verifiable long-term budgetary effects on growth and on the sustainability of public finances. This guidance (commonly referred to as the "investment clause") is specified and formalised through this Communication to take better account of country-specific situations, in line with the text and spirit of the Pact […] Member States in the preventive arm of the Pact can deviate temporarily from their MTO or adjustment path towards it to accommodate investment, provided that: their GDP growth is negative or GDP remains well below its potential; the deviation does not lead to an excess over the 3 % deficit reference value and an appropriate safety margin is preserved; investment levels are effectively increased as a result; the deviation is compensated within the timeframe of the Member State's Stability or Convergence Programme. Eligible investments are national expenditures on projects co-funded by the EU under the Structural and Cohesion policy, Trans-European Networks and the Connecting Europe Facility, as well as national co-financing of projects also co-financed by the European Fund for Strategic Investments" (European Commission, 2015, emphasis added).[a]

[a] European Commission (2015), *Making the Best Use of the Flexibility within the Existing Rules of the Stability and Growth Pact*, Strasbourg: European Commission, https://eur-lex.europa.eu/legal-content/EN/TXT/PDF/?uri=CELEX:52015DC0012&from=EN (Accessed October 15, 2021).

Many have suggested that Europe seriously needs to consider the implementation of a true golden rule, not least the conservative German council of economic experts that explicitly endorsed the principles of the golden rule, arguing that "the requirement of a general debt prohibition would be economically as absurd as banning private individuals or companies from borrowing" (SVR, 2007).[24] In the classic theory of public finance, dating back to Musgrave (1939),[25] the golden rule refers to the potential differentiation between current spending and investment spending: the first should be financed by tax revenues, whereas budget surplus or debt issuance should serve the second, with capital depreciation considered as current government expenditure. In practice, only clearly identified investment spending can be linked to debt. This premise is based on the fact that financing of expenditure which is intended to produce its effects over a long period of time, sometimes decades, cannot take place in a single budget year, but must be spread over a number of years. Furthermore, if investment promotes future growth, higher fiscal revenues will cover the financing costs.[26] Given the potential of future benefits, it is then justified that future generations contribute to financing such investments via the servicing of the debt. As Truger (2016)[27] explains, it is correct that in this way future generations inherit the burden of public debt, but in exchange they receive a corresponding public and/or social capital stock. Any failure to allow for debt financing of future generations' benefits will lead to a disproportionate burden for the present generation through higher taxes or lower spending, thus creating

24 Sachverständigenrat zur Begutachtung der gesamtwirtschaftlichen Entwicklung – SVR (2007), *Staatsverschuldung wirks am begrenzen, Expertise im Auftrag des Bundesministers für Wirtschaft und Technologie*, Wiesbaden: Sachverständigenrat zur Begutachtung der gesamtwirtschaftlichen Entwicklung.

25 Musgrave R. A. (1939), "The Nature of Budgetary Balance and the Case for Capital Budget", *American Economic Review*, No. 29, pp. 260-271.

26 The balanced budget rule refers to the Ricardian equivalence assumption, i.e. a deficit today will create expectations by individuals – who are supposed to be perfectly rational and have full information – about future tax increases to finance debt servicing. Thus, with a balanced budget rule, expectations change, and interest rates fall with benefits in terms of financing costs and releasing resources for investment.

27 Truger A. (2016), *The Golden Rule of Public Investment – A Necessary and Sufficient Reform of the EU Fiscal Framework? Hans*-Böckler-Schiftung Working Paper No. 168, https://www.boeckler.de/pdf/p_imk_wp_168_2016.pdf (Accessed October 15, 2021).

incentives for the under provision of public investment to the detriment of future generations. Given the special nature of public investment, its exclusion from the SGP rules would allow for government deficit to finance it, and not through taxes.

Unfortunately, the European framework for fiscal policy goes in the opposite direction. The Fiscal Compact (title III of the Treaty on Stability, Coordination and Governance in the Economic and Monetary Union) reaffirms the SGP tenet of the medium-term balanced budget, as it foresees that the structural budget balance of a country, i.e. net of the economic cycle, must not exceed 0,5 % of GDP, while the gap between its effective debt ratio to GDP and the 60 % reference value must be reduced at a rate of 5 % per year. As Blanchard and Giavazzi observed the SGP "contains a serious error: the way governments are expected to account for public investment" (Blanchard and Giavazzi, 2004, p. 3).[28] If net public investment were excluded from the definition of the budget that is relevant for the fiscal rules desirable outcomes might follow, in particular a substitution of current expenditure with an equivalent amount of public investment, instead of a cut in demand.

In the past the European Commission considered the golden rule on investment to be an "indiscriminate approach [that] could easily put in danger the prime objective of the SGP by undermining the sustainability of government debt" (European Commission, 2012b, p. 25),[29] while on the other hand it recommended that "For the countries with high deficits, the budgetary consolidation strategy, based on expenditure restraint, should not be achieved at the expenses of the most 'productive' components of public spending (such as public investment, education and research expenditures)" (Barbiero and Darvas, 2014, p. 5). Given such a schizophrenic stance what is unclear is how to preserve public investment, while at the same time meeting the prime objective of austerity.

---

28 Blanchard O. and Giavazzi F. (2004), *Improving the SGP Through a Proper Accounting of Public Investment*, No 4220, CEPR Discussion Papers.

29 European Commission (2012b), *Blueprint for Deep and Genuine Economic and Monetary Union – the Launching a European Debate*, Bruxelles: European Commission, https://eur-lex.europa.eu/LexUriServ/LexUriServ.do?uri=COM:2012:0777:FIN:EN:PDF (Accessed October 15, 2021).

4.7 A functional approach to the golden rule

Although very sensible, the golden rule has always faced a number of objections, from a practical point of view, beyond the issue of the hierarchy of priorities. The main argument against its operationalisation concerns the selection of potential candidates to be subjected to the rule; here, there is a risk of morally hazardous behaviour by governments, that could resort to creative accounting in order to deduct from deficit calculations spending that would otherwise be classed as current. Therefore, practical challenges need to be considered, especially in the wake of past experiences in Europe, which met with varying degree of success, as suggested by the European Fiscal Board (EFB) (2020).[30] Both Germany and the UK had fiscal frameworks favourable to public investment, with a golden rule in place for 40 years from 1969 to 2009 in the first case, and from 1997 to 2008 in the second one.

In the UK, the adoption of the golden rule brought some positive results. The British rule required that the current budget, excluding net investment, would be at least in balance over the business cycle. Net government investment increased, while the government debt showed a mixed trend with an increase in the early 2000s that was ascribed to suspected political manipulation. In contrast, the German golden rule was anchored in its Constitution and allowed deficits applied to *gross* government investment, i.e. depreciation included. The evidence of the German case is disappointing since during the existence of the golden rule the debt ratio rose from 18 % in 1970 to 64 % of GDP prior to the financial crisis of 2008/2009, while at the same time gross public investment shrank by 5 % to 2 % of GDP. As such, despite an increase in debt levels, government capital accumulation decreased over time. Finally, in 2009 the golden rule for investment was replaced with the implementation of the debt brake, written into the Constitution, a rule that strictly limits government deficits.

Some flaws in the implementation of the rule characterised the German experience. For instance, the lack of definition on which specific investments were to be considered under the golden rule could not

30 EFB (2020), *Assessment of the Fiscal Stance Appropriate for the Euro Area in 2021* Bruxelles: European Commission, https://ec.europa.eu/info/sites/default/files/2020_06_25_efb_assessment_of_euro_area_fiscal_stance_en.pdf (Accessed October 15, 2021).

prevent potentially political interpretations of its field of application. Furthermore, a gross investment variable was chosen instead of *net* investment, thus enabling higher deficits. This specificity would have a large impact on national budgets in the Euro area, since the net investment component is negligible, while all gross investment has been replacement investment.

The core issue around the golden rule would be the identification of those public investments that yield concrete future economic benefits in terms of higher productivity and growth in the long-run. According to this pragmatic criterion, however, all public spending projects that create sufficient returns would qualify under the golden rule (like education and health care), although they are, from a mere national accounting point of view, current expenditure. Traditional investments, like tangible and intangible infrastructure, have been considered, with the conclusion that they are productive and growth-enhancing expenditure, and in particular when considering the scope for improvement in the quality of infrastructure, like transport, observed in many Eurozone countries. All these observations suggested adopting a gradual approach in the selection of candidates for the golden rule, the first to include traditional investments, while other expenditures, that would be rational from the point of view of productivity but suffer from difficulties in implementation for statistical or other reasons, may follow in a second phase (Truger, 2016). In particular, spending on education and health care, when considered an investment in social capital, is considered by many to be a beneficial expenditure for long-term growth, with a high private and public rate of return, although reliably estimating this is a difficult task.

The EFB (2020) considered that deficiencies shown up from prior experience, as well as all the caveats that need to be addressed in a more favourable approach to public investment, should not disqualify golden rules more generally. The starting point should be a common agreement on the EU's objectives; should these be the most growth-friendly expenditures in the long term, or expenditures with a specific social or environmental intent. Economic, social and environmental priorities, in part made even more urgent by the pandemic, can provide a chance to pursue a functional, rather than merely accounting, differentiation of expenditure items. In this view, the boundary between current and capital expenditure would not be so clear-cut, while expenditure eligible for the golden rule would be defined in political terms. In this exercise, a link between the national golden rule and the European budget should be central, with a commitment by Member States to preserve those items necessary for urgent policies defined centrally at European level; these would not be limited to traditional investments, such as infrastructure for the environmental and digital sectors, but also include current expenditure in social sectors such as those that promote active labour participation, as well as spending in the health sector to support the development of new vaccines.

Chapter 5

The Covid-19 crisis and solidarity in Europe

5.1 Solidarity in Europe

The question of economic growth in an economic union is linked to that of solidarity. On the one hand, solidarity between Member States of the EU is at the heart of the process of European integration, in the context of a continuous tension between renouncing national sovereignty – driven by a push for cooperation – and the maintenance of prerogatives of strategic interest of governments. On the other hand, the greatest progress towards closer cooperation has mainly been made in the economic sphere, through the creation of the single market. In it, the centralisation of competences mainly responds to the need to contain the effects of competition between countries due to the presence of national regulatory differences. In essence, the objective has been to guarantee the *level playing field* within the market. In the academic debate, it has been observed that the kind of solidarity on which the EU is based today has more to do with interdependence between countries, that has been more precisely created through economic integration (*de facto solidarity*),[1] rather than through a spontaneous feeling (*affective solidarity*) that inspired the original treaties (Fabry, 2010).[2]

The EU originated from a decision of its members to pool selected aspects of their respective sovereignty, in a process whose evolution has

---

1 The Schuman Declaration states that "Europe will not be made all at once, or according to a single plan. It will be built through concrete achievements which first create a de facto solidarity.", 9 May 1950, https://europa.eu/european-union/about-eu/symbols/europe-day/schuman-declaration_en (Accessed October 15, 2021).

2 Fabry E. (2010), *European Solidarity: Where Do We Stand? Should We Foster It and How? Synthesis of the 2010 Edition of the European Think Tank Forum Palais Pedralbes – 30 September and 1 October 2010*, Paris: Institute Jacques Delors, https://institutdelors.eu/wp-content/uploads/2018/01/cr-forum-think-tanks-barcelone-2010-en.pdf (Accessed October 15, 2021).

been expressed both in the choice of European policies, and in the availability and financing of these policies. These are in effect two sides of the same coin, the EU budget, which is the operational tool that supports and accompanies the major steps in the EU's evolutionary process (Paramithiotti and Zatti, 2015). Since the 1980s, the EU budget has been the instrument capable of holding together the process of economic liberalisation on the one hand, and on the other the objective of social integration between countries with different starting conditions. This synthesis, in which integration and solidarity are linked, is adeptly summarised in Delors' own words: "competition which stimulates, cooperation which strengthens and solidarity which unites" (Delors, 2012).[3] Today, cooperation and solidarity are aspects that need to be strengthened, although they are being developed in new dimensions. On the one hand, the financial crisis has produced a new impetus in the coordination of national fiscal policies, without however generating the missing piece of European economic policy, i.e. an autonomous fiscal capacity, endowed with taxation powers, on which a completed fiscal union would be based. The Covid-19 crisis, on the other hand, has stimulated an appetite for greater *de facto solidarity*. The risk of market fragmentation generated by the lockdown measures has threatened a tightly interdependent system, where, in the words of Angela Merkel, "It is essential for Germany, as an export nation, that its EU partners also do well [...] It is in nobody's interest for Germany alone to be strong after the crisis."[4]

5.2 EU budget functions: Between theory and reality

To assess areas in which there is more room for solidarity in Europe, it might be useful to use the theory of fiscal federalism. The principle of fiscal federalism is to find ways through which different levels of government and different governments at the same level interact, through

---

3 Delors J. (2012), *For a Revival of Europe*, Paris: Institute Jacques Delors Tribune, https://institutdelors.eu/wp-content/uploads/2018/01/socialisteuropeanalternative_j_delors_ne_april2012.pdf (Accessed October 15, 2021).

4 *Merkel: Germany must help other EU states get back on their feet,* euractiv.com with Reuters, 13 May 2020, https://www.euractiv.com/section/economy-jobs/news/merkel-germany-must-help-other-eu-states-get-back-on-their-feet/ (Accessed October 15, 2021).

coordination or competition, and try to allocate the optimal level of public resources accordingly (Vaneecloo, 2006).[5]

Based on a functional breakdown of the economic role of the state, fiscal federalism seeks to establish which levels of government should be responsible for three functions:

- the *stabilisation* function, intended as a response to the need to sustain demand following shocks that causes a slowdown in the economic cycle. According to the prevailing approach, this function must be carried out centrally, for three reasons (Paramithiotti and Zatti, 2015). First, decentralised authorities have at their disposal a limited range of instruments and room for manoeuvre with respect to the central level to correct the economic cycle. Second, part of the stimulus effects financed at the local level would spill over onto other economic systems, giving rise to positive externalities that make intervention at the decentralised level sub-optimal. Third, the lack of coordination between authorities may create the risk of carrying out initiatives independently, leading to asynchrony and inconsistency, thus producing sub-optimal results at an aggregate level;
- the *redistribution* function, aimed at modifying the redistribution of resources generated by the market in order to align it more closely with equity criteria. A policy of this kind conducted at a decentralised level runs the risk of favouring the emigration of tax bases and attracting categories more in need of particular social spending interventions. It should therefore be conducted centrally;
- the *allocative* function of all those goods and services (public goods) that the market may not produce, or may insufficiently produce. This should be distributed between levels of government, on the principle that it should be allocated to the level of government in whose jurisdiction the benefits of public spending take place. In practice, central government is responsible for providing goods and services consumed by the entire population, while local governments provide those goods and services that affect their own population.

---

[5] Vaneecloo C. (2006), "Fiscal Federalism Perspective(s) and the European Union. Introductory framework", in C. Vaneecloo, A. Badriotti e Fornasini M. (eds.), *Fiscal Federalism in the European Union and Its Countries. A Confrontation between Theories and Facts*, Bruxelles: P.I.E. Peter Lang.

An institutional transformation in the sense of an upward devolution of powers from Member State governments to the EU is underway in Europe, on the basis of a model of fiscal federalism that presents some features of the traditional theoretical scheme, but with distinctive characteristics typical of the European experience. The European model differs from the traditional one, since both the stabilisation and the redistribution functions are carried out mainly at a decentralised, national level, while the production of public goods should be more centralised (Tabellini, 2002).[6] These three functions, in the European reality, therefore take the following configuration:

- with the advent of the financial crisis, the stabilisation function took shape in particular through measures outside the European budget, such as the expansionary monetary policy measures of the ECB and the ESM. The latter represented an example of solidarity on the part of stronger countries towards more fragile ones, but it intervened when countries were already in a critical condition in terms of debt sustainability and, above all, was the result of an intergovernmental treaty that placed it outside the European institutional perimeter. The recent Next Generation EU (NGEU) program, that followed the Covid-19 crisis, has introduced a new stabilisation function at the central level, albeit with important limitations due to its contingent nature, a measure linked to the pandemic;
- interpersonal redistributive policies are the competence of national governments, and will probably remain at this local level of government because of the marked differences that persist between Member States in preferences regarding optimum levels of redistribution. However, most of the EU's tasks concern the sphere of territorial redistribution, through its cohesion policy, with structural and investment funds transferring resources from the EU budget to regions lagging behind in development with the aim of strengthening economic, social and territorial cohesion, or through the CAP, which provides income support to actors in the agricultural sector;
- the allocation function has little place in the European budget: defence, foreign and security policy are largely national tasks. Although there is a degree of centralisation in areas such as

[6] Tabellini G. (2002), *The Assignment of Tasks in an Evolving European Union*, CEPS Policy Brief No. 10. (Accessed October 15, 2021).

education, research and environmental policies, it is nevertheless difficult to measure the level, because the EU and national authorities often share responsibility. The single market can also be seen as a European public good, where the centralisation of competences has been strong: from the removal of barriers to trade and factor mobility to the creation of the single currency.

To understand the weight that each function holds in the EU budget, the breakdown by thematic areas of the 2014-2020 MFF, which amounts to about €1.087 bn. euro,[7] is traced out below:

- heading 1a: *Competitiveness for growth and employment* (€142,1 bn., 13 % of the budget);
- heading 1b: *Economic, social and territorial cohesion* (€371,4 bn., 34 %);
- heading 2: *Sustainable growth: natural resources* (€420 bn., 39 %);
- heading 3: *Security and citizenship* (€17,7 bn., 2 %);
- heading 4: *Europe's global role* (€66 bn., 6 %);
- headings 5 and 6: *Administration and compensation* (€69,6 bn., 6 %).

On the basis of the functional distinction of the budget, we can extrapolate that the redistribution function takes place through items 1.b (*Economic, social and territorial cohesion*) and 2 (*Sustainable growth: natural resources*), while the remaining items 1.a, 3 and 4 fall within the allocation function, especially that concerning competitiveness and the single market.

The new 2021-2027 MFF introduced significant changes compared to the previous programs. These changes were due to the coronavirus pandemic, and the countermeasures taken by the Union. The political compromise reached by the European Council in July 2020 cut some of the expenditure in European public goods, downsizing the European Commission's original proposals to increase spending in these policy areas, like Digital Europe, Horizon Europe and the Invest EU facility. In the final stage of the negotiations, the European Parliament managed to obtain a modest increase in European public goods, like research,

7 For each expenditure item, funds available and the relative weight as a % of the total budget are indicated (data from the European Commission's website, https://ec.eur opa.eu/ info/ strat egy/ eu- bud get/ spend ing/ topic/ eu- fund ing- pro gram mes- 2014- 2020 _ en) (Accessed October 15, 2021).

health, culture, external action and Erasmus+, but the general framing of the budget did not substantially change. About 73 % of the European budget will be used to support territorial redistribution, while 21 % will finance the production of European public goods.

Over the course of the last two programs before 2021, the budget has been restructured in favour of the allocation function: between the 2014-2020 MFF and 2007-2013, items related to public goods increased (by 37 %, 26,5 % and 3,3 %, respectively) while expenditure in redistribution decreased (on average by about 10 %). In spite of this, the traditional configuration of the budget has not changed in substance, remaining a substantially redistributive budget.[8]

The predominance of territorial redistribution within the European budget is justified both in terms of economic solidarity, where Member Countries consider excessive levels of disparity to be intolerable, motivated by *affective solidarity*, and political sustainability, when a balanced development between regions is identified as a necessary condition to allow the progress of the economic integration process, the *de facto solidarity* that has allowed the development of the single market.

5.3 Macroeconomic stabilisation: Risk reduction or risk sharing?

Since its creation, the EMU has been the product of an institutional compromise; while monetary policy has been completely federalised, economic policy has remained decentralised, subject to fiscal rules and intergovernmental coordination mechanisms. In renouncing monetary sovereignty, Member States gave up an important stabilisation instrument – the exchange rate – which in the past was used by periphery countries to counter recessionary crises, while the automatic stabilisers at the national level might not have operated fully in accordance with

---

8 In particular, expenditure on external action covers only 5,6 % of the budget and its allocation has increased almost insignificantly compared to the 2007-2013 MFF, while the EU action in the field of immigration falls under the already small heading of *Security and citizenship*, which also includes programmes for health, culture and justice (Fontana O. and Venturi B. (2018), *I beni pubblici europei nel bilancio dell'Unione*, Centro Studi sul Federalismo, Research Paper, http://www.csfederalismo.it/images/CSF-IAI_QFP/CSF-IAI_RP_OFontana-BVenturi_BeniPubblici_QFP_Aprile2018.pdf – Accessed October 15, 2021).

budgetary rules. This also led to divergences in the cyclical developments of various economies, which rendered the management of a monetary union difficult and ineffective. After the financial crisis, which involved asymmetric shocks for some Eurozone countries, the debate has settled around the possible creation of a stabilisation mechanism at the central level, with a provision for income transfers to alleviate the cost that the shock imposed on the citizens of that country (De Grauwe, 2018).[9]

The idea of providing the EMU with a stabilisation function emerged at the institutional level in 2012 in the document known as the *Report of the Four Presidents*[10] (of the European Council, the European Commission, the ECB and the Eurogroup), and was part of a wider debate on the creation of an autonomous fiscal capacity in the euro area. The document outlined two possible configurations for the fiscal capacity of the EMU:

- an instrument of convergence and competitiveness, aimed at supporting, through limited, temporary, flexible and targeted financial incentives, Member States entering into contractual arrangements with EU institutions;
- a centralised macroeconomic stabilisation instrument aimed at countering asymmetric economic shocks, allowing for partial absorption. This could take the form of an insurance-type mechanism between euro area countries.

Although the need to provide the EMU with a stabilisation function was recognised, the document clarified the complementarity of the two measures within a precise timeframe; contractual arrangements and related financial incentives would support a convergence process that would lead to a stabilisation instrument later.

These two concepts of fiscal capacity reflect two different ways of understanding coexistence within the EMU. Firstly, in response to the criterion of national responsibility, which each Member State must respect to lower the risk of crisis for itself and for others (risk reduction),

---

9 De Grauwe P. (2018), *Economics of Monetary Union,* Oxford: Oxford University Press.

10 President of the European Council (2012), *Towards a Genuine Economic and Monetary Union*, https://www.consilium.europa.eu/media/23807/134190.pdf (Accessed October 15, 2021). For a reconstruction of fiscal capacity at the institutional level, see Fabbrini F. (2019), *A Fiscal Capacity for the Eurozone: Constitutional Perspectives, In-depth Analysis Requested by the AFCO Committee.* DOI: 10.2861/705606.

we see measures that provide for structural reforms and, in general, policies that reduce macroeconomic heterogeneity, limit financial vulnerability, strengthen the domestic banking system and maintain prudent fiscal behaviour. Secondly, we see measures that can be linked to the search for greater solidarity and risk sharing, with the creation of mechanisms at the European level, such as the centralisation of certain expenditure and revenue items in the budget to allow counter-cyclical transfers and/or joint investment projects.

Although forms of risk sharing are normally necessary within a monetary union, fears of morally risky behaviour, and of permanent transfers, make it politically difficult to go down this path. This is all the more true in the Eurozone, for one simple reason: if the economic policy of a monetary union without a political union requires that it is not possible to determine in advance which countries are most exposed to financial risks and prolonged recessions – this could be possible in unions of countries with a certain degree of convergence – however, in the EU's EMU the contrary condition exists: "in the euro zone there is no veil of ignorance about where the greatest risks and vulnerabilities are located" (Fracasso, 2018).[11] The controversy in Europe is exacerbated by the division between creditor and debtor countries which poses a huge obstacle to the virtues of solidarity, prevents timely resolution of crises and questions the very commitment to a common destiny (Marhold, 2015).[12]

As such, it was not only convergence that was considered a political prerequisite for any risk-sharing proposal; it was seen as the (expected) outcome of the monetary integration process itself: "Before the creation of the euro, the prevailing view in European economic circles was that economic and monetary union would reduce the incidence of asymmetric shocks. Policy-induced asymmetric shocks would be largely eliminated by the adoption of a single monetary policy and of fiscal rules that would impose sound national fiscal policies" (Sapir, 2016).[13]

The debate on solidarity was re-ignited in 2017 following the initiative of French President Emmanuel Macron to move forward with the

---

11 Fracasso A. (2018), "Solidarity and Responsibility in the Euro Area: Foes or Friends?", *The Economists' Voice*, De Gruyter, Vol. 15 Issue 1, pp. 1-4, December.

12 Marhold H. (2015), "A European Common Good?", *L'Europe en formation*, n. 376, Summer.

13 Sapir A. (2016), *The Eurozone Needs Less Heterogeneity*, VoxEU CEPR, https://voxeu.org/article/eurozone-needs-less-heterogeneity. (Accessed October 15, 2021).

European project, which proposed not only the creation of a separate EMU budget, financed by genuine own resources, to be raised in the digital, environmental and financial sectors, but also the creation of a Eurozone Finance Minister. These ambitions met with robust resistance from a group of Northern countries, Member States both inside and outside the Eurozone (the *Hanseatic League*), fierce opponents of further concessions of sovereignty at the European level. In the end, the Eurogroup meeting in October 2019 opted for an EU instrument for the euro area to support structural reforms to make national economies more resilient, the Budgetary Instrument for Competitiveness and Convergence (BICC). The BICC, however, has thus far not been completed, because of developments following the pandemic.

This lack of common vision is also attributable to an ideological contrast between two opposing positions, on the one hand, the Franco-Keynesian and, on the other, the German-Ordoliberal; if the former, abandoned in the early 1980s when political economy embraced the monetarist doctrine, supports the need to complete the monetary pillar with the fiscal one, the latter, strictly monetarist, is what the whole project of the single currency is based on. This rigid contrast prevents the recognition of the fact that in order to allow *ex post* fiscal transfers to take place only in emergency situations, as advocates of risk reduction claim, it is necessary to allow *ex ante* risk sharing, but at the same time, in order to be sustainable, European solidarity requires a degree of confidence in the responsible behaviour of the states that benefit from it. The right balance could be to accept the principles of national responsibility and fiscal rigour in the long term, while allowing for greater flexibility and shared mechanisms in the short term.

5.4 Allocation of European public goods

The *de facto solidarity* of the European integration process is rooted in the development of economic integration, which has often been characterised by the creation of mechanisms for cooperation and coordination as a means for furthering integration. Within the budget, this approach placed little emphasis on an assessment of the real impact of policies (Zuleeg, 2009).[14] In recent years, the Commission has proposed to use

[14] Zuleeg F. (2009), *The Rationale for EU Action: What Are European Public Goods?*, Prepared for the BEPA Workshop on The political economy of EU public finances: designing governance for change, 5 February.

a policy-driven approach to the EU budget. The focus should be on evaluating and monitoring the concrete results achieved by expenditure items, in order to determine their role. Consequently, a more pragmatic approach implies that there is a justification of cost-effectiveness at the basis of each policy.

The UK's departure from the EU puts further pressure on change. The budget gap created by Brexit (around 12-14 bn. euros per year) poses the need to streamline a budget quantitatively weakened due to the lack of one of its main contributors. Under the policy-oriented approach, traditional budget expenditures are set to suffer the greatest cuts.

The European Treaties provide that a number of policies such as the environment, energy, TENs, are subject to shared competence between the central level and the Member States (Art. 4 of the TFEU). These are key public goods for society, which national and sub-national governments are currently most responsible for. Yet, it is widely agreed that EU action within the budget should focus more on delivering such public goods.[15]

In the past, defining exactly what European public goods are was sometimes complicated. The terms *public benefit* and *public good* were used as synonyms, thus widening the scope to include the CAP and cohesion policy in the category of public good. In economics, however, the term responds specifically to the occurrence of a market failure, in which the State could intervene to correct its functioning and avoid a sub-optimal result. Government initiative is therefore supported by a precise economic justification, i.e. greater efficiency for society. The European public goods referred to today are the fight against global warming, research and development in large-scale and risky projects, particularly in the digital sector, development cooperation and financial assistance to third countries, immigration and refugee protection policies, the defence sector and the supply of military equipment, and the defence of the values of democracy and freedom (Fuest and Pisani-Ferry, 2019).[16] They are

---

15 See for example EPSC (2019), *Delivering on European Common Goods. Strengthening Member States' Capacity to Act in the 21st Century.* DOI: 10.2872/875838; Pisani-Ferry J., (2019c), *Europe Can Take a Bigger Role in Providing Public Goods*, Bruegel, https://www.bruegel.org/2019/12/europe-can-take-a-bigger-role-in-providing-public-goods/ (Accessed October 15, 2021); Tabellini G. (2002).

16 Fuest C. and Pisani-Ferry J. (2019), *A Primer on Developing European Public Goods. A Report to the Minister Bruno La Maire and Olaf Scholz*, 3 November, https://www.bruegel.org/wp-content/uploads/2019/11/European-public-goods-primer.pdf (Accessed October 15, 2021); EPSC (2019).

different areas and policies, where the level of solidarity may vary, but it is possible to identify some common reasons why it is reasonable to delegate the control and management at the European level.

First of all, the centralisation of expenditure makes economic sense. First, in some cases public goods are not provided at national level because fixed costs are too high, but if the scale of production increases, fixed costs decrease. This is the case of Galileo, the European global satellite-based navigation system, which would never have been carried out at national level because too expensive. The concept of economies of scale applied at European level is defined as *European added value*,[17] an apparently abstract idea, although an analysis of the costs and benefits of public spending could translate it in quantitative terms. In general, public spending at any level should lead to net benefits, i.e. a positive difference between benefits and costs. At the European level, public expenditure has an added value not only in the presence of net benefits, but also if these net benefits are greater than those obtained from public expenditure by national governments (Bertelsmann Foundation, 2013).[18] In few words, a joint action is more efficient than the sum of individual country actions.

Secondly, spill over effects outside the jurisdiction where public spending takes place suggest that a supply at national level is not efficient for Europe as a whole. If one country implements an expansive measure, it not only stimulates domestic demand, but also other countries, thanks to the strong economic integration made possible by the single market. On the other side, the individual initiative may impose costs on other members greater than their benefits, possibly resulting in a negative net benefit at European level. The case of the inflow of immigrants to various

---

17 The Commission defines European added value as "the value resulting from an EU intervention which is additional to the value that would have been otherwise created by Member State action alone" (European Commission (2011), *The Added Value of the EU Budget*, p. 2, https://ec.europa.eu/info/sites/info/files/about_the_european_commission/eu_budget/sec-2011-867_2011_en.pdf – Accessed October 15, 2021). In this sense "spending at EU level means a better deal for citizens than spending at national level" (European Commission (2010), *Revisione del bilancio dell'Unione europea*, p. 5, https://eur-lex.europa.eu/LexUriServ/LexUriServ.do?uri=COM:2010:0700:FIN:IT:PDF – Accessed October 15, 2021).

18 Bertelsmann Foundation (2013), *The European Added Value of EU Spending: Can the EU Help Its Member States to Save Money?*, Exploratory Study, Gütersloh: Bertelsmann Stiftung, https://www.zew.de/en/publikationen/the-european-added-value-of-eu-spending-can-the-eu-help-its-member-states-to-save-money/?cHash=97f2540cb3f5d496e7e3e10872bf0b98 (Accessed October 14, 2021).

European countries, after Germany decided in 2015 on a policy of openness towards refugees, highlights an element that is detrimental to the provision of European public goods, namely the heterogeneity of preferences, which are the result of an historical process and do not necessarily end up converging as a result of greater economic integration (Fuest and Pisani-Ferry, 2019).

Finally, the provision of European public goods is dictated by a simple reason: necessity. On the occasion of the 60th anniversary of the Treaties of Rome, the leaders of the 27 member states affirmed:

> The European Union is facing unprecedented challenges, both global and domestic: regional conflicts, terrorism, growing migratory pressures, protectionism and social and economic inequalities. Together, we are determined to address the challenges of a rapidly changing world and to offer to our citizens both security and new opportunities [...] We will make the European Union stronger and more resilient, through even greater unity and solidarity amongst us and the respect of common rules. Unity is both a necessity and our free choice. Taken individually, we would be side-lined by global dynamics. Standing together is our best chance to influence them, and to defend our common interests and values (Council of the EU, 2017).[19]

Although the definition of the European public good evolves over time according to EU policy priorities, in the current context these priorities respond to clear emergency situations – the biggest of them is the environmental challenge – which require collective, if not global, action. In addition, the changing global geopolitical context, in which the role of the US as a supplier of global public goods has disappeared, combined with the emergence of a multipolar structure, with the entry on the scene of new powers such as China, confront the EU with the need to seek greater collaboration in order to play a role on the international stage. In all these scenarios, solidarity should be seen as an opportunity: the opposition to European reforms of the financial and fiscal system necessary to face the new global emergencies "is credited to public opinion under the guise of a defence of national interests; a misleading guise, since

---

[19] Council of the European Union (2017), *The Rome Declaration. Declaration of the Leaders of 27 Member States and of the European Council, the European Parliament and the European Commission*, Statements and Remarks 149/17, https://www.consilium.europa.eu/en/press/press-releases/2017/03/25/rome-declaration/pdf (Accessed October 14, 2021).

it is precisely the national interest that today demands a supranational approach" (Padoa-Schioppa and Iozzo, 2020).[20]

5.5 How Covid-19 crisis has prompted more solidarity

The debate about greater or lesser solidarity within the EU has recently been reignited, although it had never completely faded away. After the 2008 crisis, the nub of the question was the Eurozone and burden sharing mechanism required to accommodate asymmetric shock, like sovereign debt crisis. In contrast, Covid-19 has manifested itself as a shock, which is symmetric in nature, nevertheless with asymmetric consequences, which required a massive response.

The Covid-19 pandemic that hit the world in 2020 has had unprecedented implications on our economy and everyday life. Although not particularly deadly – at least for the healthy and the young – the virus is highly infectious and rapidly hit all the major economies of the world simultaneously. In Europe, the first response from governments was to adopt a public health system approach. In the short-term, as the capacity of any country's health system is limited in terms of number of patients that can be properly treated at the same time, the aim of the intervention was to *flatten the curve* of infected (Gourinchas, 2020),[21] through the imposition of drastic social distancing measures that culminated in months of lockdown of economic and social activities. The aim was to stretch the spread of the pandemic over time, enabling more people to receive proper health treatment. Obviously, given the complexity and the interconnectivity of our economies, the lockdown triggered a chain of events, described as both supply and demand side shock. On the supply side, both the direct reduction of numbers of workers (because of quarantine, or for care-giving reasons due to school closures), and

---

20 Padoa-Schioppa A. and Iozzo, A. (2020), *Globalizzazione e Unione europea: sfide e strategie – Profili istituzionali del Green Deal*, Centro Studi sul Federalismo, Policy Paper No. 42 (Author's translation), http://www.csfederalismo.it/images/policy_paper/CSF_PP42_APS-Iozzo_Globalizzazione-Ue_Genn2020_def.pdf (Accessed October 15, 2021).

21 Gourinchas P. O. (2020), "Flattening the Pandemic and Recession Curves", in Baldwin R. and Weder di Mauro B. (eds.), *Mitigating the COVID Economic Crisis: Act Fast and Do Whatever It Takes*, London: CEPR Press VoxEU.org eBook, https://voxeu.org/content/mitigating-covid-economic-crisis-act-fast-and-do-whatever-it-takes (Accessed October 15, 2021).

interruptions along the supply chain both domestically and internationally, produced a negative productivity shock. On the demand side, loss of income, fear of contagion and growing uncertainty caused households and businesses to consume and invest less. As a consequence, the prioritisation of the health system's needs brought about a corresponding, and inevitable, economic recession. The Covid-19 crisis has therefore led to some changes in the European economic policy framework, stressing the need for adequate macroeconomic support from the public sector, as has been unanimously argued since the beginning of the pandemic.[22]

5.6 The EU's first line of defence

In the EU public sector intervention as a result of the Covid-19 crisis can be divided in two categories. The first line of action was devoted to maintaining financial stability, and to allowing national governments to support their health systems, as well as households and the business sector. In March, the ECB launched the €750 bn. – upgraded to €1,35 tn. just two and a half months later – Pandemic Emergency Purchase Programme (PEPP), a monetary package to counter the risks to liquidity, and improve the outlook for the euro area. A massive pan-European crisis response package followed. The European Commission, the EIB and the ESM agreed to finance up to €540 bn. to help people, businesses and states throughout Europe, including liquidity support for companies, funding for the development of treatments and vaccines, and financing for employment as well as direct and indirect healthcare costs related to the pandemic.[23] At the same time the European Commission – with support from the Council – activated the General Escape Clause, which

---

[22] See the review from prominent academics released in March 2020 Baldwin R. and Weder di Mauro B. (2020).

[23] At the Eurogroup of 9th April 2020, member states decided to (1) strengthen EIB activities, in order to create a pan-European guarantee fund of €25 bn., which could support €200 bn. of financing for companies with a focus on SMEs; (2) to establish a Pandemic Crisis Support for a total volume of around €240 bn. and conditional on the support of domestic financing of direct and indirect healthcare, cure and prevention related costs due to the Covid-19 crisis; (3) to create a temporary EU loan-based instrument (Support to mitigate Unemployment Risks in an Emergency – SURE), providing funding to Member States of up to €100 bn. to cover part of the costs related to the creation or extension of national short-time work schemes.

temporarily suspended the EU's fiscal rules enshrined in the SGP. This offered the necessary flexibility to national budgets in their support of the economy, and to respond in a coordinated manner to the impact of the Covid-19 pandemic. The Commission also provided increased flexibility in the implementation of the state aid rules.

Although at the national level, Member States were given the freedom to spend, there were clear differences in the fiscal space that governments had to support their economies by fighting a shock, which, although symmetrical in nature – no country was immune to infection – had an asymmetric impact on public finances. As the Commission commented, "Many of the EU countries currently hit hardest entered the Covid-19 crisis on weaker budgetary footing and with low macroeconomic resilience due to a mix of legacy factors and policy choices. Starting positions differ according to the extent of debt overhangs from the preceding decade, fiscal deficits, private sector financial buffers and the strength of social safety nets." (European Commission, 2020c, p. 5).[24] Accordingly, the capacity of Member States to exploit this new flexibility showed stark disparities. As regards State Aid, Germany accounted for €996 bn., equivalent to around 29 % of German GDP and 52 % of all aid measures provided in the EU, followed by France (around €324 bn., 13,4 % of GDP), Italy (around €302 bn., 17 % of GDP) and Belgium (around €54 bn., 11 % of GDP) (European Commission, 2020c, p. 6).

Although the pandemic crisis itself was symmetric in nature, its effects on Member States economically was asymmetric, depending on previous conditions, not only in national fiscal positions, but also in the structure of individual economies and the quality of a state's governance. This substantial disparity in policy response is mainly a consequence of differences in previous macroeconomic conditions that risked a new existential crisis triggered by Covid-19 (Tooze and Schularick, 2020).[25] In Italy, given the disappointing GDP growth trends of the last 20 years, any new crisis could bring the public debt/GDP ratio to over 150 % of GDP, putting pressure on the country's credibility in the financial markets. In this perspective, the risk of a deepening of divergences between

---

[24] European Commission (2020c), *Identifying Europe's recovery needs*, Staff Working Document, https://eur-lex.europa.eu/legal-content/EN/TXT/?uri=SWD:2020:98:FIN (Accessed October 15, 2021).

[25] Tooze A. and Schularick M. (2020), "The Shock of Coronavirus Could Split Europe – Unless Nations Share the Burden", *The Guardian,* 25 March.

various Member States could have undermined the European project itself, were a solidarity-based approach, with relative sharing of the tax burden, not have taken over.

5.7 The long-term recovery package

With this unprecedented impetus towards solidarity, in May 2020 Germany and France proposed their European level initiative to get out of the crisis. The proposal comprised the following actions: developing a new EU approach based on strategic health sovereignty in order to pursue common R&D, stocks of medicines, prevention and reaction plans; speeding up green and digital transitions, reaffirming the principles of the EGD; enhancing the EU's economic and industrial resilience and sovereignty, and giving a new impulse to the Single Market, with a prospect of a sovereign industrial base, also based on the implementation of the IPCEIs, like for instance hydrogen technologies and systems. Finally, the most revolutionary idea by the Franco-German axis was to finance an ambitious plan aimed at investment and reforms (Recovery Fund), embedded in the MFF framework, through the Commission borrowing on markets on behalf of the EU for a substantial amount (€500 bn.), that would be disbursed in the form of grants, as is the case for structural funds. This proposal would be very beneficial in terms of national public finances, as the new common emissions would not impact on the national debts of Member States, and provide budgetary expenditure for the most affected sectors and regions. Therefore, countries would receive on the basis of their effective needs, but be responsible for the disbursement of Commission bonds on the basis of their capital key in the EU budget. This configuration represents a redistributive policy, as the difference between what a country gets and what it has to pay back represents a real positive transfer (Merler, 2020a).[26]

Although the proposal may be judged as not commensurate with real economic needs, two points are particularly in relation to progress towards a fiscal union: the issuance of common debt, and the introduction of new own resources.

---

[26] Merler S. (2020a), *EU Recovery Fund: A Franco-German Revolution*, *Algebris Policy Forum Blog*, https://www.algebris.com/it/policy-research-forum-it/eu-recovery-fund-una-rivoluzione-franco-tedesca/ (Accessed October 15, 2021).

First, the idea of issuing large amounts of Eurobonds to finance grants was finally accepted, although only temporarily, even by Germany, signalling an important political change. In 2018 Germany signed the Meseberg Declaration in cooperation with France, in which neither common debts nor transfers were foreseen. However, the *frugal four* countries (the Netherlands, Austria, Denmark and Sweden) continued to argue that the fund under discussion should be temporary and a one-off, with a sunset clause after two years, and should not lead to debt mutualisation.

In July 2020, the European Council finally reached the difficult political compromise on a recovery plan, the NGEU, amounting to €750 bn., that was negotiated along with the 2021-2027 MFF itself amounting to €1.090 bn.[27] With the agreement of the NGEU, the European Commission will for the first time make large sums available to those EU countries hardest hit by the biggest recession in 70 years, financed by issuing common European debt. The largest part of NGEU (almost 90 %) is devoted to the Recovery and Resilience Facility (RRF), providing large-scale financial grants to support Member States, with the aim of mitigating the economic and social impact of the coronavirus pandemic, and of making EU economies more sustainable, resilient, and better prepared for the challenges posed by the green and digital transitions. According to the conclusion of the European Council, the Member States will prepare national recovery and resilience plans setting out their reform and investment agendas for the next few years. As regard conditionality, the RRF plans will be assessed by the Commission, based on the criteria of consistency with the country-specific recommendations, as well as the impact projects would have on strengthening growth potential, job creation and economic and social resilience. Furthermore, the effective contribution to the green and digital transition will also be a prerequisite for a positive assessment.

Even if the mutualisation of debt was finally introduced, it is interesting to note that the issuing of Eurobonds is only linked to the NGEU plan and not to the MFF. This point is important from the perspective of the translation of a momentum in solidarity into a structural change of the European integration process. Since the debt-in-common

---

27 As agreed by the Heads of State and Governments, the NGEU would be made up of 390 billion euros in grants (quite lower than the 500 bn proposed by both the Commission and the Franco-German axes) and 360 billion euros in loans.

was presented as a temporary tool, it will be difficult to make a transition from this initiative to a system of permanent EU common issuance, linked to programs with a long-term prospects (Merler, 2020b).[28]

Furthermore, these long-term strategic programs were not sufficiently addressed in the latest EU budget negotiation process. Discussions on the 2021-2027 MFF started in 2018 with a Commission proposal focused on a *Union that protects, empowers and defends*. However, the proposal had to be updated after the coronavirus pandemic, to account for the dramatic need of intervention at the European level. A second proposal followed in May 2020, to ensure the budget could better support Europe's recovery, without neglecting the long-term issues related to the strategic agenda of the EU. A comparison between the updated Commission proposal of May 2020, and the final agreement by the European Council in July, shows an increase in appropriations for cohesion and agriculture policies (by 2,2 % and 0,9 %, respectively); *Migration and Border Management* and *Security and Defence* headings also received higher provision than in the 2014-2020 MFF, although not in line with the requests of the Commission and the European Parliament. In a similar vein, programs considered to be investments in EU common goods such as Horizon Europe and Invest EU have been cut in comparison with the revised Commission proposal (by 62 % and 81 %, respectively). Many commentators, who clamoured for a European budget with greater focus on higher European added value, have been frustrated by this result. As Enderlein tweeted "So, if I understand current #EUCO discussions correctly, some of the main proposed cuts are in: - Health (EU4Health) - Research (Horizon) - Climate transition (JTF) This is not frugal. This is stupid."[29] Covid-19 has not changed the international challenges with which the EU is confronted; many of the problems we will face in the next decade will simply be more extreme versions of what we are already experiencing today. For instance, the pandemic crisis has accelerated the pace of digital transformation, with further expansion in e-commerce

---

28 Merler S. (2020b), *Next Generation, chi ci guadagna e chi ci perde*, Lavoce.info, https://www.lavoce.info/archives/68692/next-generation-chi-ci-guadagna-e-chi-ci-perde/ (Accessed October 15, 2021).

29 Enderlein H. (2020, July 18), [So, if I understand current #EUCO discussions correctly, some of the main proposed cuts are in: - Health (EU4Health) - Research (Horizon) - Climate transitition (JTF) This is not frugal. This is stupid.]; Retrieved from https://twitter.com/henrikenderlein/status/1285295837380304896 Accessed December 2, 2021).

and increases in the pace of adoption of telemedicine, video-conferencing, online teaching, and fintech (Susskind et al., 2020).[30]

With the advent of the Covid-19 crisis the debate about the role of a Eurozone budget or budget line in respect of fiscal capacity has changed. The creation of a fiscal capacity came in the form of the NGEU, which is both an instrument for stabilisation, mainly aimed at investment, and an instrument for convergence and competitiveness, through reforms, as the BICC was intended to be in the agreement of the Eurogroup. In context, however, the BICC has turned out to be an inadequate tool to respond to a crisis. First, with a provision of €17 bn. over the whole seven year financial programming cycle, it is clearly too small to provide the necessary funding to countries. Furthermore, the BICC lacks some of the fundamental features that were planned for the NGEU, since it did not follow a risk-sharing approach, as a major part of the fund would have returned to contributor countries, nor did it envisage any form of borrowing capacity.

A second point concerns the possibility of deepening on-going discussions about genuine European own resources. In July 2020 the European Council agreed that over the coming years the EU would work towards reforming its own resources system with the introduction of new sources of financing, with proposals that have been discussed for years; these issues have now gained extreme urgency and importance. The possibility that the proceeds of new own resources would be used for repayment of NGEU borrowing is a point in favour for an acceleration in the implementation of new fiscal resources, that could possibly replace national contributions in a period of mounting national debt. In Chapter 8 we analyse the own resources issue, and offer some proposals on possible solutions.

In conclusion, the political result achieved with the NGEU is important because it provided the Union with the stabilisation function that was deemed necessary to complement the imperfect institutional architecture of the Eurozone (Saraceno, 2020).[31] In a federation, like the US, the

---

30 Susskind D., Manyika J., Saldanha J., Burrow S., Rebelo S. and Bremmer I. (2020), "How will the World Be Different After Covid-19?", *Finance & Development*, June, Vol. 57, No. 2, pp. 26-29, https://www.imf.org/external/pubs/ft/fandd/2020/06/how-will-the-world-be-different-after-COVID-19.htm (Accessed October 15, 2021).

31 Saraceno F. (2020), *La riconquista*, Roma: LUISS University Press.

central government should support a country or a region that is affected by a crisis through automatic stabilisers, like unemployment subsidies or deposit insurance. In contrast, in the Eurozone this central mechanism was absent, at least during the sovereign debt crisis; the hardest hit countries had to commit themselves to respecting restrictive fiscal rules, that had pro-cyclical effects on their economies, without such compensatory transfers from the central budget. The Covid-19 crisis created the conditions for a change of attitude towards solidarity, with a major breakdown of the taboo of transfers. On the other hand, the allocation of European public goods was sacrificed. Creel et al. (2020)[32] have pointed to the fact that there has been a lot of discussion about financing, but little about the sort of concrete projects into which the EU should be putting public money. They proposed combining two pillars: a national leg, similar to the agreed Recovery Fund, with grants for a total of €500 bn., targeted at those states with the most pressing needs arising from the pandemic; and a European pillar – three times bigger – that would finance projects with a genuine European value-added, and promote longer term goals, and also avoid the risks of coordination and duplication between twenty-seven national actors. In this field, EU-wide solutions with a strategic long-term horizon could include: a European health policy responsible for investment in human capital to match the demands of health skills and the supply of drugs and health commodities; European green transport infrastructures, like a high-speed railway network; and projects under the EGD, to decarbonise the economy while being socially sustainable. This list is only a starting point, and could be enlarged to encompass other strategic directions for the EU's future long-term investment policy. In the next chapter we examine some of these options.

[32] Creel J., Holzner M., Saraceno F., Watt A. and Wittwer J. (2020), *How to Spend It*, IMK Policy Brief No. 92, June, Düsseldorf: Hans-Böckler-Stiftung, Institut für Makroökonomie und Konjunkturforschung, https://www.econstor.eu/bitstream/10419/224266/1/p_imk_pb_92_2020.pdf (Accessed October 14, 2021).

Chapter 6

The European Social Green Deal

6.1 The new development strategy for climate change

Climate change is the challenge our generation has to face. The Paris Agreement, adopted at the Conference of Parts 21 (COP21) climate talks in December 2015, sets out a global aim to limit average global surface temperatures to well below 2°C above pre-industrial levels. It adds that there should be efforts to limit this to 1,5°C.

The EU has already started to modernise and transform its economy with the aim of reaching a net zero emission economy by 2050, as it first defined in the 2018 communication *A Clean Planet for all* which committed the EU to the goal of reducing GHG emissions by 40 % (compared to 1990 levels) by 2030 (European Commission, 2018).[1] Between 1990 and 2018 greenhouse gas emissions reduced by 23 % in EU as a whole (Fig. 6.1). However, this target has more recently been revised, since current climate policy will only reduce emissions by 60 % by 2050, a trend that is not enough to reach the ultimate objective, the limitation, by the middle of the century, of increases in temperature compared to pre-industrial level well below the 2°C.[2] In fact, above this threshold, a *Hothouse Earth* scenario could develop, with effects on the planet that

---

1 European Commission (2018), *A Clean Planet for All. A European Strategic Long-term Vision for a Prosperous, Modern, Competitive and Climate Neutral Economy*, Bruxelles: European Commission, https://eur-lex.europa.eu/legal-content/EN/TXT/PDF/?uri=CELEX:52018DC0773 (Accessed October 15, 2021).

2 As the Commission observed, the Intergovernmental Panel on Climate Change (IPCC) issued in October 2018 its Special Report on the impacts of global warming of 1,5°C above pre-industrial levels and related global greenhouse gas emission pathways. Based on scientific evidence, the Report demonstrated that human-induced global warming had already reached 1°C above pre-industrial levels, and was increasing at approximately 0,2°C per decade. Without stepping up international climate action, global average temperature increase could reach 2°C soon after 2060 and continue rising afterwards (European Commission, 2018).

could run out of control, making large-scale irreversible climate impacts more likely, with damage to economic, food, water and energy systems. These could, in turn trigger conflicts and migratory pressures; in essence, climate change could undermine security and prosperity in the broadest sense.According to the Intergovernmental Panel on Climate Change (IPCC)'s 2018 Special Report on Global Warming, possible responses to climate change fall into three categories: mitigation, adaptation and remediation. Mitigation means measures to reduce carbon emissions (for example, through decarbonisation of energy and transport systems or through changes in consumption patterns) or to enhance carbon sinks (like afforestation or reforestation); adaptation comprises measures that make the human population more resilient to the effects of climate change, like flood control measures and changing land use and even relocation of cities; remediation means measures to counteract the effects of GHG emissions, like global warming (an example is through stratospheric aerosol injection) (Coffman et al., 2020).[3] Over the next few decades, mitigation, adaptation and remediation will all be major sources of investment opportunities, particularly for institutional investors. For the moment, mitigation measures like the electrification of transport, and reducing building's energy consumption are the most important areas, and the most readily achievable, although requiring substantial planning; adaptation and remediation will become more urgent areas of investment, in particular if the efforts of limiting global warming are to stick to the 2° or even the 3°C scenario.

The EU strategy defined in 2018 provided a comprehensive set of concrete actions, ranging from energy efficiency of buildings to the deployment of electricity from renewable sources, from the circular economy to increase recycling rates, and from reducing demand for raw materials to carbon capture and storage systems. The effectiveness of these proposals will depend both on the speed of their implementation, and on the willingness, and capacity, of citizens to take an active part in these changes. An important element of the transition therefore concerns public acceptance of certain modes of production, and new lifestyles and consumption patterns, which adds further complexity.

---

3 Coffman D., Cardinale R., Meng J. and Mi Z. (2020), "Ecological Transition", in Saraceno F. and Cerniglia F. (eds.), *A European Public Investment Outlook*, Cambridge: Openbook Publishers.

In December 2019, soon after the Paris Agreement's inception, the European Commission proposed an upward revision of climate goals, and raised the emission reduction target to 55 % by 2030 and further explored how the EU intended to meet the carbon neutral target (see Fig. 6.1). President Ursula von der Leyen launched the long awaited EGD, which outlined the roadmap and actions to achieve the goal of making Europe the first continent with zero environmental impact by 2050. The development strategy adopted by the Commission replaced the Europe 2020 Strategy, and fully incorporated the need to respond to the growing pressures arising from the climate challenge. The EGD, while looking far ahead, calls for concrete action in the immediate future with initiatives in different areas which, while responding to the environmental challenge, could also be an opportunity to give the European economic development model an environmental and social friendly direction.

To be successful, the EGD will have to act as a forum for dialogue between diverse but complementary sectors, actors and problems, with a common interest in protecting the planet. Such an approach goes by the

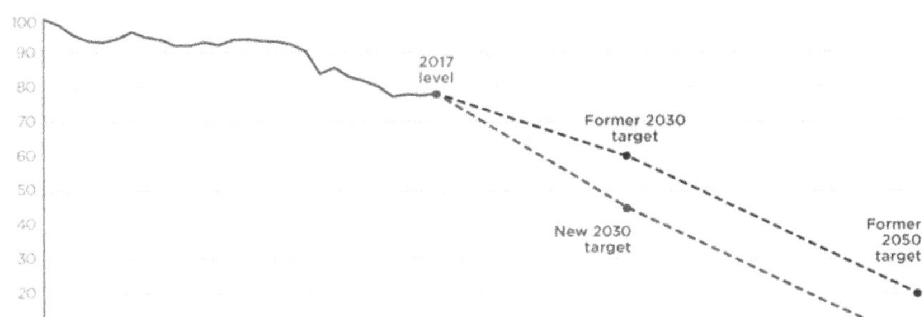

Fig. 6.1: EU28 Greenhouse gas emission, actual, 1990-2017 and long-term targets (index 1990=100)

Note: Former 2030 and 2050 target refers to 2018 communication *A Clan Planet for all*, while new targets to 2019 EGD.

Source: Pisani-Ferry (2019b), *A Credible Decarbonization Agenda Can Help Strengthen Europe's Economy*, Real Time Economic Issues Watch, Peterson Institute for International Economic, https://www.piie.com/blogs/realtime-economic-issues-watch/credible-decarbonization-agenda-can-help-strengthen-europes

name of green industrial policy; in using this term, Rodrik and Altenburg (2017)[4] warn that while industrial policy is a well understood concept, the range of policies the 'green' variant covers goes well beyond industry itself, embracing entire economies, and not just manufacturing industry. Industrial policy can be defined on the basis of different objectives: the economic (improving efficiency); environmental (ensuring sustainability); social (increasing equity); and political (protecting specific interests), nevertheless, they can overlap and coordinate with each other. Modern green industrial policy encompasses all measures that correct the allocation dynamics of the market, bringing them back into a broader project of socially desirable structural transformation, the direction of which is well defined in environmental terms. With this in mind, the EGD will have to provide for a system of incentives and disincentives, favourable legislation, and complementary infrastructures. It should also seek a strong social consensus, be aware of the costs of the transition, and allow fiscal and monetary policy to follow a coordinated action.

6.2 The four pillars of the EGD

In line with Rodrik and Altenburg's approach, the EU recognised the need to rethink clean energy policies in all sectors of the economy, and recognised the importance of pushing the level of ambition higher. As already mentioned, after an initial commitment to reduce greenhouse gas emissions by 40 % by 2030, the EU Commission is expected to increase the targets by 2030 to between 50 % and 55 % compared to 1990 levels. Accordingly, a wide range of instruments and new policies are foreseen by the EDG through four main pillars: carbon pricing, sustainable investment, a new industrial policy, and a fair transition (Belladonna and Gili, 2020).[5]

4 Rodrik D. and Altenburg T. (2017), "Green Industrial Policy: Accelerating Structural Change towards Wealthy Green Economies", in Altenburg T. and Assmann C. (eds.), *Green Industrial Policy, Concept, Country Experiences*, UN Environment; German Development Institute (DIE), https://www.un-page.org/files/public/green_industrial_policy_book_aw_web.pdf (Accessed October 15, 2021).

5 Belladonna A. and Gili A. (2020), *How the European Green Deal Will Drive the Next Generation*, ISPI Commentary, 24 June, https://www.ispionline.it/it/pubblicazione/how-european-green-deal-will-drive-next-generation-eu-26494 (Accessed October 14, 2021).

The first pillar is based on the *polluter pays* principle, which translates into an effective carbon pricing mechanism to get the right price for pollution. All the reforms to be carried out by the Commission must therefore ensure effective carbon pricing throughout the economy. This will encourage changes in consumer and business behaviour, and facilitate an increase in sustainable investment, thanks to the internalisation of pollution costs for fossil fuel energies. At the EU level, there is currently only one mechanism within the industrial sector and power plants to contain emissions through prices: the Emission Trading Scheme (ETS). It is a cap-and-trade system; the number of allowances to be allocated and their recipients are set below a ceiling (cap), within which private operators in the industry buy at auction or receive free emission rights, based on the allowances received, which they can then trade. One aspect of the ETS that has been criticised is the partial coverage of emissions; despite a gradual increase, less than half of the allowances in the ETS are sold, while the rest are granted free of charge to operators most prone to the risk of relocating to other jurisdictions (i.e. *carbon leakage*) with lower levels of environmental protection. To counter this, the EU intends imposing carbon pricing at the border for selected sectors (through a carbon border adjustment mechanism), a tariff on imports commensurate with the quantity of CO_2 emitted during the production of the imported goods, with the aim of reducing carbon leakage. This would make it possible to avoid the use of a free allocation of permits, and ensure equal treatment between domestic and foreign production.[6]

Sustainable investments are the second driver of a transition towards a sustainable economy. Estimates of the investment needed to achieve climate and energy targets vary from an order of magnitude of around €260 bn. (about 1,5 % of 2018 GDP), as reported by the European Commission (2019c),[7] to

---

6 For a comprehensive analysis on carbon pricing and its implications in Europe, see Majocchi A. (2018), *European Budget and Sustainable Growth. The Role of a Carbon Tax*, Peter Lang.

7 European Commission (2019c), *United in Delivering the Energy Union and Climate Action – Setting the Foundations for a Successful Clean Energy Transition*, Bruxelles: European Commission, https://eur-lex.europa.eu/legal-content/EN/TXT/PDF/?uri=CELEX:52019DC0285&from=EN (Accessed October 15, 2021).

According to Commission's estimate, the investment needs per sector would be: €125 bn. for the residential sector, €71 bn. for the service sector, €21 bn. for the transport sector, €21 bn. for power generation, €13 bn. for the power grid, €4 bn. for the industrial sector, and €2 bn. for boilers.

€1.000 bn. per year (European Court of Auditors, 2017).[8] The intention of the Commission is to deploy an Investment Plan for a sustainable Europe that is expected to generate €100 bn. a year until 2030. It will combine dedicated financing to support sustainable investments and proposals for an improved enabling framework that is conducive to green investment. However, the generation of effective investment will be conditional on private finance deciding to invest in environmentally sustainable projects. Many efforts are being made in this direction to mobilise sustainable finance, with capital flows redirected towards green investments. In order to establish a link between finance and environmental sustainability, a comprehensive *Sustainable Finance Action Plan*, was launched in 2018 with measures capable of directing, in a clear and transparent way, sums of private capital towards uses with a real impact on the climate. Among the measures, the implementation of a single classification system (known as *taxonomy*), helps by making it clear to the markets which type of activity can be considered truly sustainable, in accordance with the objectives of environmental policy. This should also create a standard for European green bonds, which finance projects with a positive impact on the environment. These have been present on the market since 2007, but there is still no certificate to validate their green nature. In concert with these efforts, the EIB is pursuing its *metamorphosis* to align its activities with the objectives of the Paris Agreement of 2015. From 2021 fossil fuel-based energy projects will no longer be the subject of the Bank's lending activities. At the EU budget level, on the other hand, while the 2014-2020 MFF devoted at least 20 % of the budget to climate-related expenditure, the new program aims to reach 30 %.

The third pillar is represented by a new EU industrial strategy the Commission recently adopted (European Commission, 2020a).[9] The strategy intends addressing the unsolved twin challenges of green and digital transformations, putting the latter at the service of the former, as the digital sector has to contribute to the EGD, both as a source of clean technology solutions, and by reducing its own carbon footprint.

---

8 European Court of Auditors (2017), *EU Action on Energy and Climate Change*, p. 58, Luxembourg: Publications Office of the European Union. DOI: 10.2865/38310.

9 European Commission (2020a), *A New Industrial Strategy for Europe,* https://eur-lex.europa.eu/legal-content/EN/TXT/PDF/?uri=CELEX:52020DC0102&from=EN (Accessed October 15, 2021). In 2021 the strategy was then further developed to take into account the effects of the pandemic on the competitiveness of the European economy with a view to strengthening the EU's strategic autonomy.

However, carbon neutrality cannot be reached at the expense of the competitiveness of European industry, considering the growing geopolitical tensions with China, and also with the US. To overcome the challenge of making the whole European economy sustainable while maintaining its industrial competitiveness, the EU needs to become a global innovation powerhouse in energy, mobility and construction technologies. For the EU it will be crucial to invest in R&D in more coordinated and synergic way within member countries to avoid overlapping, and to profit from economies of scale.

The fourth pillar of the EGD is the Just Transition Mechanism (JTM), intended as a compensation scheme to counter the adverse distributional effects of the transition. It will draw on sources of funding from the EU budget, along with EIB loans. One component of the mechanism will be a dedicated fund, the Just Transition Fund (JTF) that will finance regions with high employment in coal, lignite, oil shale and peat production, as well as territories with greenhouse gas-intensive industries, which could be severely impacted by the transition. The Commission recognises that without considering the distributional effects, the EDG will have scarce chances of success. Managing the transition will lead to significant structural changes in business models, skills requirements and relative prices.

Reaching the long-term target by 2050 would require a specific decarbonisation strategy based on the recognition of priorities by sector, according to the technologies available, as well as clear targets and timelines for various measures, since not all sectors would reach the goal at the same time. First of all, the bulk of emissions in the EU is divided into five macro sectors: transportation (28 %), industry (26 %), power (23 %), buildings (13 %), agriculture (13 %), while fossil fuel combustion represents the biggest source of emissions, accounting for 80 % (D'Aprile et al., 2020).[10]

The decarbonisation pathway has to follow a specific sequence in which sectors reach net-zero. This order is based on interdependencies between and among sectors, relative costs, and the maturity of the technology required in each sector. Based on these factors, the first sector

---

10 D'Aprile P., et al. (2020), *Net-zero Europe. Decarbonization Pathways and Socio-economic Implications*, McKinsey & Company, https://www.mckinsey.com/business-functions/sustainability/our-insights/how-the-european-union-could-achieve-net-zero-emissions-at-net-zero-cost (Accessed October 14, 2021).

to reach net-zero would be power, then transportation and buildings, followed by industry and agriculture. Decarbonising power production could be achieved quickly, because most of the technology for generating renewable power is already mature.

6.3 Public investment and climate debt

To coincide with the signature of the 2015 Paris Agreement, the European Energy Union was introduced to meet the EU's energy and climate targets for 2030. The energy strategy aimed at addressing different aspect related to energy, these can be understood as follows:

- the diversification of Europe's sources of energy ensuring energy security through solidarity and cooperation between member countries;
- a fully integrated energy market, to enable the free flow of energy within the EU through adequate infrastructure, without technical or regulatory barriers;
- the support of breakthroughs in low-carbon and clean energy technologies through the prioritisation of research and innovation needed for the energy transition.

To achieve these goals, in those sectors not covered by the ETS, (i.e. buildings, transport and agriculture), the open method of coordination was applied to the Energy Union, along with a governance structure that resembles that of the Eurozone. Each Member State has to present its 10-year integrated National Energy and Climate Plan (NECP) for the period from 2021 to 2030, to demonstrate in a clear and transparent way how it intends to contribute to the general effort. The NECPs covering the first period, from 2021 to 2030, will have to ensure that the Union's 2030 targets are met. In detail, EU targets at the aggregate level refer to: – at least 40 % cuts in GHG emissions (compared with 1990 levels); – at least 32 % share for renewable energy; – and at least 32,5 % improvement in energy efficiency. The system was built on a iterative process between each Member State and the Commission, meaning that if the latter considers that a country has not pledged a sufficient contribution in its draft NECP to contribute fully towards EU targets, or if at any point in time a country were to fall behind schedule in delivering those targets, it can issue recommendations to that country and ask it to fall back in line. This process is similar to the European Semester, introduced during the sovereign debt crisis to coordinate national fiscal policies of Euro area countries, where the Commission assesses the compatibility of national budget plans with respect to the European aim of sound fiscal policy.

A crucial question is how to respond to the very long-term goal of net-zero emissions in Europe, in a coordinated and shared manner, if the efforts of some national governments are not commensurate with realistic needs.

After an extensive process of preparation and coordination at the national level, and constant dialogue between Member States and EU institutions, national governments have recently presented their final plans. The plans, if fully implemented, would lead Europe to surpass the targets of GHG reduction, and consist both of policy tools and an investment agenda that provide business and investors with a forward-looking framework. According to a final assessment of the Commission, national planning has shown mixed results. In most fields Union targets are expected to be met, renewable energy and emission reduction targets should be reached by 2030, at least at the aggregate level; under planned measures contained in NECPs the share of renewable energy could reach a level of nearly 33 %, while energy efficiency will fall short of the desired level with a 3 % gap (European Commission, 2020b).[11] The assessment shows that the reduction for primary and final energy consumption will reach about 29 %.

However, the aggregate figures mask differences between countries in their efforts in energy and climate policies, and prevent the EU from being more ambitious. In fact, the targets set for energy efficiency and renewable energies are compatible with a reduction of emission of 40 %, a threshold that does not align with what would be required on the basis of the scientific evidence.

One way to quantify the constraints posed by climate change is the concept of the carbon budget. This is predicated on the idea that the quantity of CO_2 that can be released in the atmosphere is limited, if a temperature change threshold has to be respected, be it 2° or 1,5° C above pre-industrial level. Given the fact that there is an almost linear

---

[11] European Commission (2020b), *An EU-wide Assessment of National Energy and Climate Plans*, Bruxelles: European Commission, https://eur-lex.europa.eu/legal-content/EN/TXT/PDF/?uri=CELEX:52020DC0564&from=EN (Accessed October 15, 2021).

relationship between cumulative emissions of CO_2 and global average temperature increases, it is possible to quantify the total amount of global emissions remaining (i.e. the carbon budget) before temperatures reach a given threshold. If climate policy is committed to a target of 1,5°C above pre-industrial times, as the IPCC recommends, a reduction of 65 % on 1990 levels by 2030 is needed (Wildauer et al., 2020).[12] According to preliminary estimations by Guéret et al. (2018),[13] for nearly all EU countries the carbon budget is almost exhausted with on average only 10 years remaining.

These results indicate that a significant current share of capital stock in the business sector, residential and tertiary buildings, means of transportation, etc., has to be considered as stranded assets, and needs to be retrofitted. In monetary terms, this huge effort can be translated into a kind of climate debt, which gives us a measure of how much we should pay to respect the climate constraint. For countries highly affected by the limits of the carbon budget, the carbon debt is quite important, amounting to nearly 50 % of EU GDP to stay below a looser threshold of 2°C in the next few years.[14] While it is difficult to be precise about these estimates, they appear large enough to suggest that when environmental aspects are taken into consideration, the macroeconomic situation of a country may change: "a country may seem in a sustainable and prudent situation – a low public deficit, a public debt stable at a low ratio to GDP – but may be facing a wall due to climate change unpreparedness"(Guéret et al., 2018, p. 7).

This coincidence of an unsatisfactory assessment of national climate policy planning, and recommendations by science for urgent action, lead us to recognise that political consensus will, first and foremost, make it difficult to achieve the overarching public sector investment plan that

---

12 Wildauer R., Leitch S. and Kapeller J. (2020), *How to Boost the European Green Deal's Scale and Ambition*, Greenwich Papers in Political Economy, Greenwich: University of Greenwich, https://www.jku.at/fileadmin/gruppen/108/ICAE_Working_Papers/wp111.pdf (Accessed October 15, 2021).

13 Guéret A., Malliet P., Saussay, A. and Timbeau, X. (2018), *An Explorative Evaluation of the Climate Debt,* OFCE Policy briefs 45, https://www.ofce.sciences-po.fr/pdf-articles/actu/OFCE-Policybrief45Eng.pdf (Accessed October 15, 2021).

14 As the authors themselves warn the interpretation of this high quantification must be done carefully: it is the net present value of costs to be paid in order to reach the 2°C target, without any consideration on how to do it.

can overcome the magnitude of the problem. After years of fiscal consolidation leading economic growth strategy, the economic recession caused by the pandemic threatens public funds for transition even more. It is true, for example, that the Covid-19 crisis negatively impacted on energy demand, but this is not the result of structural changes and will not be permanent. The EU has been called on to support Member States in financing more public investment, and in creating the conditions for greater private sector involvement.

6.4 Financing the EGD

It is evident that to cope with climate change substantial investment will be required. At the national level, the NECPs submitted to the Commission show that the priority areas for reforms and investments include: the renovation of the building stock and access to affordable housing; the decarbonisation of industry and renewable energy; sustainable mobility; energy system integration, including infrastructures, batteries and renewable hydrogen. As regards the building sector – a key priority, given that buildings are responsible for 40 % of energy demand and 36 % of total emissions – Member States have identified the need to collectively invest around €130 bn. per year in order to reduce energy consumption in the building stock. However, the rate of renovation for energy savings observed in the EU, of between 2012 and 2016 of 1 % energy saved, is not sufficient to achieve decarbonised buildings: a tripling to 3 % primary energy savings per year would be needed, corresponding to about €800 bn.[15] The magnitude of the investment actually required substantially differs from the amounts governments have made available in their NECPs.

In the Commission's proposal, the financial pillar of the EGD will be an comprehensive program, the Sustainable Europe Investment Plan, which overall would be capable of amassing €1.000 bn. by 2030. Basically, it is a scheme that mainly draws on a combination of various extant EU funding sources, like the Cohesion Policy, the CAP, InvestEU, with

---

[15] European Commission (2019a), *Comprehensive Study of Building Energy Renovation Activities and the Uptake of Nearly Zero-energy Buildings in the EU, Final Report*, https://op.europa.eu/en/publication-detail/-/publication/97d6a4ca-5847-11ea-8b81-01aa75ed71a1 (Accessed October 15, 2021).

the cooperation of the EIB to leverage private financing – and sources coming from ETS funds.[16]

The JTM is a key pillar of the EGD, targeting specific regions, as climate neutrality will require a fundamental restructuring of their economies, structural changes in business models and new skill requirements. Its method of financing basically replicates the Juncker Plan, as it will be based on a range of instruments: the JTF, used primarily to provide grants within the EU budget; the dedicated transition scheme under InvestEU to crowd-in private investments, and a new just transition public sector loan facility with the EIB to leverage public financing. Altogether, the components of the JTM could help mobilise investment in the regions most exposed to transition challenges, in the order of €100 bn. over the programming period 2021-2027.

A crucial question remains; whether the EGD, as launched by the Commission, will be sufficient in terms of financial allocation. Before trying to answer the question, it is relevant to note that estimating the financial needs also depends on underlying assumptions about the expected results for emission reductions, as well as the approach adopted to calculate such reductions.

As discussed, it is estimated that limiting global warming to 1,5°C above pre-industrial levels – the average global temperature has already increased by 1°C – requires a substantial upgrading of existing capital stock. The Commission has estimated the additional annual investment expenditure required to meet two different scenarios. In order to reach a GHG reduction of 40 % (relative to 1990 levels) by 2030, the amount of investment would be €260 bn., while in order to limit the global temperature increase to 1,5 °C further annual investments of €175–290 bn. will have to be made before 2050. However, other projections are critical of such estimates, and take a more conservative approach on the way to reduce emissions. To be precise, EGD's 2050 carbon neutral objective

16 The EU ETS Modernisation Fund and Innovation Fund, both financed outside the EU's long-term budget, will channel additional money to the green transition. The Innovation Fund will support investments in scaling up break-through low-carbon technologies and processes in renewable energy and energy intensive industries, including carbon capture, use and storage, and energy storage, while the Modernisation Fund will support investments in modernising the power sector and wider energy systems, boosting energy efficiency in ten lower-income Member States. It can also support the re-skilling and up-skilling of the people affected.

is defined in terms of net emissions, meaning that positive emissions are allowed as long as they are offset by negative emissions; these are derived from removing CO_2 from the atmosphere, and storing it on land, underground or in the oceans. Unfortunately, although plenty of these technologies have been proposed (from re-forestation to carbon capture and storage) none are ready to be rolled out around the world, or, in some cases, even been shown to work at scale (Carbon Brief, 2016).[17] An over-heavy reliance on negative emissions is risky, because of the uncertainties involved in large scale deployment of associated technologies. Therefore, adopt an absolute zero emission goal is recommended.

Taking these issues into account may lead to different outcomes in the investment gap. Some studies, like Wildauer et al. (2020), find that annual investment requirements of about €800 bn. in the EU are required for a successful transition over the coming decades, suggesting that the EGD substantially underestimates investment needs. In particular, of Wildauer's estimated €800-900 bn. per year investment (that may come from redirecting investments that would otherwise have funded carbon-intensive sectors, or from additional capital outlays), nearly half of the total capital would go to transportation (€11,8 tn.), followed by 30 % to buildings (€8,4 tn.), 9 % to power (€2,5 tn.), 3 % to agriculture (€935 bn.), and 1 % to industry (€350 bn.), while about 14 % (€3,4 tn.) of the total investment would fund improvements in energy transmission and distribution infrastructure.

The two levels of action, national and European, as depicted by the NECPs and the Sustainable European Investment Plan, will probably not be enough to meet the financial needs to tackle climate change. Even the additional, new resources brought in by the NGEU, with an increase in the JTF of €40 bn., and the InvestEU scheme by another €15 bn., do not solve the problem of the limited size of the European budget in general. In order to mobilise further capital, especially from the private sector, targeted interventions will be needed, from green finance taxonomy[18] to price measures, such as carbon pricing or cap-and-trade system.

---

17 Carbon Brief (2016), *Explainer: 10 Ways 'negative emissions' Could Slow Climate Change*, 11 April, https://www.carbonbrief.org/explainer-10-ways-negative-emissions-could-slow-climate-change (Accessed October 15, 2021).

18 The specific way the EU has developed a classification of projects that would be helpful for investors in order to recognise true green projects.

6.5 Carbon pricing

For some years now, there have been discussions about reforming the EU budget, not only on the expenditure side but also on the revenue side. One strategy to increase the EU's budget would be to introduce genuine own resources, and justify their creation by linking these to EU policies that promote the production of European public goods. This window of opportunity for change has come about with the ambitious EGD programme with its huge investment needs. One proposal has been to introduce a carbon tax as a means of discouraging the use of fossil fuels, while at the same time generating revenue for public budgets. One caveat: this solution would be optimal from an environmental point of view, but difficult to implement politically and socially.

For Baranzini et al. (2017)[19] carbon pricing is the most important tool to combat climate change. It would incentivise the transition from fossil fuels to clean energy – making carbon intensive fuels more expensive – and give a clear signal to the markets of the political support for an ecological transition. According to the World Bank, carbon pricing is an instrument that captures the external costs of GHG emissions, like damage to crops, health care costs, and ties them back to their sources through a price, usually in the form of a price on CO_2 emitted. It can be implemented in two ways, as a quantity system (like a cap-and-trade mechanism) or as a pricing system (i.e. a carbon tax). Although there are differences between the two, the need to price carbon is acknowledged from all corners of the world, and in society, not only from *Fridays For Future*, or similar ecological movements, but also from the business sector.[20]

---

[19] Baranzini A., van den Bergh J. C. J. M., Carattini S., Howarth R. B., Padilla E. and Roca J. (2017), "Carbon Pricing in Climate Policy: Seven Reasons, Complementary Instruments, and Political Economy Considerations", *WIRE's Climate Change*, Vol. 8, No. 4. DOI: doi.org/10.1002/wcc.462.

[20] In October 2018 a group of global companies asked for a strengthening of carbon pricing in Europe, proposing that European governments: firstly, progressively implement a carbon price floor in the power sector to complement an efficient EU-ETS price signal and secondly, initiate a trajectory for a rising carbon price on fossil fuels. They added that "The rising carbon price should be part of a tax or similar measure on transport and heating fuels paid by all households and businesses. Significant revenues collected by the governments could be used to mitigate the impacts on most vulnerable consumers but also to foster public policies supporting investments in clean transport and a decarbonised heating/cooling sector."

At the Community level only the industrial sector, and power generation plants, are covered by a carbon pricing mechanism, the ETS. Critics of the ETS point to the fact that more than half of total EU emissions (55 %), i.e., from the construction and domestic sectors, agriculture and transport, are excluded from the ETS. Furthermore, even within the ETS framework itself, there is a problem of partial coverage of emissions. In fact, less than half of the allowances in the ETS are auctioned, while the rest are allocated for free to operators most exposed to the risk of relocation to jurisdictions with a lower level of environmental protection.

In sectors not covered by the ETS scheme, Member States can decide whether to apply a carbon tax as a measure of environmental protection, which at the same time represents a source of fiscal revenue. In the EU the carbon tax is raised in a number of countries, although with different rates: Sweden (with a rate of €112 per tCO_2 [tonnes of CO_2]), Finland (€67), France (€48), Denmark (€26), Ireland (€25), Slovenia (€18), Portugal (€9), followed by Poland, Estonia and Latvia with less than €4 per tCO_2. Germany has decided to introduce carbon pricing of €25/tCO_2 on transport and domestic heating from 2021. In sum, the carbon pricing system in EU is complex, partly based on a market mechanism, partly on taxation, and reflects different levels of ambition among the Member States.

A further aspect linked to GHG mitigation efforts concerns the risk of carbon leakage; this is the risk that a EU-wide carbon price may lead countries with highly energy-intensive industries to move their plants to countries with lower environmental protection, and then to import the necessary goods. For this reason, introducing a carbon price at the border, via a Carbon Border Adjustment (CBA) would put domestic and imported goods on an equal footing, so that European production does not suffer fiscal damage. The CBA would therefore be based on a rate equivalent to that paid by European companies, to (a) avoid infringing the World Trade Organization (WTO) rules of non-discrimination and (b) provide the prerequisite for political acceptance by Member States of a carbon price applied at the European level. Crucially, the CBA would take the form of a customs duty, commensurate with the CO_2 content of all goods imported into the EU by producer countries that do not

---

See *Global companies call for more action* of November 2018, https://orsted.com/-/media/WWW/Docs/Corp/COM/News/Carbon-pricing-declaration-november-2018.pdf (Accessed October 15, 2021).

apply a cost to emissions. As such, the CBA could be introduced as part of the Community's customs policy, which is an exclusive competence of the Union.

The proposed introduction of a CBA can gather support for at least three reasons. First, foreign trade is an important source of emissions. Emissions from domestic production have shown a decreasing trend in Europe, but the point of view of consumers should also be taken into account, as ultimately it is the demand by households, governments and companies that contributes indirectly to emissions, irrespective of where production takes place. A large proportion of goods produced in China, a major CO_2 emitter, are exported to the EU, where consumers benefit from cheaper products. For some countries, such as Italy, France and Sweden, more than 30 % of emissions for which they are responsible come from imports, with the balance from national production.[21] A CBA could reduce the negative impact of international trade on global emissions, discouraging carbon leakage.

Second, the existing ETS could provide a useful infrastructure. In this case, implementing a CBA could be based on an extension of the ETS, where importers would be subject to the same obligation as domestic producers to return permits based on the carbon content of imported goods. The practical advantages would be to avoid the unanimity vote in the Council required for a genuine European tax,[22] and to benefit from existing technical and political capital (Mehling et al., 2019).[23]

Finally, the introduction of a CBA could generate substantial revenues for the EU budget. According to a study by the Austrian Institute for Economic Research, the revenue generated by such a measure could

---

21 Ritchie H. (2019), *How Do CO2 Emissions Compare When We Adjust for Trade?*, Our World in Data, https://ourworldindata.org/consumption-based-co2 (Accessed October 15, 2021).

22 Given its nature of customs duty related to an EU exclusive competence, the revenues generated from a CBA will constitute an own resource intended to finance the European budget. Therefore, a CBA will not require an *ad hoc* decision for the creation of a new own resource, in accordance with the procedure described in Art. 311 of the TFEU, which provides for a unanimous decision of the Council, after consulting the European Parliament, approved by all the Member States in accordance with their respective constitutional rules.

23 Mehling M., van Asselt H., Das K. and Droege S. (2019), *What a European 'carbon border tax' Might Look Like,* VoxEU CEPR, https://voxeu.org/article/what-european-carbon-border-tax-might-look. (Accessed October 15, 2021).

be substantial, as it could potentially finance one-third of the EU budget by 2027, even in more conservative scenarios (Krenek et al., 2019).[24]

The introduction, or strengthening, of carbon pricing would not only be the most effective measure to incentivise the markets in a transition from fossil fuels to clean energy, and give a clear signal to the markets of the political support of the EDG. However, given the public goods nature of environmental protection, it is important that public finance also plays its part, through investment in research and development, and infrastructure, particularly in electricity, transport and social housing, such as thermal insulation in public buildings and social housing.

6.6 The green golden rule

The decline in public investment in recent years has been driven by tight fiscal budgets, and a change in spending priorities with a re-prioritisation of public spending away from investment towards current expenditures (Bubbico et al., 2020).[25] Indeed, in Europe the need for public investment at the national level has to contend with the constraints of the Maastricht fiscal pillar rules. These rules have been criticised for their complexity, short-sightedness and anachronism.[26] The fundamental difference between current economic conditions and those of 1997, when the SGP was designed, has been the fall in interest rates: in such a situation, the objective of a structural deficit tending towards zero prevents national governments from benefiting from the opportunity of borrowing

24 Krenek A., Sommer M. and Schratzenstaller M. (2019), *Sustainability-oriented Future EU Funding. A European Border Carbon Adjustment*, WIFO Working Papers, No. 587, https://www.wifo.ac.at/jart/prj3/wifo/resources/person_dokument/person_dokument.jart?publikationsid=61931&mime_type=application/pdf (Accessed October 15, 2021).

25 Bubbico R. L., Brutscher P. and Revoltella D. (2020), "Europe Needs More Public Investment", in Saraceno F. and Cerniglia F. (eds.), *A European Public Investment Outlook*, Cambridge: Openbook Publishers.

26 A famous proposal for reforming the fiscal finance and governance in the EMU's architecture was formulated by fifteen Franco-German economists (Bénassy-Quéré, A., Brunnermeier M. K., Enderlein H., Farhi E., Fratzscher M., Fuest C., Gourinchas P.-O., Martin P., Pisani-Ferry J., Rey H., Schnabel I., Véron N., Weder di Mauro B., and Zettelmeyer J. (2018), *Reconciling Risk Sharing with Market Discipline: A Constructive Approach to Euro Area Reform*, CEPR Policy Insight 91, https://cepr.org/sites/default/files/policy_insights/PolicyInsight91.pdf). (Accessed October 14, 2021).

at real interest rates which are now basically negative to finance public investment. From a theoretical point of view, if the growth rate in the euro area were low, but still higher than long-term interest rates on public debt, it would be possible to maintain the stability of debt-to-GDP ratios, while creating deficits. This is the situation that characterises the Eurozone as a whole today. In this context, "Why wouldn't EU citizens accept channelling debt-financed public investments into environmental research, renewable energy, clean transportation systems, and other efforts to contain climate change, when financial conditions would make such investments collectively profitable?" (Pisani-Ferry, 2019a).[27]

A recourse to public debt would also be justified by the type of expenditure it would cover. Supporting public investment through debt issuance, besides making economic sense, could bring double benefits: it could stimulate growth in the long term by creating the conditions to attract further investment from the private sector; and strengthen climate action with much-needed transport (rail network and electric car) and social infrastructures, amongst others.

The idea of creating debt to support the energy transition must also encompass concerns about intergenerational justice, which leads to the following dilemma: it is better (worse) to bequeath the burden of an economic debt, in some cases already very high, or that of an environmental debt, understood as the accumulation of past environmental impacts of natural resource depletion and environmental degradation, to which future generations have not contributed, but with which they will have to reckon? This trade-off can be solved by choosing to put economic debt at the service of the priority of reducing climate debt. There is one option that can be taken, not only by countries with enough room for manoeuvre to allow fiscal expansion to make investments, but by the Eurozone as a whole. This option means going beyond the current investment clause (see Section 4.6), which only exceptionally allows investment debt to be exempted from fiscal rules in times of economic recession, and introducing a green golden rule to allow public investment to finance the energy transition. In its communication on the EGD the European Commission did recognise the importance of 'greening' national public budgets, preferred to discuss this within the context of wider economic governance and fiscal rule reform. The benefits would go beyond the

---

[27] Pisani-Ferry J. (2019a), "When Facts Change Change the Pact", *Project Syndicate.*

environmental sphere. Fears of a global slowdown, due to the trade tensions between the US and China, and more recently, to the lockdown caused by the Covid-19 pandemic, suggest a need for change in budgetary rules, towards a more favourable attitude on public investment, that can stimulate production towards domestic rather than foreign demand.

6.7 A green monetary policy

After the financial crisis, central banks in high-income countries embarked on ambitious QE programmes of financial asset purchases in an attempt to stimulate investment in the real economy. In the Eurozone, the ECB has created €2,6 tn. of new money since 2015 in the context of its QE program, without considering the PEPP, that increase money injection by further €1,85 tn. This expansive monetary policy firstly comprised a certain amount of financial assets that were purchased by the ECB and secondly new liquidity that was created and put at the disposal of commercial banks, in the hope that these would in turn increase lending to the real economy. However, for the purposes of ecological transition, there is no evidence that the credit created by commercial banks flowed to low-carbon sectors; on the contrary, if anything, QE schemes implemented since the financial crisis may be perpetuating society's high-carbon lock-in. As a European institution, should the ECB contribute to the EGD and do more to prevent climate change? In 2018, Benoît Cœuré discussed this in a speech on the relation between monetary policy and climate change, and reminded us that "without prejudice to its primary objective, the ECB shall support the general economic policies in the Union" (Cœuré, 2018).[28] Indeed, a high level of protection and the improvement of the quality of the environment are not only among the EU's general policies, but figure at the top of its agenda for the next decade as a cross-sector strategy.

The idea of a green QE program has gained appeal over the last few years. It has been proposed as an effective strategy in the fight against global warming, while acknowledging that it cannot by itself prevent severe climate change, since other types of environmental policies and

---

28 Cœuré B. (2018), *Monetary Policy and Climate Change*, conference in Berlin, November 8, https://www.ecb.europa.eu/press/key/date/2018/html/ecb.sp181108.en.html (Accessed October 14, 2021).

strategies are necessary (Dafermos et al., 2018).[29] However, the ECB could make its monetary policy green, through the purchase on the secondary market of assets that are linked to low-carbon projects. Green bonds are an example of such assets, and they going through a period of rapid expansion.[30] Different actors, including private firms and governments, can issue green bonds. In particular, the ECB's purchase of bonds issued by development banks would be an effective way of implementing green QE, given the latter's role in supporting the process of economic development, usually providing lending for activities that commercial banks are unwilling to finance, or on more favourable terms (Campiglio et al., 2017).[31] The market for green bonds has developed rapidly in recent years, with global issuance rising from less than €1 bn. in 2008 to more than €120 bn. in 2017, while euro-denominated net green bond issuance has increased ten-fold since 2013, reaching more than €40 bn. in 2017 but soon after decreasing. As regards Europe, on the one hand the European Commission has recently issued €12 bn. of green bonds on financial markets to finance the green parts of NGEU. This represents the world's largest green bond issuance to date. On the other hand, the ECB holds green bonds amounting to 3,5% of its own funds portfolio, which has a total market value of €20.8 billion, and it plans to increase this share over the coming years.

Therefore, it is possible that the ECB may already be implementing an indirect and unplanned form of green QE through the purchase of, for instance, the EIB's bonds, whose proceeds are then used to finance low-carbon projects. However, one main reason against this proposal is the fear of breaching the narrow mandate of the ECB, that of price stability. In his speech, Cœuré also warned about the need to carefully weigh up all relevant considerations, and determine the strategies that would be

---

[29] Dafermos Y., Nokolaidi M. and Galanis G. (2018), *Can Green Quantitative Easing (QE) Reduce Global Warming?*, FEPS Policy Brief, https://www.feps-europe.eu/attachments/publications/feps%20gperc%20policybriefgreenqe.pdf (Accessed October 14, 2021).

[30] As the ECB reports, the term *green bond* refers to debt securities whose proceeds are used to finance investment projects with an environmental benefit (ECB (2018), Economic Bulletin, Issue 7/2018).

[31] Campiglio E., Godin A., Kemp-Benedict E. and Matikainen S. (2017), "The Tightening Links Between Financial Systems and the Low-Carbon Transition", in Arestis P. and Sawyer M. (eds.), *Economic Policies Since the Global Financial Crisis,* pp. 313-356, London: Palgrave Macmillan.

both legal and effective in promoting environmental protection, without interfering with price stability. In fact, climate change is a typical supply side shock, which is less easy – when compared to a demand shock – for central banks to accommodate, as these pull output and inflation in opposite directions.[32] In addition, green QE might overburden central banks with additional responsibilities, and potentially compromise their effectiveness in maintaining price stability.

One possible solution to prevent QE from potentially fuelling inflation could for the ECB to replace public and corporate sector bonds when they come to maturity with the issue of new green bonds, to finance environmental projects, thus keeping the money base unchanged (De Grauwe, 2019).[33] There is another controversial aspect, the risk that the ECB might be overburdened with additional responsibilities that would imply a political decision-making process. However, the recognition that climate change could pose a risk to the macroeconomic financial system could introduce a more proactive, interventionist, role for the ECB in the green bond market, without the need to change its mandate (Campiglio et al., 2018).[34] If climate-related financial risks are intrinsic to the stability of the financial system, this could ultimately justify the implementation of measures to mitigate these risks in all central bank operations.

---

32 Climate change supply shock is characterised by droughts and heat waves leading to crop shortfalls, putting upward pressure on food prices, while hurricanes and floods destroy production capacity, thereby raising input and output prices, or on the other hand, unusually cold winters can be seen as malign productivity shocks – that is, they may raise input prices for the same level of output.

33 De Grauwe P. (2019), *Green Money without Inflation,* Social Europe, https://socialeurope.eu/green-money-without-inflation (Accessed October 15, 2021).

34 Campiglio E., Dafermos Y., Monnin P. et al. (2018), "Climate Change Challenges for Central Banks and Financial Regulators", *Nature Climate Change*, Vol. 8, No. 6, pp. 462-468, https://doi.org/10.1038/s41558-018-0175-0. The authors find two types of climate-related financial risks. The first is represented by the possible damage and undesired modifications to the production and consumption process brought about by disruptive phenomena produced by climate change. These can have large impacts on the assets of households and businesses as well as on the balance sheets of their insurance companies and the commercial banks they have borrowed from. The second refers to the potential disruption brought by the low-carbon transition itself. In this sense, the phasing out of fossil fuels will have an impact on the market valuation of the world's largest fossil companies, whose financial stocks will suffer price reductions that will have a cascading effect on the various investors.

In order to establish the link between financial and environmental sustainability, the European Commission has launched a comprehensive *Action Plan: Financing Sustainable Growth*, with measures capable of clearly and transparently directing the amount of private capital towards uses with a real impact on the climate. Among the measures identified, the plan identified the implementation of a single classification system, which makes it clear to the markets which type of activity can be considered truly sustainable, in accordance with the objectives of environmental policy.

The process of taking due account of environmental and social considerations when making investment decisions, leading to increased investment in longer-term and sustainable activities, is at the core of the action plan for sustainable finance adopted by the Commission. Accordingly, Environmental, Social and Governance (ESG) criteria should be integrated into the monitoring of financial institutions decisions to invest, and consider the risks that such factors may pose to financial stability.

Fundamental to the hypothesis of increasing periodic purchases of green bonds, a decision that is in the hands of the ECB, is the controversial issue of defining what can be labelled as a climate-friendly investment, and therefore financeable through the issuance of such bonds. For this reason, efforts towards a clear and detailed taxonomy system should take high priority; this would serve to identify investments consistent with environmental sustainability. Such a classification would also be useful for the transparent application of the green golden rule (see Section 6.6) in the selection of green investments.

6.8 The EIB as the EU's Climate Bank

The EIB is perhaps one of the lesser-known European institutions in public debate. In fact, it has been described as the "neglected institution" within the complex European architecture (Robinson 2009).[35] However, after the financial crisis, and the sharp decline in investment, the EIB has been re-evaluated, and its growth in importance has coincided with a period in which the EU budget has been under pressure on a broad front.

---

[35] Robinson (2009), "The European Investment Bank: The EU's Neglected Institution", *Journal of Common Market Studies*, Vol. 47, Issue 3, pp. 651-673.

The EIB is the world's largest multilateral borrower and lender, with €55 bn. of financing, mainly through lending, provided within the EU in 2019 (EIB, 2020, p. 60).[36] With its financing capacity, the EIB's activity has a potentially significant effect on EU policy making; it is the dominant source of EU finance for many projects, such as transport infrastructure. It must also be noted that through the leverage effect made possible by matched funding – loans are granted on the basis that additional funding is provided by Member States, agency or private actors receiving the loans – it is clear that it has had a very significant effect on EU expenditure policy. In particular, as Robinson reports, since 2007 the EIB's declared ambition has been not so much to increase the volume of its financing, but rather "to contribute effectively, through a more selective choice of projects, to achieving the Union's objectives and to mobilise funds from other sources for such projects" (Robinson, 2009, p. 661).

In the aftermath of the financial crisis, the focus has been on regaining investment levels in both small-medium enterprises and infrastructure, while at the same time the EIB has begun to embark on a process of change consistent with the EU's ecological transition. The EIB's intention to become a climate bank has been evident for some time; in 2015 it adopted the Climate Strategy, with which environmental issues become the guiding principle for all the bank's operations, particularly those relating to lending. The Strategy was reinforced more recently, when the EIB Board of Directors adopted the new Energy Lending Policy (ELP), which envisages phasing out the Bank's support for energy projects that depend on fossil fuels from 2021, in line with the Paris Agreement, to make "financial flows consistent with a path leading to low greenhouse gas emissions and climate resilient development" (Art. 2.1(c) of Paris Agreement). At the political level, President Emmanuel Macron has advocated a new role for the EIB in his appeal *Pour une Renaissance européenne*, in which he envisages European scientific progress based on the ecological challenge.

The EIB is contributing to the general effort needed to mobilise the funding of €260 bn. per year (the amount estimated by the Commission) by devoting a higher share of its financing activity to climate–related

---

36 EIB (2020), *Statistical report 2019*, Luxenbourg: European Investment Bank, https://www.eib.org/attachments/general/reports/eib_statistical_report_2019_en.pdf (Accessed October 15, 2021).

investment, with an increase from 25 % in 2012 to 31 % in 2019. The aim of the recent ELP is to allocate 50 % of lending activity to environmental protection projects by 2025, through operations focused on energy efficiency investments, especially in residential buildings, for the production of energy from renewable sources, and to support technological innovations and new energy infrastructure. The EIB manages a budget of €600 bn., with a subscribed capital of €240 bn., of which only €25 bn. is paid-up capital, (investments by EU Member States, according to their economic weight within the EU at the time of their accession). However, under its Statute, the EIB is authorised to have maximum loans outstanding equivalent to two and a half times its subscribed capital. This means that the EIB has already exhausted its lending capacity, and if asked to do more, with more complicated and riskier projects for climate and digital purposes, the capital base would have to be strengthened.

A crucial aspect in making the fight against climate change effective will be to translate emission reduction targets into well-defined criteria for the selection of projects. The ELP seems to have moved in this direction, since, for example, it stipulates that only power generation projects with CO_2 emissions below a certain threshold are eligible for lending. In addition, a review is needed of the carbon pricing values that the EIB usually applies when carrying out an economic assessment of submitted projects. As things stand, these values are out of line with the parameters defined in the scientific evidence to allow for fuel switching. According to the High-Level Commission on Carbon Prices (chaired by Nicholas Stern and Joseph Stiglitz), the level of carbon pricing, consistent with the achievement of the most ambitious containment target of under 1,5° C by 2030, is between €44 and €88 per tCO_2.

6.9 Beyond GDP: Sustainability as an economic policy

The ecological crisis has led us to rethink economic growth in terms of sustainability, prompting a debate on reforms that try to combine two agendas. On the one hand, civil, academic, and political actors aim to go beyond economic growth as a collective horizon, and, on the other, at articulating environmental challenges alongside social issues.

With respect of the first agenda, we must acknowledge that combining the dimensions of economic prosperity with those of environmental and social sustainability is one of the cornerstones of the EU's development strategy. The EGD is a clear demonstration of this, as it aims to radically transform the way we produce and consume. And, in addition, when it comes to the measurement of well-being, the EU is making efforts to promote the use of new indicators that can go beyond the mere calculation of GDP.

In 2007, the European Commission, together with the European Parliament and other international partners, launched the *Beyond GDP* conference with the aim of identifying the most appropriate indices for measuring progress. As the then Commission President José Manuel Barroso said, "GDP is an indicator of economic market activity. It is not designed to be an accurate measure of well-being" (Beyond GDP, 2007).[37] GDP measures the monetary value of what is produced, and represents prosperity derived from consumption. However, it is not able to differentiate between activities on the basis of their social and environmental impact. While GDP is a useful tool for economic policy, it is as such ill-suited to tell much of the story of what is of most concern today, such as climate change, inequality, or the quality of public health.

In the years of the financial crisis, initiatives proliferated to develop indicators of well-being and sustainability in all their dimensions. The High-level group of experts (known as the Stiglitz-Sen-Fitoussi Commission), appointed by the then French President Nicolas Sarkozy, was just one example of many efforts to increase the multidimensionality of well-being, and to raise awareness of its profound implications for policy making. One of the main limitations of the research is the difficulty of translating into a single number – as comparable and objective as possible – the amount of data collected in different areas, that is difficult to synthesise into an indicator as immediate as GDP, without the risk of dispersing the underlying information. In Europe, it was not only France that showed such vision and initiative. Italy is one of the countries at the forefront of multidimensional measurement on the international scene, with the introduction in 2013 of BES (*Benessere Equo e Sostenibile* – Equitable and Sustainable Well-Being) indicators. At the EU level, some progress has been made with the introduction of a set of indicators the

---

[37] Beyond GDP (2007), *Summary Notes from the Beyond GDP Conference Highlights from the Presentations and the Discussion*, International Conference 19-20 November, https://ec.europa.eu/environment/beyond_gdp/download/bgdp-summary-notes.pdf (Accessed October 15, 2021).

complement macroeconomic analysis of the labour market. However, these are auxiliary measures that do not change the traditional approach to GDP and the focus on economic variables.

The effective implementation of alternative measures to GDP within the European context has so far also proved difficult due to political factors, such as the absence of a strong narrative to support them in the public debate, along with a lack of a clear political imperative from which the impetus for institutional change might be derived. Overcoming these obstacles requires institutions to stimulate more debate about the kind of society that citizens want, as well as ensuring that new analytical tools are incorporated into decision-making processes. In this respect, the role of additional indicators is at least twofold. Firstly, they serve to better monitor and assess the progress of our society towards certain politically shared goals; secondly, they can guide economic policy, with particular reference to fiscal policy choices.

Picking up on the first point, it should be noted that the EU has adopted the SDGs of the United Nations 2030 Agenda, which provide benchmarks in various areas, including environmental sustainability and social inclusion, for which countries should strive. Through the development of the SDG Index we know – not too surprisingly – that there is a clear contrast between the better-positioned Northern EU countries and those in the South and East.[38] What is most worrying is not only that no Member State is on track to achieve all the SDGs, but especially that the worst performance is in areas of environmental sustainability, including responsible consumption, climate action, protecting life below water and on land, fighting hunger due to unsustainable diets and farming practices. Using the SDG Index, it is also clear that for a given state their position in the traditional ranking based on GDP size may change when other dimensions of well-being are taken into account. For example, Italy, one of the richest countries in the EU, drops to seventeenth place, having yet to achieve any of the seventeen SDGs.

From this perspective, and considering the political capital that the Commission continues to invest in the EGD, there is an urgency to complement policy making with indicators that go beyond GDP. President

[38] See *Performance of European Countries against the SDGs. Part 1*, https://eu-dashboards.sdgindex.org/chapters/part-1-performance-of-european-countries-against-the-sdgs (Accessed October 15, 2021).

von der Leyen has expressed her intention to link the European Semester – the cornerstone of economic governance among Member States – to the SDGs. The Semester was created in 2010 during the Eurozone crisis as a tool to monitor not only *ex post* but also *ex ante* the public finances of countries through specific recommendations. At least until the outbreak of the pandemic, the fiscal rules of the SGP provided the guide to policy making. The pandemic led to a temporary suspension of the pact, which will have an impact on its reform process. The reform of the fiscal rules, already on the table before the pandemic crisis, could be the occasion to recognise a preferential status to SDGs-oriented public spending, decoupling the huge investments needed to combat climate change from the financial sustainability rules.

6.10 The decoupling of GDP growth and the welfare state

In a recent contribution, Éloi Laurent (2021)[39] has tried to answer a crucial question: can we build a socio-ecological transition that is decoupled from the diktat of economic growth? Although the question seems quite radical, the author illustrates the reasons why such a transition may seem possible.

The post-war decades in Europe, and in Western countries in general, were characterised by a combination of economic growth and social policy, in which the two dimensions went hand in hand, although neglecting the ecological impact of economic prosperity. This link, formalised by Nobel prize Gunnar Myrdal has, however, changed over time. The idea that economic growth is at the basis of the development of the welfare state by financing social protection does not reflect the logic of the nexus between them.

The coupling of economic growth and social protection is referred to as the socio-economic paradigm, also known as social democracy. This combination has proved to be virtuous thanks to a cumulative process, where economic growth was fuelled by the increase in labour productivity and employment, which in turn has enabled social progress by

---

[39] Laurent É. (2021), *From Welfare to Farewell: The European Socio-ecological State Beyond Economic Growth*, ETUI Working Paper No. 4, https://www.etui.org/publications/welfare-farewell (Accessed October 15, 2021).

reducing inequalities and extending social protection to all stages and domains of the economic life cycle. However, this old coupling has been destabilised by the effects of neoliberalism that has broken the virtuous circle between economic growth and welfare state. Two mechanisms work in the socio-economic paradigm. First, the relation between GDP growth and employment, supposed to be positive in the past, is no longer valid. Even in the Eurozone this decoupling holds true, with periods of real GDP growth alongside increasing rates of unemployment. In the context of welfare this implies the lack of the guarantee that when GDP grows so does employment, allowing social contributions to increase and social policy to be properly financed.

Second, a similar disconnection holds for the relation between GDP growth and household income, hampering states' capacity to finance social policy through taxation. Here the problems are related to various factors. Here we can cite, among others: increasing inequality, that prevents national income growth from translating into household income growth; and tax competition, which diverts large amounts of national income and prevents the taxation of more mobile tax bases (such as corporate profits) that contribute to GDP but do not participate in the financing of social policy.

One conclusion from the facts as outlined is that the focus should not be on GDP growth, as this does not support employment growth and equality, but rather on human development, where wealth is defined in terms of quality of life. In more recent times, GDP growth has been more associated with productivity gains (in practice, the quality of labour supply) than with labour supply (the quantity of workers employed). This implies that as part of a human development strategy, the welfare state should intervene more in policy areas that have an effect on improving labour productivity, like public health and education. However, one important point to stress is that "the major goal of increasing labour productivity is not enrichment but to enable people to avoid spending their lives working. It allows the volume of working hours to be reduced at a constant standard of living, which frees human life from the burden of labour. The goal of labour productivity is therefore human well-being, not growth, which appears as a by-product of human well-being" (Laurent, 2015, p. 15). [40]

---

[40] Laurent E. (2015), *Social-Ecology: Exploring the Missing Link in Sustainable Development*, Documents de Travail de l'OFCE 2015-07, Paris : Observatoire Francais des Conjonctures Economiques (OFCE).

This perspective has little to do with the prevailing narrative in Europe, that of seeking increases in labour productivity as a contributing factor in increases in external competitiveness, within an economic framework based on export growth.

6.11 Energy transition and the social dimension

If ecological transition is defined in terms of a human development strategy and human survival, then it would be appropriate to make it clear that the EDG should not be understood as a mere instrument for economic growth, but should also serve to modify market allocation mechanisms towards sectors suitable for transition; this might mean a reallocation from fossil fuels to renewable sources, or from speculative to sustainable finance. It is true that the economic aspect should not be overlooked; there are good indications that economic savings, in terms of avoided climate damage, could result from the transition. Although it is very difficult to estimate the present and future costs of climate change, because of uncertainty over the level of temperature increases that will be actually reached according to studies, the costs for Europe will be high, and above all will rapidly increase over time; as such, any delay in the environmental field may well lead to an escalation of the costs of continued inaction, due to the unpredictability of ecosystems once certain thresholds are exceeded (COACCH, 2018).[41] However, the economic argument for using the EGD as a policy option to combat the recession, although relevant, must leave room for one of the essential elements in the implementation of the EDG, namely its impact on society, understood both on workers directly involved in fossil fuel-intensive sectors, and on the most vulnerable households in general.

In the case of workers, the literature suggests that the renewables sector is more labour-intensive than traditional energy sources. In theory, the shift towards low emission technologies should lead to net job creation, both in the short and long term, with new waves of investment in innovation that will generate demand for skilled labour (Fankhaeser et al.,

---

41 COACCH (2018), *The Economic Cost of Climate Change in Europe: Synthesis Report on State of Knowledge and Key Research Gaps. Policy brief by the COACCH project*, https://www.ecologic.eu/sites/files/publication/2018/2811-coacch-review-synthesis-updated-june-2018.pdf (Accessed October 14, 2021).

2008).[42] In practice however, in the European context, some regions are still linked to coal exploitation; hence the employment aspect is a crucial factor. There are some 440.000 workers throughout Europe, most of them in Poland, who could either be relocated to other sectors or to jobs with similar skill requirements (e.g. in precious and base metal mines), or leave the labour market through early retirement schemes. In addition, local economies traditionally dependent on coal mining may be diversified by converting mining sites for the use of renewables, such as wind or solar parks, or by promoting sports or cultural services as alternative activities (Alves Dias et al., 2018).[43] The cases of Saarland and the Ruhr region in Germany provide an example of a strategic approach towards a gradual industrial restructuring process with the support of workers.[44] In these cases, in parallel with supporting and restructuring the steel and coal industries, other industries (automotive and tourism) were established. Other key elements of the transition have led to major investment in R&D, the creation of universities and research centres (in IT, biotechnology and medicine), the establishment of technology parks, a support for technology transfer, and targeted support for SMEs. Trade Unions were also important in facilitating negotiated phase-outs from the dependency on the coal industry. Finally, structural regional policy and the use of European Structural Funds and Cohesion Fund played a crucial role.

6.12 The socio-ecological nexus

Usually, reflections on sustainable development have focused on the one hand on the potential of the green economy, where interactions between the economy and the environment are considered, and, on the other hand, on concepts of inclusive development, where the mutual relations between the economy and people are considered. What is absent

---

42 Fankhaeser S., Sehlleier F. and Stern N. (2008), "Climate Change, Innovation and Jobs", *Climate Policy*, Vol. 8, Issue 4, pp. 421-429.

43 Alves Dias, P., Kanellopoulos, K., Medarac, H., Kapetaki, Z., Miranda Barbosa, E., Shortall, R., Czako, V., Telsnig, T., Vazquez Hernandez, C., Lacal Arantegui, R., Nijs, W., Gonzalez Aparicio, I., Trombetti, M., Mandras, G., Peteves, E. and Tzimas, E. (2018), *EU Coal Regions: Opportunities and Challenges Ahead*, *JRC Science for Policy Report*, Luxembourg: European Commission.

44 Galgóczi B. (2014), "The Long and Winding Road from Black to Green: Decades of Structural Change in the Ruhr Region", *International Journal of Labour Research*, Vol. 6, issue 2, pp. 217-240.

here is a third link, between the environment and the social dimension, in particular if the latter is characterised by high levels of inequality. "Environmental risk is certainly a collective and global horizon, but it is socially differentiated": Laurent (2015, p.3) uses these terms to sum up the link between environmental challenges and social inequalities. The impact of the environmental crisis is not the same for everyone, but varies according to individual socio-economic status.

In this approach, inequality has consequences that make it more difficult to combat environmental challenges. It has been shown, for example, that poorer households are less likely to change their waste reduction habits and recycling practices. On the contrary, household consumption tends to become ostentatious in an attempt to imitate the lifestyle of the wealthiest households, in a society where the consumption pattern of the wealthiest population is culturally dominant. Causal links also work in the opposite direction, from the environmental to the social sphere. The emergence of exceptionally warm temperatures produces, through reduced yields, price increases for consumers, with regressive effects for households with lower incomes. Or, as the French experience of the movement of the *gilets jaunes* tells us, attempts to introduce or increase environmental protection measures encounter such resistance from society that they require forms of compensation based on income, if not also on geographical location. In general, the people most vulnerable to climate change are usually the poorest, with poor health, living in precarious housing, with low levels of education and unstable jobs, and living in areas with non-resilient health systems.

In the EU about 118 million people (23,5 % of the total) are at risk of poverty or social exclusion, are living in households with low incomes, suffer from material deprivation, and are limited by very low work intensity. Because of their economic-social-cultural status, these categories are also the most resistant to changes in behaviour, as well as towards new forms of environmental taxation, given the regressive effect of such taxation on income.

This picture demonstrates the need to support social investment, through welfare services that enable people to stay active in the labour market, and reduce the risks of poverty or social exclusion. From this perspective, it is important to provide social infrastructure (health, education and housing) that creates and maintains the conditions for active participation in society, for example, by raising awareness of environmental education and providing facilities for the treatment of pollution-related diseases. These services can play a key role in alleviating the burden that addressing the environmental challenge can place on social conditions, and hence reduce the conditions for resistance to change. Particular attention will have to be paid to situations of energy poverty, where an estimated 50 m. households in Europe are affected; thanks to the renovation of social housing, co-financed with the European level, it would be possible to achieve greater energy efficiency and thus savings in energy consumption.

6.13 Social investment and infrastructure

Contemporary economic, social, and environmental challenges offer an ideal opportunity to re-evaluate the role of the welfare state. One aspect of the debate examines the idea of social investment as a framework to understand welfare state changes, and re-design accordingly. The idea of social investment originated partly as a reaction to neoliberal prescriptions that dominated the social policy debate in the 1980s and 1990s. Neoliberalism considers social policy primarily as a cost factor, adopting the perspective of a trade-off between equality and efficiency, thus advocating strong limits to state intervention. In contrast, the social investment perspective emphasises the two-fold role of the welfare state, that is to promote and advance both equality and efficiency. In doing so, this latter approach tries to provide a conceptual framework that translates these welfare state objectives into a fundamentally changed socio-economic environment, where efficiency improvements combine with equality (Leoni, 2016).[45]

Social investment consists of a mix of policies that aim both to repair the damage caused by crisis, and to prepare individuals and households to increase their resilience to new social risks. It combines income support measures, social services for the family, and education and training policies to increase the employability of the individual – intended as the set of personal skills and resources with which the worker can defend himself against changes in the labour market, like the fragmentation of contracts and working careers (Esping-Andersen, 2002).[46]

---

[45] Leoni T. (2016), "Social Investment as a Perspective on Welfare State Transformation in Europe", *Intereconomics* Vol. 51, pp. 194-200.

[46] Esping-Andersen G., Gallie D., Hemerijck A. and Myles J. (2002). *Why We Need a New Welfare State*, Oxford: Oxford University Press.

In 2013, the Commission launched its Social Investment Package, with the aim of avoiding the waste of human capital resulting from prolonged periods of inactivity. This emphasises the productive function of social policy, which must simultaneously create the conditions for increasing people's productivity, and guarantee financial stability. If successfully applied, the *preventive measure* of social investment should, in the long run, prevent national welfare systems from incurring the costs of *remedial measures*. Therefore, these policies can represent investments, which in the medium- and long-term generate returns by enhancing welfare and avoiding benefit dependency.

According to Hemerijck (2014),[47] there are three types of social investment policies: flow, stock and buffer measures, respectively referring to actions concerning the critical transition from the period of school to that of work, the improvement of the quality of human capital, and the implementation of a universal minimum income. In this framework, social infrastructure plays a critical role; this can be broadly defined as long-term physical assets in the social sectors that enable goods and services to be provided. In order to generate benefits in terms of positive spill over for society, as well as in economic activity, they should be high quality, otherwise they can prolong existing inequalities. Growing demand, and increased costs for more social infrastructure, has to face constraints in terms of public debt overhang that squeeze public resources for investment. In addition, an ageing population, in-work and out-of-work poverty, inequality, and the misery of a generation of young people who have difficulties finding a job or career, put further pressure on the need for social policy and its financing. By 2060, the over-65s will account for almost 30 % of the EU population, and for each elderly person there will only be two workers, compared to the current four. The ageing of the population should also be seen in relation to another fact, with gloomy prospects in the long-run; the risk of ending up in poverty in Europe is increasing, particularly for the young (18-24 years old). This is partly due to the high proportion of NEETs (Not in Employment, in Education or Training) for whom finding a job and feeling involved in society is increasingly difficult.

---

[47] Hemerijck A. (2014), "Social Investment 'stocks', 'flows' and 'buffers'", *Rivista delle Politiche Sociali*, Vol. 1, No. 1, pp. 9–26.

A good starting point on the path towards strengthening the European social dimension is the European Pillar of Social Rights, launched in 2017. Bringing together new and old labour market and social security rights, the document aimed to set out the EU standard to which member countries should strive. As such, the Pillar established twenty rights, including: the right to education, training, and lifelong learning; the right of children to receive care and education during early childhood; the right for all to health care, and the right to social housing. While across all cases the Pillar calls for high quality services at affordable prices, the Pillar is not *per se* a legally binding instrument for Member States, as social policy is an exclusive national competence. The concrete realisation of social rights is therefore left to the will of member countries, according to the role that social policy has in their public spending.

Keeping in mind all these considerations, in 2018 a *High Level Task Force on Investment in Social Infrastructure in Europe*, chaired by Romano Prodi and Christian Sautter, was commissioned to draw attention to the role of social infrastructure. The Task Force's report underlined the fact that investment in social infrastructure – education, health and personal care, social housing – both private and public, is far from reaching the level needed to cater for the EU's current population, nor is the investment always appropriate in view of changing needs and expectations over the coming decades. The minimum infrastructure gap in social infrastructure investment is estimated at €100-150 bn. per year, and will reach a total gap of over €1.500 bn. by 2030. This projection, however, does not include further pressures that the pandemic crisis exerts directly on health systems, and indirectly on the risk of poverty.

The group also identified a greater involvement of private capital in the social sector to bridge the infrastructure gap. The point is that "There is an obvious asynchronicity between the financial industry's willingness to have infrastructure financing as a fully-fledged *'asset class'* to invest in and the time needed to build all the missing parts of the underlying framework" (Fransen et al., 2018, p. 44).[48] Long-term institutional investors seek low-risk, inflation-linked, long-term financial instruments to match their long-term liabilities. However, the conditions required to

---

[48] Fransen, L., del Bufalo G. and Reviglio E. (2018), *Boosting Investment in Social Infrastructure in Europe. Report of the High-Level Task Force on Investing in Social Infrastructure in Europe*, Luxembourg: Publications Office per the European Union. DOI: 10.2765/794497.

permit such instruments have not yet been reached; prudential regulations and accounting standards are a prerequisite to making infrastructure investment more attractive to long-term investors and to banks.

Investments in the social infrastructure differ from those in the economic infrastructure, with the latter often dependent on the cash flows such activities produce. However, this does not mean that the social infrastructure will not attract private finance; to increase the size of public/private investment and innovation in those sectors major changes and new initiatives are needed, like for example, the well-established practice in the EU of blending, i.e. using financial instruments (loans, guarantees, equity) alongside limited public resources to mobilise a larger volume of investment. The report also envisaged the launch of a European Social Infrastructure Agenda by 2022, to be followed by a new public-private Fund for Social Investment that should be able to issue Euro Social Bonds, that suit the investment needs of long-term institutional investors.

Chapter 7

An investment plan for Africa

7.1 Synergies of EU–Africa Cooperation

In a rapidly evolving global context, the EU is looking more and more closely at relations of mutual cooperation with Africa, with the awareness that the two Continents have much to gain from closer cooperation. A change of pace took place at the 2007 Africa – EU Summit in Lisbon with the launch of the Joint Africa – EU Strategy (JAES), setting out the intention of both partners to move beyond a donor-recipient relationship toward long-term cooperation on jointly identified, mutual and complementary interests. Although, more than 10 years later, the Strategy has not produced the expected results, the narrative of wanting to overcome the traditional partnership based on development aid is still very much alive.

In September 2018, the European Commission launched a *New Africa-Europe Alliance*, focused on the creation of sustainable investment and jobs (European Commission, 2018b).[1] The Alliance is mainly an economic and financial plan that fits into the vision already defined by broader international frameworks, such as the UN Agenda 2030 and its SDGs, and the 2015 Paris Agreement. At the centre of the initiative is, on the one hand, the deepening of economic integration and trade relations, both within the African continent and with Europe, and on the other a comprehensive plan for strategic investments on the African continent. The two initiatives are closely linked, as investment, especially in infrastructure, is essential to promote economic activity and allow trade, while at the same time investors need a strong, positive investment

---

1 European Commission (2018b), *Communication on a New Africa – Europe Alliance for Sustainable Investment and Jobs: Taking Our Partnership for Investment and Jobs to the Next Level*, Bruxelles: European Commission, https://eur-lex.europa.eu/legal-content/EN/TXT/PDF/?uri=CELEX:52018DC0643&from=EN (Accessed October 15, 2021).

climate, which depends on economic prospects and the existence of product and service markets.

In the JAES, Africa called for the recognition of a partnership "based on a Euro-African consensus on values, common interests and common strategic objectives", guided by the principle of "interdependence between Africa and Europe, ownership and joint responsibility" of various challenges that both continents are facing. Europe's quest is both for new markets – investment opportunities in which to make use of excess savings that underpin its macroeconomic situation, and for a shared management of the migration issue, in which the Alliance is part of a more comprehensive approach. In contrast with the EU, Africa is a fast-growing continent, with a young population, that is taking steps toward greater internal economic integration. Its development must build on the diversification of its economy, and investment, new technologies and economic models that can help Africa embark on a path of sustainable development with new jobs, especially for the young entering the labour market.

The EU is the Africa's biggest investor, with its Member States holding FDI stock worth €239 bn. in 2018.[2] The strong economic progress over the last two decades, and the inherent potential for the future of Africa, suggests opportunities for greater investments, while at the same time pursuing objectives coherent with the *Social* EGD.

7.2 African trade, between *old* and *new* friends

Promoting the Africa economic integration process, at both the regional and continental levels, is necessary to provide markets that demand investments. The African continent has embarked on the creation of a Continental Free Trade Area; through the removal of tariff and non-tariff barriers on goods and services, the aim is to facilitate intra-African trade, promote regional value chains to enable the integration of the African continent into the global economy, boost industrialisation, competitiveness and innovation, and ultimately contribute to Africa's economic development and social progress. The EU is actively supporting, in the perspective of a more ambitious objective, a project intended

2 Eurostat website https://ec.europa.eu/eurostat

to create a comprehensive continent-to-continent free trade agreement with Africa (European Commission, 2018b).

Although trade relations between the two partners are important, they are still limited and subject to increasing competition from other players, in particular China. For Europe, the African continent is the fourth-ranked trading partner, with a share of European international trade of 7,5 % (as an average between import and exports), after Asia (41 %), other European non-EU countries (24 %) and North America (19 %) (Eurostat, 2019b).[3] For Africa, the EU remains the largest trading partner: in 2017, 37 % of exports and 35 % of African imports (with a total value of €243 bn.) were with the EU. At the national level, the EU's main African trade partners are South Africa, Algeria, Morocco and Nigeria, accounting for more than half of total African trade with the EU.

In terms of products, the EU's major imports from Africa are above all energy products, in particular crude oil, for which Africa is second only to Russia, followed by food and live animals. The main products Africa requires from the EU are machinery and vehicles, in particular motor vehicles. This imbalance in trade flows – raw materials against manufactured goods – places Africa at the bottom of the value chain, with Europe at the top; this nevertheless reflects the production structure of African economies, highly dependent on raw materials.

Europe's trading prominence in the African continent is however being challenged, as there are signs of a change in the relative weight of international trade partners. In recent years, the trend has been toward a decrease in trade relations with Europe, considered the continent's "old friend"; trade with new partners has grown, namely the BRICS (Brazil, Russia, India, China, South Africa), and in particular China, which from 2017 has now become the continent's "new friend", just behind the EU, with a total volume of $101 bn.[4] Alongside this, trade relations between African countries themselves, considered "good" friends as internal trade

---

3 Eurostat (2019b), *The European Union and the African Union. A Statistical Portrait,* Luxembourg: Publications Office of the European Union, https://ec.europa.eu/eurostat/documents/3217494/9767596/KS-FQ-19-001-EN-N.pdf/376dc292-0d2d-4c66-9a36-5bc63c87466c?t=1556886137000 (Accessed October 15, 2021).

4 Data from Ministry of Commerce People's Republic of China, http://english.mofcom.gov.cn/article/statistic/lanmubb/AsiaAfrica (Accessed October 15, 2021).

is less vulnerable to external shocks, remain stable, albeit at lower levels (Sandrey 2015).[5]

7.3 Intra-African trade between *good* friends

The African Continental Free Trade Agreement (AfCFTA), signed in March 2018, represents the continent's most ambitious integration initiative. Its main objectives are: the creation of a single continental market for goods and services, with free movement of business, people, and investments; the expansion of intra-Africa trade across the Regional Economic Communities (RECs) and the continent in general; and the enhancement of competitiveness and support of economic transformation. Intra-African trade is in fact still relatively underdeveloped, accounting for less than 20 % of the continent's total trade. The main actor in intra-African trade is South Africa. For some countries like Morocco, Nigeria and Egypt, intra-African trade is a small part of their international trade, while for others, like Zimbabwe, Uganda and Tanzania, the share of trade within Africa is about half of their total volume. Agricultural products traded within the continent account for 19 %, while the rest is dominated by non-agricultural goods, like mineral fuels, oils and gas, gold and diamonds, all commodities that play an important role in the intra-African trade balance (Tralac, 2019).[6]

One of the reasons for this low level of trade between *good friends*, i.e., African countries themselves, is the dependence of domestic economies on the production of raw materials, with a specialisation limited to one or a few products. Such a structure does not facilitate internal trade relations, due to a low level of complementarity between economies, and above all does not permit the creation of internal value chains, which would allow greater diversification of production. On the contrary, low diversification exposes domestic economies to the impact of price fluctuations and natural disasters for agricultural products, in particular.

5 Sandrey R. (2015), *The African Trading Relationship: New, Old and Good Friends*, Tralac ebook, https://www.tralac.org/publications/article/8223-africa-s-trade-relations-old-friends-good-friends-and-new-friends.html (Accessed October 15, 2021).

6 Tralac (2019), *The African Continental Free Trade Area, a Tralac Guide – 5th edition*, https://www.tralac.org/documents/resources/booklets/2878-afcfta-a-tralac-guide-5th-edition-june-2019/file.html (Accessed October 15, 2021).

Although African countries have seen their GDP growing, the effects of fluctuations in world market prices for raw materials, and in particular the decline in prices of crude oil and natural gas, have curtailed the economic output of a number of countries. Nevertheless, African GDP growth rates in 2017 outstripped the growth rates of the best performing EU countries, with almost 4 % on average for Africa, compared to less than 2 % for EU.

Other obstacles limit the development of intra-African trade. For example, the dominance of protectionist trade policies between African countries, in contrast to Europe's greater openness to imports, helps to create an imbalance in external trade relations. Although the great majority of African countries belong to the WTO, trade policies are, in most cases, protectionist. In most African countries effective tariff rates are very high, between 6 % and 17 % (Dabrowski and Myachenkova, 2018),[7] which are not only higher than those applied in the EU and US, but also in developing countries like those belonging to the Association of South East Asian Nations (ASEAN-5), their competitors. Even being part of one or more of the eight RECs does not offer many reduced tariff preferences, or indeed an incentive for regional trade, which remains stagnant. Finally, non-tariff barriers also contribute to discrimination against intra-continental trade as compared to trade with external partners, while the free movement of people within the continent is difficult. In this respect, the creation of an African passport, which is fundamental to the free movement of people, is being discussed within the African Union.

7.4 Complementary policies to African integration

An important ingredient in African economic integration is the introduction of a common currency. The Treaty of Abuja, in establishing the African Economic Community, provided for the creation of the African Central Bank by 2025 and a new single currency, the *Afro*, which will be achieved through the creation of regional monetary unions, each with the adoption of different currencies linked to the euro, pound and

---

[7] Dabrowski M. and Myachenkova Y. (2018), *Free Trade in Africa: An Important Goal But Not Easy to Achieve*, Bruegel Blog Post, https://www.bruegel.org/2018/04/free-trade-in-africa-an-important-goal-but-not-easy-to-achieve/ (Accessed October 14, 2021).

dollar. Achieving a single African currency would represent an important political result, with the *Afro* becoming a symbol of African unity, as well as producing benefits in terms of greater trade integration. However, an assessment of the costs that would result should not be neglected, such as the loss of states' ability to use individual monetary policy to respond to asymmetric shocks. While monetary unions can deliver low inflation and greater stability in good times, the absence of a nominal exchange rate anchor may mean that African economies would remain vulnerable to persistent real exchange rate misalignment; this makes a focus on issues of fiscal flexibility all the more important . A monetary union needs to coordinate the fiscal policies of its member countries; but different countries, with their structural differences, may need different fiscal stabilisation at different times. A solution might be a mechanism of transfers to member countries in the event of a negative shock, aiming at supporting employment or investments. However, the experience of the euro itself shows the difficulties in building a stabilisation instrument, the product of a lack of solidarity required to assemble fiscal resources.

Economic integration through trade liberalisation needs to create complementarities between its member countries, and therefore requires measures to correct regional imbalances that may arise. Some limited progress has been made towards creating financial support to compensate for further economic integration. For example, the Economic Community of West African States (ECOWAS), a community with a very wide diversity of economies in terms of size, development and resources, has equipped itself with the Bank for Investment and Development (EBID). This operates through two subsidiaries, the European Regional Development Fund (ERDF) and the ECOWAS Regional Investment Bank (ERIB). The ERDF focuses on the public sector, particularly financing basic economic infrastructure and poverty alleviation projects, while the ERIB concentrates on promoting the private sector as an engine of sustainable growth.

The risks to which the most vulnerable economic actors, such as local manufacturers, are exposed need to be balanced with support for the creation of employability, such as technical, entrepreneurial or even simply basic literacy skills; essentially education, training and support for small and micro-enterprises to adapt to new structural market conditions. In Africa, in addition to unemployment, there is a problem of the misalignment of skills, known as skills mismatch, i.e. inconsistencies between what is learned at school and what is required in the labour market. To counter this trend, the EU has made available in the period 2014-2020, through its Pan-African Program (one of the main EU financial instruments for the implementation of the 2007 Joint Strategy), about €230 m, to provide young people with market-oriented skills, modernise higher education, improve mobility within the continent and with Europe, and support technological innovation.[8]

7.5 Steps forwards more EU-Africa integration

The long-term goal within the New Alliance is to create a comprehensive continent-to-continent free trade agreement between the EU and Africa. The Commission intends to exploit, to the greatest extent, the Economic Partnership Agreements (EPAs) African countries have with the EU. However, this action may have problematic implications in terms of achieving greater intra-African integration through the AfCFTA, to which the EU gives its full support.

Firstly, the EPAs are negotiated between the EU and five different blocs which, in most cases, do not correspond to the eight existing RECs, recognised as the building blocks of the African Union. Therefore, there is a risk that the provisions of the EPAs will complicate the adoption of Common Internal Tariffs, which in turn is a critical step toward the consolidation of RECs into Custom Unions (Karingi et al., 2015).[9]

Secondly, the institutional framework, set up under the Cotonou Agreement between the EU and ACP Group (African, Caribbean and Pacific Group of State) is complex. The hybrid solution proposed by the EU post-Cotonou seeks to frame relations between Africa and the EU through an *African Pillar* within the ACP-EU framework; however, the role of the AU here is unclear. Whereas the ACP Group is traditionally a tool to facilitate the delivery of traditional Official Development Assistance (ODA), the AU is in reality seeking a partnership relationship with the EU that goes beyond development aid (Medinilla and Bossuyt,

---

8 See the Multi-annual Indicative Programme 2014-2017 and 2018-2020, https://ec.europa.eu/europeaid/regions/africa/continental-cooperation/pan-african-programme_en

9 Karingi S., Mevel S. and Valensisi G. (2015), "The EPAs and Africa's Regional Integration", *Bridges Africa*, Vol. 4, N. 6, pp. 14-16.

2019).[10] This divergence between institutional actors could lead to solutions of greater or lesser symmetry in future trade relations between the two sides of the Mediterranean.

Thirdly, the impact of EPAs on intra-regional trade could prove controversial. The gradual opening up of trade with Europe could end up granting more favourable treatment to a number of EU imports over comparable African products. Therefore, unless the various RECs decide to reduce their respective tariffs, European products may end up substituting intra-African exports. However, apart from tariffs, numerous non-tariff barriers add to the protective measures that can effectively stop cross-border trade in goods and, especially, in services. The Agreement establishing the AfCFTA also explicitly provided for efforts to progressively eliminate non-tariff barriers to trade.

Trade liberalisation, within the RECs, intra-African, and between the EU and Africa, is an essential step for a strong partnership between the two continents, and should evolve toward a new approach that seems to be emerging in the New Alliance, at least in its intentions. International trade today has a different meaning than in the past; it is no longer a question of producing something in one country and selling it in another, but rather of cooperating across borders to minimise production costs and extend market coverage (African Development Bank – AfDB, 2018a, p. 55).[11] The value chain model – the series of activities from production to distribution – has taken on a global dimension, in which intermediate stages can be carried out in different countries. The objective of integration between the two continents should lead to African economies, even the least developed, becoming part of the value chains between the two continents, in a view to a relationship of equals, not only inspired by the principle of *trade, not aid*, but also of *co-production* and the sharing of resources. This means supporting a model for African countries focused not only on the export of commodities, as is currently

---

10 Medinilla A. and Bossuyt J. (2019), *Africa-EU Relations and Post-Cotonou: African Collective Action or Further Fragmentation of Partnerships?*, ECDPM Briefing Note 110, https://ecdpm.org/wp-content/uploads/BN-110-Africa-EU-relations-post-CotonouAfrica-EU-relations-and-post-Cotonou-african-collective-action-fragmentation-partnerships-ECDPM-March-2019.pdf (Accessed October 15, 2021).

11 AfDB (2018a), *African Economic Outlook 2018*. African Development Bank, https://www.afdb.org/fileadmin/uploads/afdb/Documents/Publications/African_Economic_Outlook_2018_-_EN.pdf (Accessed October 14, 2021).

the case, but also on their processing on the ground, encouraging technology transfer, which could enable them to align with European quality standards and the creation of regional value chains.

A similar idea is suggested by *La Verticale*, and aims at creating a new economic partnership between Africa and Europe, based on sustainability and solidarity (Guigou J.L., Beckouche P., 2017).[12] With the crisis of multilateralism and the domination on the geopolitical scene of the G2 (US and China), Europe has an interest in working towards integrating its southern regions with Africa, for reasons of geographic, cultural and linguistic proximity, and for the synergies that could derive from it. On the one hand, European countries could find youth, labour force, new markets and investment potential in the South, while on the other side Africa could benefit from technology, institutional stability, modern governance and the provision of infrastructure.

7.6 Investment in Africa: Financing and critical aspects

The creation of new investment is vital for development, and the Africa-EU Alliance strongly relies on private (domestic and foreign) investment in Africa. However, the current picture of investment in the continent is unpromising; since 2009, FDI inflows to Africa account for less than 5 % of the total inflows worldwide (United Nations Conference on Trade and Development - UNCTAD, 2016).[13] Furthermore, they tend to fluctuate year to year, and uneven at the regional level, with a few countries, namely South Africa, Nigeria, Kenya, Egypt and Morocco, attracting more than half of the total FDI. Nevertheless, Europe plays a major role in the continent; in cumulative terms, as of 2016 European countries held approximately 40 % of FDI stock, although multinational enterprises, in particular from France and United Kingdom, have been divesting because of rising instability in many African countries.

Investment in infrastructure is also fundamental for greater economic integration between countries, but currently infrastructure in transport, water, energy and ICT in Africa is lacking. Recent estimates

---

12 Guigou J. L. and Beckouche P. (2017), *Afrique Méditerranée Europe: La Verticale de l'avenir*, Bruxelles: Nevicata.

13 UNCTAD (2016), *World Investments Report 2016*, https://unctad.org/system/files/official-document/wir2016_en.pdf (Accessed October 15, 2021).

suggest that the annual financial gap for infrastructure (the difference between the amount needed to develop Africa's infrastructure and the amount actually invested) ranges from $68 to $108 bn. (AfDB, 2018b).[14] Additionally, financing needs vary by sector, with water facing major challenges, with an 81-84 % shortfall in its annual requirement, while the transport gap is relatively negligible (8 %). The lack of infrastructure is a major obstacle to economic development and trade. For example, in the presence of a restrictive visa policy, the development of digital communications could favour distance relationships between people as well as online commerce platforms. However, only one in five Africans has regular access to the internet. Other problems relate to the cost of electricity, which is four times higher than industrial rates elsewhere in the world, or travel times along key export corridors, some two to three times higher than those in Asia (AfDB, 2018b).

According to the Infrastructure Consortium for Africa (ICA), a total of $100,8 bn. was committed to Africa's infrastructure operations in 2018. This is a substantial increase (24 %) over the level committed in 2017 ($81,6 bn.) (Fig. 7.1). Almost half of the increase observed in 2018 resulted from the inclusion, for the first time, of stand-alone commitments made by the private sector, while in previous years, commitments by the private sector were only gathered in the context of PPPs. In cumulative terms, the largest share was made up of public investments by African governments themselves (37 %), followed by China (26 %), ICA members (20 %),[15] the private sector (12 %), and other sources (6 %)[16] (Fig. 7.2). About $6 bn. came from Europe, both from EU institutions and Member States, with the EIB providing €2,2 bn.,

---

14 AfDB (2018b), *Annual Report 2018,* African Development Bank Group, https://www.afdb.org/fileadmin/uploads/afdb/Documents/Generic-Documents/AFDB_Annual_Report_2018_and_Appendices_-English.pdf (Accessed October 14, 2021).

15 ICA members are the G8 countries, two G20 countries (Kingdom of Spain and Republic of South Africa), the World Bank Group (WBG), the African Development Bank Group (AfDB), the European Commission, the EIB and the Development Bank of Southern Africa (DBSA).

16 This category includes the Arab Co-ordination group (like Arab Fund for Economic and Social Development and the Islamic Development Bank) and countries like India, Japan and South Korea.

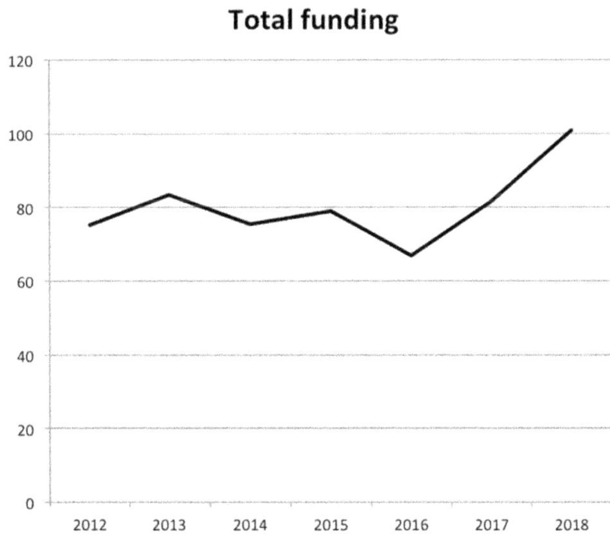

Fig. 7.1: Total funding (2012-2018, $bn.)
Sources: ICA

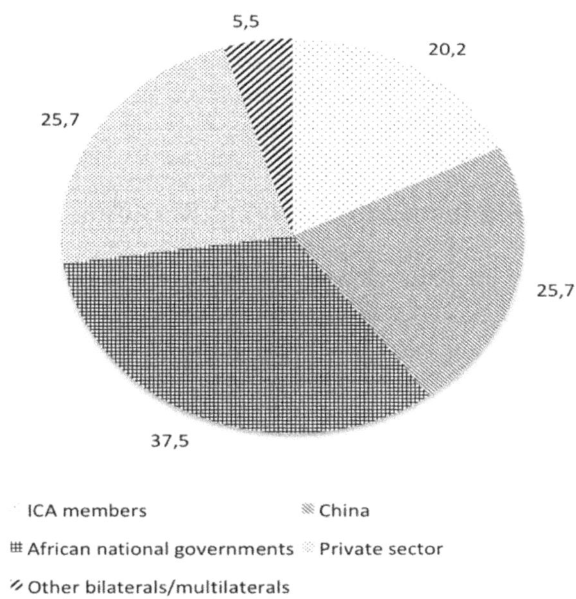

Fig. 7.2: Where the funding come from (% of total)
Source: ICA

the EU-AITF $200 m., and at the national level, France and Germany with contributions of $1,9 bn., and $1,6 bn. respectively.

At the sectorial level, energy was the main destination of funds (43,5 % of the total) followed by the transport (32,3 %), water (13,2 %) and ICT (7 %) sectors. Finally, the financing trend by region saw West Africa as the main destination, with increasing financing since 2013 (25,7 % in 2018), North Africa (19,9 %), East Africa (14,2 %), Southern Africa (13,7 %) excluding Republic of South Africa, that alone receives 17 %, while Central Africa continues to remain the least attractive for investors (7 %).

In conclusion, closing this gap has for many years been given a high priority in many African countries, whose governments are generally the main contributors to total infrastructure spending. However, foreign investors are needed to meet Africa's substantial investment requirements effectively. Institutional investors, such as insurance companies, pension funds, and sovereign wealth funds have more than $100 tn. in assets under management globally. Seen from this perspective, a small fraction of excess global savings and low-yield resources would be enough to plug Africa's financing gap, and finance productive and profitable investments. However, insufficient stock and the poor quality of infrastructure are not just the consequence of limited resources; these can also be partly attributed to a shortage of bankable projects and effective institutional arrangements capable of attracting investors.

7.7 Alternative form of financing: Blending finance

Foreign financing of development relies on a variety of sources, both public, such as ODA, and private, such as FDI. For some countries, such external financing has been a substantial resource, indicating a strong dependence on foreign aid. As regards the private sector, Africa can only manage to attract a very small share of total global investment. Notwithstanding this, for some years there have been developments in the way that financing resources have been used. The UN 2030 Agenda for Sustainable Development placed new emphasis on the blending of traditional ODA or other philanthropic resources, tools foreseen by the Millennium Development Goals (MDGs), with other resources of private investment; this blend can finance sustainable development, resulting in positive outcomes for both investors and communities. The underpinning rationale is the concept of *additionality*, where the blending of public finance leads to an additional result than would not otherwise happen.

Furthermore, the blending of finance encourages an exchange of knowledge between private operators, who have entrepreneurial skills but are not very familiar with the context in which projects are carried out, and public institutions, which can provide the missing information. The reasons for the unattractiveness of investment are many, firstly there are structural and institutional flaws, like corruption and the lack of rule of law and an independent legislative power. Then there are projects that are insufficiently profitable, despite potentially high economic, environmental and/or social benefits, projects with excessive risk profiles, or projects located in already heavily indebted countries, meaning that they have to comply with IMF requirements for loans.

The EU has, since 2007, been pushing the blending agenda in Africa as an instrument to support its external policy objectives. This was achieved through the creation of the EU-Africa Infrastructure Trust Fund (EU-AITF), which became in 2015 the Africa Investment Facility (AfIF), mainly funded by the European Development Fund (EDF). Between 2007 and 2015, total investments of €57 bn. were made (€7 bn. a year), based on a public contribution of €3,4 bn. in sectors such as energy, transport, water and sanitation, and private sector development. In September 2017, the AfIF was transformed into the Africa Investment Platform (AIP) and became an integral part of the European Fund for Sustainable Development (EFSD), the new EU initiative for investment in Africa and countries adjoining the EU, the neighborhood, also known as the External Investment Plan.

7.8 The European EIP

One of the key elements of the EU's initiative in Africa is an investment plan to crowd-in private investment. In 2017 the EU launched the European External Investment Plan (EIP) with the aim of attracting more investment into the EU *Neighbourhood* and in Africa. The initiative allowed the EU to export the PPPs model already consolidated with the Juncker Plan; indeed, the EIP is developed through the multi-level and multi-sector approach of the three pillars.

The first element of the EIP is the financial pillar, which provides for the establishment of the EFSD, whose rationale is to use limited public resources (€4,1 bn.) to attract substantial funding from the private sector, and thus leverage the expected total amount (up to €88 bn.). The EFSD consists of both pre-existing blending facilities (€2,6 bn. coming from the former AfIF and the Neighbourhood Investment Facility) and a new guarantee instrument of €1,5 bn.[17] By 2020, the EFSD is expected to have leveraged €44 bn. of actual investment, which, if national contributions were added, could double. As regards the guarantee, the Commission has distributed the entire amount through four areas of intervention as follows: sustainable energy and connectivity (39 %), financing for small and micro-medium enterprises and agriculture (33 %), digitisation (14 %), and sustainable cities (11 %). Most of the EU investment program for Africa is devoted to the production of renewable energy in urban and rural areas, and to the support of entrepreneurial activities, in particular very small-scale projects and those in fragile contexts.

Awareness that the African continent can look forward to a future of expansion has led to a change in the West's perception of developing countries, which aim to become the new (future) players in the global economy. From this perspective, development aid has become insufficient, and no longer fulfils its function, to create political and economic partnerships between equals, as advocated by the JAES. The EFSD, therefore, follows the new trends of development finance, promoted both by the UN Agenda 2030 and by the G20; to achieve the ambitious SDGs, traditional aid is no longer sufficient, but it is necessary to use the PPPs, in which limited public resources are the driving force behind other forms of financing from the private sector.[18]

An important role is played by *soft infrastructure*; these collateral initiatives range from technical assistance, to support for reforms that improve the business environment. For this reason, the EIP includes two

---

17 Half of which comes from the Community budget (€350 m.) and the EDF (€400 m.), and half are contingent liabilities in case of need (€750 m.) (European Commission (2017c), Questions and answers about the European External Investment Plan, https://ec.europa.eu/commission/presscorner/detail/en/MEMO_17_3484 - Accessed October 15 2021)

18 The EU is not new to the use of innovative financial instruments (blending facilities), such as EFSD (Große-Puppendahl S. and Bilal S. (2018), "What Is the European External Investment Plan Really About?", *ECDPM Briefing Note* n. 101 Bruxelles: ECDPM - Accessed October 2021). For example, the Africa Investment Facility

other pillars. One concerns technical assistance from financial institutions, such as the EIB, which as the EU's development bank will provide local authorities with the necessary advice to design and promote projects attractive to the private sector. The other provides for the promotion of a more investment-friendly political, regulatory, and business environment in the beneficiary countries.

By putting three areas of intervention under the same programme, the EU can take a leading role in the international arena in the field of development aid, approaching the issue from various points of view. In practice, however, this approach can be problematic in its implementation. Firstly, all three pillars, although interlinked, have different timescales of implementation; the success of the whole Plan, however, cannot be separated from the sum of the three pillars. Secondly, because the components of the EIP belong to different actors, with interests and priorities that may be at odds with each other. As regards the involvement of the private sector, it is clear that its profit-seeking behaviour can favour the implementation of projects in certain geographical areas of the continent, to the detriment of other, less attractive areas. South Africa, Nigeria, Kenya Egypt, and Morocco attract collectively more than half of total FDI to Africa. The risk of geographical concentration could lead to accentuating inequalities between the most advanced and least developed countries, with underdeveloped financial markets. In this sense, the third pillar – that of dialogue with partner countries to promote legal, political and institutional frameworks better suited to creating economic stability and respect for fundamental rights – is probably the most relevant as it would strength the effectiveness of the first two pillars, albeit with results emerging in the long run. Building strong and lasting political relations with African countries is fundamental, and must be strongly and purposefully promoted over time by the EU. Moreover, it is not just the rule of law, an independent judiciary and predictable taxation that are key factors influencing investors' decisions; peace and stability also form part of these considerations. Otherwise, the high cost that private investment would face – thought to be around

(€648 m.) is the main regional platform in Africa, combining contributions from the EU with other resources provided by financial institutions for development and private donors. At the sectoral level, there are platforms such as the Electrification Financing Initiative (launched in 2015, with €75 m. allocated by the EU) and the Agricultural Financing Initiative (set up in 2016, with €200 m.).

three times higher in fragile contexts – would discourage new initiatives (EPSC, 2017).[19]

7.9 Critical aspects of the EIP

In spite of giving new names to regional blending facilities, the total allocation of the EFSD consists of resources that are not new, but result from their reclassification, and will be split between Africa and the Neighborhood. In 2017, €5,6 bn. was approved for blending projects in Africa, mostly in the transport and energy sectors, thus almost in line with what happened before the introduction of the EFSD, with the EU-AITF and AfIF. Effectively, the only new element of EFSD is the guarantee component, that shifts the focus toward de-risking instruments, instead of subsidising interest rates to increase the affordability of loans. This will represent the main tool through which the EU will seek to support investment in the most difficult contexts, such as conflict-affected and least developed countries. In fact, one of the critiques often made of traditional aid is that the allocation of resources is concentrated on middle-income countries and on certain sectors, neglecting the objectives of poverty reduction, thus increasing disparities between countries. The EFSD guarantee should instead generate investment in rural areas and in small/micro-businesses.

Investment plans involving Africa must not overlook the role played by the informal sector in the region. According to the ILO, non-agricultural employment in the informal economy accounts for 66 % of total employment in sub-Saharan Africa, and 52 % in North Africa. If the informal sector is recognised as "a vibrant, entrepreneurial part of the economy which can stimulate economic growth and jobs", which represents the dominant share of many sectors, such as manufacturing and trade, then it should be included in the debate. Sparks and Bannet (2010) [20] suggest stimulating the transference of the informal sector into the formal by removing barriers to greater participation. For example, they propose literacy and vocational training programs aimed

---

19 EPSC (2017), *The Makings of an African Century*, Strategic Note, Issue 23, https://www.prospectivayestrategia.cl/pdf/strategic_note_issue_23.pdf (Accessed October 15, 2021).

20 Sparks D. L. and Barnett S. T. (2010), "The Informal Sector in Sub-Saharan Africa: Out of the Shadows to Foster Sustainable Employment and Equity?",

at the informal sector, as well as the provision of special social benefits, such as health care, in return for a small contribution, and to increase the funding capacity needed to start up new, or expand existing businesses.

However, the EFSD does not allocate new resources with respect to past needs; the investment gap in Africa, not least in infrastructure, needs huge financial resources that Europe alone cannot furnish. However, a closer partnership with Africa will require more attention from Europe with a substantial increase of available funding for both the improvement of African infrastructure, and in specific sectors, like manufacturing and energy. The partnership could produce strategic benefits at various levels: in terms of new markets for goods, services, and capital, given the long-term period of stagnation; and provide a source of young, connected and skilled workers, to counter an ageing European population. Not least, the partnership could create business opportunities for European companies to ensure greater access to electricity in Africa, while tackling climate change as broadly as possible, as the reduction of European CO_2 emissions alone cannot solve this environmental issue. The ambitious EGD absolutely must contain an African component as an integral part of the challenge to climate change.

Energy is a key vector for development; just think of the potential implications for education that the possibility of shifting activities, such as studying, to after dark, thanks to the availability of electric light. At the same time, the demand for energy services across the continent will surge in the coming decades in line with the demographic boom (Sartori and Colantoni, 2019).[21] From this perspective, the development of African countries will require a different approach, in contrast to the *business as usual* scenario. Bold actions, embedded in a transformative agenda, are needed to concurrently increase the likelihood of meeting SDGs by 2030, and tackling climate change. Accelerated renewable energy growth, (wind and solar), associated with new development models in African countries are two key policy actions that could bring us all onto a pathway toward smart sustainable development within global

---

International Business & Economics Research Journal (IBER), Vol. 9, No. 5, https://doi.org/10.19030/iber.v9i5.563

[21] Sartori N. and Colantoni L. (2019), "Empowering Africa", in Colantoni L., Montesano G. and Sartori N. (eds.), *Empowering Africa. Access to Power in the African Continent*, Bern: Peter Lang.

boundaries (Randers et al., 2018).[22] Unlike the energy model developed in Europe, Africa, with a dispersed rural area and a large informal sector, can best be served by a decentralised approach based on small solar panels and batteries in rural areas, and micro-grids in urban areas. In this sense, through the EIP, Europe could respond to the growing demand for energy, by supporting major private investments in solar panel systems, especially in view of the ongoing revolution in reducing costs of renewables.

In addition, as Majocchi (2020)[23] affirmed, in the light of the EU's ongoing efforts to progressively curb its use of fossil fuels and promote the exploitation of renewable resources, the inexhaustible source of solar energy available in Africa could also be exploited by European countries. But of course this would require technological innovation and massive flows of investment. A project of this kind has been launched by the Desertec Foundation with a plan to power Europe from solar power plants in the Sahara Desert. The idea is very appealing, and originated from the finding that in just six hours, the world's deserts receive more energy from the sun than humans consume in a year. However, the investment needed to translate the Desertec concept into a profitable business project – estimated at €400 bn. – as well as internal tensions between the Foundations and Desertec industrial consortium about the location of the ultimate users of this energy (should this benefit African or European countries?), have made it impossible to continue with this ambitious project.

The Desertec experience tells us that in such large-scale initiatives it is crucial to understand which kind of approach should be taken. A top-down approach, without community involvement, does not guarantee that such schemes will help alleviate poverty, reduce unemployment or preserve a safe environment and, above all, does not exclude the risk

22 Randers J., Rockström J., Stoknes P., Golüke U., Collste D. and Cornell S. (2018), *Transformation Is Feasible – How to Achieve the Sustainable Development Goals within Planetary Boundaries – A Report to the Club of Rome, for Its 50 Years Anniversary*, report to the Club of Rome from Stockholm Resilience Centre and BI Norwegian Business School, https://www.stockholmresilience.org/download/18.51d83659166367a9a16353/1539675518425/Report_Achieving%20the%20Sustainable%20Development%20Goals_WEB.pdf (Accessed October 15, 2021).

23 Majocchi A. (2020), "A Green New Deal for Europe and Africa", in Majocchi A. (ed.), *A Green New Deal for Europe and Africa,* Bruxelles: Peter Lang.

of perpetuating situations of exploitation (Hamouchene, 2020).[24] Conversely, for the Desertec Foundation, the core concept of such initiatives should be that regions like the Sub-Sahara, with particularly sunny conditions, be preferred sites for solar power plants, but with only a small fraction of the electricity demand of highly industrialised countries being covered by imports from sun-rich regions (Desertec, 2013).[25] As the International Energy Agency (IEA) observed

> It would seem unacceptable, for example, if all solar electricity were exported overseas while local populations and economies lacked sufficient power resources. Newly built plants will have to fulfill the needs of the local population and help develop local economies. Meanwhile, the returns from exporting clean, highly valued renewable electricity to industrialised countries could help cover the high initial investment costs of CSP beyond the share devoted to exports (IEA, 2010, p. 39).[26]

7.10 Migration management in the long-term perspective

Politically, the EIP is framed as part of the EU's response to the perceived migration crisis, and therefore tries to address the root causes of migration through a long-term strategy to contain migratory pressures.[27] Apart from the consideration that the bulk of African migration takes place within the African continent itself, results in terms of reduced

[24] Hamouchene H. (2020), *Desertec: What Went Wrong?*, EcoMENA, https://www.ecomena.org/desertec (Accessed October 15, 2021).

[25] Desertec Foundation (2013), *Principles, Criteria and Indicators for the Evaluation of Renewable Energy Power Plants, Version 1.0*, https://www.desertec.org/wp-content/uploads/2019/01/DESERTEC-Criteria.pdf (Accessed October 15, 2021).

[26] IEA (2010), *Technology Roadmap – Concentrating Solar Power*, Paris: IEA, https://iea.blob.core.windows.net/assets/663fabad-397e-4518-802f-7f1c94bc2076/csp_roadmap.pdf (Accessed October 15, 2021).

[27] The fund is framed as aiming to "address specific socio-economic root causes of migration, including irregular migration, and to contribute to the sustainable reintegration of migrants returning to their countries of origin and to strengthening of transit and host communities" (European Union (2017), *Regulation of the European Parliament and of the Council Establishing the European Fund for Sustainable Development (EFSD), the EFSD Guarantee and the EFSD Guarantee Fund*, Bruxelles: European Commission, https://eur-lex.europa.eu/legal-content/EN/TXT/PDF/?uri=CELEX:32017R1601&from=EN - Accessed October 15, 2021).

migration may not emerge very soon, in the light of Africa's ongoing demographic transition. In fact, it has been observed in the literature that once economic growth has been triggered in a country, this can increase pressures to emigrate, defined in the literature as the *migratory hump*: the increase in per capita income is accompanied by an increase in the level of education, which, however, does not correspond to immediate adequate employment opportunities in the local context.[28] Migration is only reduced when certain levels of general socioeconomic well-being are reached, which, for the majority of the African sub-Saharan countries, where most of the (above all irregular) migration to Europe originates today, can only take place over decades. Financing investments is one way to create local development and contain migration in the very long term, but it requires the complementary management of migration flows which takes into consideration a foreseeable increase, rather than a reduction, over the next decades. In the same way, demographic projections of Europe and Africa suggest an asymmetry between the two continents, in which migration could play an important role. According to forecasts, by 2100 Africa's population will reach 4,2 bn., with an average age of 35 years, while the population in Europe is not destined to change much, remaining around 600 m., with a tendency to decrease.

One of the inventive proposals of the European Commission for the EU 2021-2027 MFF was to allow more flexibility to adjust for emergencies. In this vein, and on the basis of a *crisis mode* displayed by EU institutions and Member States in tackling the migration question, the EU created the African Trust Fund (ATF) in 2015. This spends mainly on migration management and control, through the securitisation of migration, to the detriment of development and poverty reduction objectives (Barana, 2017).[29] The risk of such management of the *migration crisis* is first to feed the perception of Africa as a source of migrants to Europe,

---

[28] The development-migration link is complex and suffers from other factors, such as population growth, inequality, the emulation effect, whether or not there are obstacles to migration and credit restrictions (see Angenendt S., Martin-Shields C. and Schraven B. (2017), *More Development, More Migration? The "Migration Hump" and Its Significance for Development Policy Co-operation with Sub-Saharan Africa*, SWP Comment 2017/C 40, https://www.swp-berlin.org/publications/products/comments/2017C40_adt_etal.pdf – Accessed October 14, 2021).

[29] Barana L. (2017), *The EU Trust Fund for Africa and the Perils of a Securitized Migration Policy*, IAI Commentaries 17, https://www.iai.it/en/pubblicazioni/eu-trust-fund-africa-and-perils-securitized-migration-policy (Accessed October 14, 2021).

and, as a consequence, to divert funds formerly allocated to European development cooperation, since most of the ATF's resources come from the EDF.

From this perspective, current EU migration policy, based on the closure of borders, and the outsourcing of management in return for economic aid, should seek more coherence with the economic framework set by the EIP, leaving room for measures to increase the potential for legal migration, associated with an idea of mobility within a broad geographical continuity between Africa and Europe. Objective 10.7 of the SDGs aims to "facilitate orderly, safe, regular and responsible migration and mobility of persons, including through the implementation of well-managed and organised migration policies". Examples of this could be European programs to regularly employ low-skilled workers in Europe, perhaps in the form of seasonal workers, usually employed in the informal sector.

7.11 The presence of the *new* friend China

China's presence in Africa began in the late 1960s, with the Chinese decision to financially support the Tanzanian government's project to build the Tazara railway line between Tanzania and Zambia. Since then, China has become a significant foreign provider of finance for major infrastructure projects. Between 2000 and 2014, it provided around $86 bn. in loans to African countries. This commitment has been strengthened through the periodic Forums on China-Africa Cooperation (FOCAC), with an increase from $6 bn. per year in the period 2000-2014 to $20 bn. per year in the current phase. Although China is catching up in accumulating investment in Africa, it must be remembered that these investments are still in their early stages, compared with those amassed by European countries, that continue to be the largest investors in Africa, not only in terms of stock but also in terms of flow (Garcia-Herrero and Xu, 2019).[30] However, the approach which China takes in pursuing its interests in Africa has some interesting implications for Europe.

---

[30] Garcia-Herrero A. and Xu J. (2019), *China's Investment in Africa: What the Data Really Says, and the Implications for Europe*, Bruegel Blog post, https://bruegel.org/2019/07/chinas-investment-in-africa-what-the-data-really-says-and-the-implicati ons-for-europe/ (Accessed October 15, 2021).

First, China's BRI-related infrastructure program mainly operates by lending to national governments through project finance, which in some cases has given rise to problems of excessive external debt.[31] At FOCAC 2018, the Chinese government indicated that of the $60 bn. promised, a reduced share will be in the form of loans, while on the other hand, financing will increase in the form of donations and loans at preferential rates, showing signs of a correction of the risk of a debt trap. President Xi Jinping has encouraged the participation of Chinese private companies in the financing program, although limited to Chinese capital. However, given the large investment needs and the expected population boom in next decades, China's presence in Africa does not pose a risk of crowding out Europe's initiatives.

Second, the way in which China makes infrastructure investments abroad differs from traditional donors, as China is willing to finance projects in the proximity of rural towns and villages that are generally passed over by development finance. Although this approach has had positive effects in terms of reducing inequalities between regions, it can lead to negative consequences, such as local corruption or cases of environmental degradation caused by the lack of a preliminary analysis of the social and environmental impact of projects (Bluhm R. et al., 2018).[32]

Third, as Chinese investments have grown, the stability of the region has also become a concern from the Chinese point of view. At FOCAC 2018, a fund was launched to promote cooperation in the areas of peace and security, public order, and the fight against terrorism. As in the EIP, the question of investment is therefore part of a broad, and multidisciplinary strategy, which offers not only mutual economic opportunities, but also the provision of the soft infrastructure required to reduce risk and encourage the emergence of more private investment.

---

[31] The case of Sri Lanka, which formally handed over the port of Hambantota with a 99-year lease in order to repay its debts to China, or Kenya, which similarly guaranteed a mortgage in favor of China on the port facilities of Mombasa in the event of non-payment of the debt, are examples of the risk of losing control of strategic commercial nodes.

[32] Bluhm R., Dreher A., Fuchs A., Parks B., Strange A. and Tierney M. (2018), *Connective Financing: Chinese Infrastructure Projects and the Diffusion of Economic Activity in Developing Countries*, Aid Data Working Paper No. 64, http://docs.aiddata.org/ad4/pdfs/WPS64_Connective_Financing_Chinese_Infrastructure_Projects_and_the_Diffusion_of_Economic_Activity_in_Developing_Countries.pdf (Accessed October 14, 2021).

Fourth, the impact of any external intervention in Africa, whether European or Chinese, should be appraised in terms of effective jobs created. Investment by China in Africa is particularly concentrated in transport and energy infrastructure, as such securing both access to resources, and the use of China's excess capacity in construction and transportation, two of China's strategic objectives in Africa (Garcia-Herrero and Xu, 2019). In the light of the demographic boom, it is essential that any program of investment in Africa should take job creation into consideration, with higher attention paid to the more labour-intensive sectors, such as manufacturing, which will in turn contribute to making the local economy more diversified and less commodity dependent.

Finally, the issue of debt sustainability, largely due to the emergence of China as one of the main financiers of African infrastructure (Procopio, 2020),[33] is becoming more evident with the fiscal requirements posed by the Covid-19 pandemic, leading to a new degree of tension on the use of financial resources. On the one hand, governments will need considerable resources to spend on health care, and to support people facing the consequences of the pandemic. On the other hand, however, they are contractually bound to pay their debts, or risk losing access to international financial markets.

The debt situation in low-income countries, like sub-Saharan countries, was high risk even before the pandemic crisis. One reason for the increased debt levels has been a change in the composition of debt from concessional, to market-based loans from private and public lenders. The higher interest rates of the non-concessional loans increased the debt burden in these countries. Public debt in sub-Saharan Africa jumped by more than 6 % to 58 % of GDP in 2020, the highest level in almost two decades. External debt stocks to exports increased from 88 % in 2009 to 153 % in 2019. In addition, declining government revenues, low FDI, and reduced inflows of remittances have exacerbated the situation. Heavily indebted countries are obliged to use already scarce financial resources to service their debts, although these resources are required for other purposes, like education, health, and social security systems. In this situation, high debt service payments prevent countries from

---

[33] Procopio M. (2020), *The International Politics around Africa's Debt*, ISPI Dossier, https://www.ispionline.it/it/pubblicazione/international-politics-around-africas-debt-27020 (Accessed October 15, 2021).

making investments in economic development that are necessary to support growth.

To help cope with the severe economic consequences of Covid-19, and safeguard debt sustainability at the same time, the international community, in particular the G20 countries, has a key role to play in providing short-term liquidity and debt relief to sub-Saharan countries. The IMF and the Word Bank have established two processes for providing timely liquidity to developing countries: the Debt Service Suspension Initiative (DSSI), and the Common Framework for Debt Treatments beyond the DSSI.

These initiatives have both pros and cons (Berensmann et al., 2021).[34] One advantage is that they also include non-members of the creditor countries' Paris Club. Since the share of bilateral official loans from non-Paris Club members to DSSI – eligible countries significantly increased in the past decade, like in the case of China, this is an important aspect. On the other hand, however, the Common Framework is not a comprehensive instrument for sovereign debt restructuring; private creditors have not yet committed to granting debt treatment on comparable terms.

The IMF has also backed an unprecedented, and by far the largest in the institution's history, new allocation of Special Drawing Rights (SDRs) of $650 bn. (1 % of global GDP) with the aim of increasing their reserves and liquidity, without adding to their debt burden.

A critical aspect of this allocation is that SDRs are allocated according to countries' quotas within the IMF, and the quota formula depends heavily on countries' aggregate GDP. As a consequence, barely 3 % of the $650 bn. went to low-income countries, 30 % went to middle-income emerging markets and nearly 60 % was allocated to high-income countries. The IMF Managing Director Kristalina Georgieva welcomed this operation although acknowledging that it will be crucial that IMF will "identify viable options for voluntary channelling of SDRs from wealthier members to support our poorer and more vulnerable countries to help their pandemic recovery and achieve resilient and sustainable growth, which will also help boost global economic recovery." (Georgieva,

[34] Berensmann K., Ordu A. and Senbet L. W. (2021), *Covid-19 Crisis: G20 and Debt Sustainability in Sub-Saharan Africa*, ISPI Commentary, https://www.ispionline.it/en/pubblicazione/covid-19-crisis-g20-and-debt-sustainability-sub-saharan-africa-29953 (Accessed October 14, 2021).

2021).[35] A viable option would be to allocate the European countries' quotas to a fund for the development of African countries in a similar way as the NGEU, where disbursements would be conditional on the achievement of certain priority objectives, like tangible and intangible infrastructures in strategic sectors for African development.

35 Georgieva K. (2021), *IMF Managing Director Kristalina Georgieva Welcomes the Executive Board's Backing for a New US$650 Billion SDR Allocation*, Press Release 21/208, https://www.imf.org/en/News/Articles/2021/07/08/pr21208-imf-managing-director-kristalina-georgieva-executive-board-backing-new-us650b-sdr-allocation (Accessed October 15, 2021).

Chapter 8

The long and promising road to genuine European own resources

8.1 The EU budget: A reform from both the revenue and expenditure sides

The issue of financing the EU's budget has been at the centre of the debate over the EU reform process for some years. Current discussions concern not only the revenue side of the budget, that is, how and to what extent it should be financed, but also the expenditure side, that is, how the budget should be spent.

As regards the sources of revenue, Art. 311 of the TFEU states that "The Union shall provide itself with the means necessary to attain its objectives and carry through its policies. Without prejudice to other revenue, the budget shall be financed wholly from own resources." It is then the Own Resources Decision (ORD) which specifies the European sources of revenue, which basically are:

- traditional own resources, mainly from customs duties and sugar levies;
- VAT-based own resources, consisting of the application of a uniform rate to VAT assessment bases, harmonised and determined for all Member States according to EU rules;
- own resources based on Gross National Income (GNI), resulting from the application of a uniform rate to the sum of the gross national incomes of all Member States. This rate is adjusted every year in order to achieve a balance between revenue and expenditure.

GNI-based own resources finance about two thirds of the EU budget. This source provides some benefits in terms of transparency, predictability, and fairness. Moreover, as the distribution of the burden among Member States is proportional to their respective economic weight, it encourages Member States to think of the budget in accounting terms on the basis of net balances, i.e. to look at the difference between what is paid through European public coffers and what is received in the form of European policies.

Therefore, introducing new and genuine European own resources that do not come from the Member States' coffers, but are directly allocated to the EU, can help to reduce the prevailing logic of *juste retour*. To this end, it is also crucial to link the introduction of new and genuine own resources to their use. Indeed, on the expenditure side there is a lively debate on the redefinition of tasks within the EU. Both the European Parliament and the Commission believe that the EU budget as it stands today no longer reflects Europe's strategic priorities. Traditional policies, such as cohesion and agricultural policies, should be scaled down to leave more room for the provision of European public goods, with which to respond to new global challenges linked to the fight against climate change, the digital transition, and the security of its citizens.

The HLGOR (2016) noted that the net balances approach, by which Member States look at the EU budget, does not take into account the principle of European added value. This value is particularly strong for some EU policies, whose benefits transcend the borders of the country where the money is spent and spread to most if not all Members States. The introduction of new own resources would be justified precisely to support the production of European public goods with high added value.

As already mentioned in Chapter 5, the Covid-19 pandemic has opened a new phase in the integration process, which redefines the terms of European fiscal capacity. The nature and scale of the economic crisis caused by the coronavirus pandemic has called for a response that affects not only the countries of the Eurozone – since it is no longer a crisis peculiar to the euro – but the Union as a whole. From an institutional point of view, the measures adopted in Europe against the pandemic go well beyond the previous decisions of the Eurogroup with respect to the BICC, as they provide for the creation of a spending capacity –NGEU. Financed by new European debt, this is in addition to the 2021-2027 MFF and dedicated to the recovery following the pandemic.

In fact, the NGEU would be financed by common European bonds of €750 bn., issued on the market by the Commission on behalf of the EU. To allow this operation, and to preserve the Union's excellent credit rating, the own resources ceiling for payments will be changed permanently from 1,29 % to 1,46 % of EU GNI, with a temporary increase of the ceiling by a further 0,60 percentage points, intended exclusively for borrowing operations of the NGEU.

This increase, partly necessary to fulfil the common NGEU obligations, will be financed through the gradual introduction of new European own resources, which the inter-institutional agreement between the European Parliament, the Commission and the Council has already defined with a roadmap for 2021 through to 2026. In the first phase, a new resource consisting of a share of revenues from national contributions, calculated on the basis of the weight of non-recycled plastic packaging waste, will be introduced, while at the same time a carbon border adjustment mechanism and a digital levy will be presented by the Commission. The border mechanism will be accompanied by a proposal for an own resource based on the ETS, with its extension to the aviation and maritime sectors. These new own resources are expected to be introduced by January 2023. In the second phase, from 2024, the Commission will propose additional new own resources, which could include a financial transaction tax, a contribution linked to the corporate sector or a new common corporate tax base, with a view to introducing these by 2026.

The introduction of new European own resources will therefore be needed to prevent an increase in the payment ceiling, leading to an increase in national contributions. However, the revenue from new own resources collected directly by the EU, and thus having the nature of federal resources, could be used for several purposes. It could cover the cost of the common debt issued to finance the NGEU, estimated at between €15 and €29 bn. per year until 2058. Part of the revenue could be used for a structural reinforcement of the MFF, that could better target EU programmes that support European public goods for the benefit of all member countries. In particular, the financing of both a vast *Social* EGD and the EIP *with Africa* proceeds in this direction.

In these terms, the link between genuinely European own resources, whose tax base goes beyond national borders, and European policies whose effects extend to all member countries, would become even stronger. Finally, the issue raised by President Macron in his 2017 speech at Sorbonne University of an additional Eurozone budget, in which countries that have already joined the monetary union decide to take further steps in the integration process, should not be underestimated.

8.2 New European own resources

The introduction of European taxes could take place without a real transfer of fiscal sovereignty from the national to the European level. In other words, it may be possible to introduce a specific own resource that would be justified by the achievement of EU objectives, through an amendment of the ORD, whereby the new tax would first be established on a legal basis and then included as a new own resource. However, this would only be possible through the special legislative procedure set out in Art. 311 of the TFEU, i.e. by a unanimous decision of the Council of the EU, on a proposal from the Commission, after consulting the Parliament. Before entering into force, the decision would have to be approved by each Member State in accordance with their respective constitutional requirements (in most cases, the responsibility for ratifying the ORD lies with the national parliament, whilst in some others, the government decides). Given the complexity of this procedure, EU own resources are deemed to have a *quasi*-Treaty status (D'Alfonso, 2021).[1]

Another possibility for change could be through the way decisions on taxation are made. One way to move from unanimity to qualified majority voting for taxation would be through the *passerelle clauses* contained in the Treaties, which allow the Council to adopt measures in the field of taxation, hitherto subject to unanimity, by qualified majority voting, or through the ordinary legislative procedure (Art. 48 of the TFEU). In 2019, the Commission invited Member States to reflect on the possibility of introducing a more democratic and efficient way of voting on common taxation (European Commission, 2019b).[2] However, the procedures of the *passerelle clauses* stipulate that the European Council has to take the initiative, should indicate the scope of the intended change in the decision-making process, and should notify national parliaments. If none of the national parliaments oppose this decision within six months, then the European Council may adopt it by unanimity, after obtaining the consent of the European Parliament.

---

1 D'Alfonso A. (2021), *National ratification of the Own Resources Decision*, EPRS Briefing, https://www.europarl.europa.eu/RegData/etudes/BRIE/2021/690520/EPRS_BRI(2021)690520_EN.pdf (Accessed October 14, 2021).

2 European Commission (2019b), *Towards a More Efficient and Democratic Decision Making in EU Tax Policy,* https://ec.europa.eu/taxation_customs/sites/taxation/files/15_01_2019_communication_towards_ a_more_efficient_democratic_decision_making_eu_tax_policy_en.pdf (Accessed October 15, 2021).

The political difficulties linked to the introduction of new resources therefore call for exploring new legal avenues to circumvent the unanimity requirement. In this regard new developments have emerged. The European Commissioner for the Economy, Paolo Gentiloni, has repeatedly emphasised that the Commission should carefully examine the possibility of using Art. 116 of the TFEU as a legal basis for introducing new own resources. This provision states that

> where the Commission finds that a difference between the provisions laid down by law, regulation or administrative action in Member States is distorting the conditions of competition in the internal market and that the resultant distortion needs to be eliminated, it shall consult the Member States concerned. If such consultation does not result in an agreement eliminating the distortion in question, the European, Parliament and the Council, acting in accordance with the ordinary legislative procedure, shall issue the necessary directives. Any other appropriate measures provided for in the Treaties may be adopted.

Thus, the way forward to introducing new European taxes could be to address the distortion of the conditions of competition in the internal market.

A further aspect to be considered is that new European taxes could lead to an unequal distribution of the additional fiscal burden among the various Member States. This issue is similar to that of rebates, i.e. the discounts granted since the 1980s to the UK and then to some other net contributor countries, who were concerned about their excessive contributions to the EU budget. In the context of an overall reform of the budget, on both the revenue and the expenditure sides, these compensation mechanisms should be abandoned. Firstly, with the exit of the UK, the initial assumption that triggered the logic of *juste retour* and rebates will disappear. Secondly, with a budget more oriented towards European public goods that serve the wellbeing of all citizens, the logic of national net balances is no longer valid. This should be replaced by the search for European added value, i.e. the greater convenience and effectiveness for all Member States in assigning new competences in certain areas to the European level.

However, in case of an excessive burden, we could refer to the compromise solution suggested by the Monti report on own resources:

> [...] any correction mechanism on the revenue side should be abolished. The balance between own resources has to be so that we can avoid any

correction mechanism. In case of any excessive burden caused by one or another own resource on a Member State, it could be alleviated by means of a specific compensation limited in duration and amount, and preferably calculated in terms of lump sums. Such an approach would make the own resources system simpler and fairer (HLGOR, 2016, p. 13).

Despite these political difficulties, the only way to consistently increase the European budget requires overcoming the logic of fair return by finding new alternative sources of revenue to national contributions. In a recent paper Fontana and Gasbarro (2021)[3] argue that new and genuine European own resources could be recovered in those areas where strong negative externalities for society arise, i.e. gambling, tobacco consumption, polluting carbon dioxide emissions, tax avoidance and financial transactions. If the general framework were considered, the combined effect on the revenue and expenditure sides could be summed up in the following sentence: *taxing the bad to finance the good*, referring to the taxation of negative externalities produced by certain behaviours and the promotion European public goods.

8.3 Gambling

In order to describe and quantify the legal gaming sector in Italy, reference is generally made to: turnover, the total amount bet by the players (in 2018 it was €106,8 bn.); pay-outs (€87 bn.), the total amount won; expenditure (or gross margin) (€18,9 bn.), the difference between turnover and pay-outs, corresponding to the actual losses of players; and revenue from taxation (€10,4 bn.). In recent years, gaming turnover in Italy, as in the rest of Europe, has experienced significant growth, reaching an amount of over €354 bn. in the Eurozone, as of 2018.

In Italy, the tax rate is around 10 % of turnover, a relatively modest percentage when compared to the taxation on income from labour, with a rate ranging from a minimum of 23 % to a maximum of 43 %. Nevertheless, gambling represents one of the most profitable sectors of the Italian economy; it is approximately twice as much as other leading

3 Fontana O. and Gasbarro L. (2021), *European Fiscal Capacity and New Own Resources: Proposals and Scenarios*, CSF Research Paper, June, http://www.csfederalismo.it/images/Research_paper/CSF-RP_Fiscal-Capacity-Own-Resources_O.Fontana-L.Gasbarro_June2021.pdf (Accessed October 15, 2021).

sectors, such as engineering (€46,7 bn. in 2018) and textile-fashion (€54 bn.), with only agribusiness coming closest (€132 bn. in 2017).

Taxation of the gaming sector, both in Italy and the rest of the major European countries, is not uniform for different types of games. For example, traditional games, such as lotto and lotteries, are subject to a tax levy corresponding to the residual fiscal margin, whilst other sectors, such as betting and new-generation games, have different rates and tax bases depending on the type of game. Similarly, in the main European countries, the taxation systems are structured on a tax base that can be represented by the turnover or the gross margin. There are also differences in terms of the tax rates applied, although these are on average higher in Italy.

Given the complexity of the gaming taxation framework, it does not seem realistic to introduce a levy at the European level, which would interfere with the existing systems in the Member States. As such, a linear surtax with a standard rate on top of the national systems, without changing their internal structure, could be a viable solution to implementing a European levy on gaming. Irrespective of the amount won by a player or the type of game, the surtax could take the form of a withholding tax on the amount of the pay-outs at the time when this amount is distributed. There is therefore no exemption threshold on pay-outs, as this surtax will be levied on all of them. Assuming a 10 % tax rate on all pay-outs realised in the Eurozone countries (2018 data), the revenue that could be realised would amount to €28,8 bn. (Tab. 8.1). In the case of a 15 % tax rate, the revenue would rise to €43,3 bn. For the EU, the revenue would rise to €33,9 bn. (10 % rate), and €50,9 bn. (15 % rate), calculated on the amount of pay-outs, roughly estimated on the basis of the economic weight of non-Euro countries (about 15 % of EU GDP).

8.4 Tobacco

The intention of European legislation in the tobacco sector is to harmonise taxation applied at the national level. Tobacco taxation seeks to achieve a twofold objective: on the one hand, to provide stable revenue for Member States' coffers; on the other hand, to increase the level of health protection of individuals and thus reduce the negative externalities of tobacco consumption. Tobacco taxation has two components: an *ad*

Tab. 8.1: Author's simulation of a 10 % and 15 % over-taxation of pay-outs in Eurozone countries (2018 data, € m.).

	Turnover	Pay-outs	Revenues from surtax of 10 %	Revenues from surtax of 15 %
Italy	106.800	87.800	8.780	13.170
Germany	65.978	52.713	5.271	7.907
France	47.936	37.603	3.760	5.640
Spain	42.687	34.055	3.406	5.108
Finland	12.050	10.291	1.029	1.544
Netherlands	13.264	10.685	1.069	1.603
Ireland	8.011	6.822	682	1.023
Belgium	12.787	10.980	1.098	1.647
Austria	10.585	9.161	916	1.374
Portugal	8.995	7.253	725	1.088
Greece	11.085	9.175	918	1.376
Slovakia	3.893	3.273	327	491
Slovenia	3.628	3.168	317	475
Latvia	3.153	2.834	283	425
Estonia	1.208	1.057	106	159
Lithuania	1.159	1.015	102	152
Cyprus	411	278	28	42
Luxembourg	345	254	25	38
Malta	301	204	20	31
Total EMU	**354.276**	**288.621**	**28.862**	**43.293**
Total UE	**416.700**	**339.500**	**33.950**	**50.925**

valorem component, i.e. a percentage applied to the price; and a specific component, i.e. a fixed amount based on quantity, regardless of price.

Within the EU, Member States may prefer a different type of taxation (specific and *ad valorem*),[4] but they must respect common parameters when determining the level of taxation to be applied domestically.

4 The effect of taxation on price varies according to the type of taxation. *Ad valorem* taxes, being proportional to the sales price, do not directly affect price determination, whereas the weight of specific taxes varies according to price, because if the price of tobacco increases, the tax burden on tobacco itself decreases, thus providing an incentive to maintain high prices, which is necessary to counteract cigarette consumption, i.e. one of the two objectives of taxation.

According to EU guidelines, taxation must be mixed, i.e. be composed of a part of specific taxes and a part of *ad valorem* taxes.[5] In addition, reference values for the minimum tax burden on tobacco are set. This mechanism should ensure that prices, although different between Member States, do not fall below a certain threshold, so as not to encourage tobacco consumption, and that when consumption falls, tax revenues for Member States remain stable through a gradual increase in taxes.

Prices per packet of cigarettes vary widely across Europe, ranging from a minimum of €2,86 per packet in Bulgaria, to a maximum of €13 in Ireland, one of the countries with the highest price in the world. In general, the highest price countries are Australia (€19,39) and the United Kingdom (€12,23), while the United States (€7,10 euro) still has a higher price than the European average of €5,6 per pack.[6]

In line with the Commission's intention to discourage unhealthy consumption by applying an additional cost on cigarette consumption, an EU surtax of €0,05 per cigarette should be introduced through the national tax system, and independently of current prices. Based on 2018 consumption figures, this would generate revenues of €15,5 bn. for the euro area and €22 bn. for the EU (Tab. 8.2). Even after the application of the EU surtax, the average price in Europe would remain below that of the most ambitious countries in terms of tobacco taxation. Although we have not estimated the revenue effect of a surcharge on e-cigarettes, we believe that this segment should also be included in taxation.

8.5 CO_2 emissions

The EU has been working for a number of years towards combatting CO_2 emissions which are largely responsible for global warming. This commitment is enshrined in the EGD, with the goal of net zero emissions by 2050. Among the various measures outlined by the Commission, forms of carbon pricing are crucial to driving the transition to a

---

5 Council of the European Union (2011), *Directive 2011/64/EU on the Structure and Rates of Excise Duty Applied to Manufactured Tobacco*, https://eur-lex.europa.eu/legal-content/EN/TXT/PDF/?uri=CELEX:32011L0064&from=en (Accessed October 14, 2021).

6 Data available on www.numbeo.com, *Price Rankings by Country of Cigarettes 20 Pack (Marlboro) (Markets)*, https://www.numbeo.com/cost-of-living/country_price_rankings?itemId=17&displayCurrency=EUR

Tab. 8.2: Author's simulation of a European surtax of €1 per pack on cigarette consumption in the EU and the Eurozone (2018)

	Price per packet (€)	**Consumption of cigarettes (thousands)**	**Revenues from surtax €0,05 per cigarette (€ m.)**	**Price per packet after surtax (€)**
Ireland	13	1.763.336	88	14
France	10	40.232.403	2.012	11
Finland	7,7	3.890.085	195	8,7
Netherlands	7	11.134.964	557	8
Belgium	6,75	9.443.837	472	7,75
Germany	6,4	74.360.153	3.718	7,4
Sweden	6,18	5.431.203	272	7,18
Denmark	6,04	5.281.339	264	7,04
Malta	6	532.056	27	7
Italy	5,5	67.402.620	3.37	6,5
Austria	5,5	11.831.567	592	6,5
Spain	5	44.810.363	2.241	6
Portugal	5	10.589.379	529	6
Greece	4,5	13.043.843	652	5,5
Estonia	4,5	1.551.664	78	5,5
Slovenia	4,1	3.550.336	178	5,1
Hungary	4,03	8.309.404	415	5,03
Latvia	3,98	1.940.496	97	4,98
Croatia	3,96	6.270.259	314	4,96
Rep. Ceca	3,96	21.221.296	1.061	4,96
Lithuania	3,95	2.801.043	140	4,95
Romania	3,93	2.623.258	1.312	4,93
Slovakia	3,91	7.003.123	350	4,91
Poland	3,71	42.898.820	2.145	4,71
Bulgaria	2,86	13.902.690	695	3,86
Luxemburg	n.a.	3.001.399	150	n.a.
Cyprus	n.a.	1.245.097	62	n.a.
Total EMU		**310.127.764**	**15.506**	
Total UE		**439.675.355**	**21.984**	

zero-emission economy. In reality, it is a matter of getting carbon prices right, through the application of a tax rate on fossil fuels, which would be based on the amount of CO_2 produced during combustion. This step would thus encourage the transition to the use of clean energy.

At the EU level, only the industrial sector and power generation plants are regulated through the ETS, a mechanism for limiting emissions introduced with the 2003/87 Directive. An oft critiqued aspect of the ETS is its partial coverage of emissions. Although a gradual increase is envisaged, less than half of the allowances in the ETS are currently sold, whilst the remainder are given free of charge to those operators most at risk of relocating to less environmentally friendly jurisdictions (*carbon leakage*). The price of allowances sold on the ETS auction has been rising in recent months, reaching over €50 tCO_2, which is in line with the scientific community's call for a steady and gradual increase in carbon pricing.

More than half of total emissions (55 %) are excluded from the ETS, in particular those from the agriculture, transport, construction and residential sectors. It is up to Member States to decide whether to apply carbon pricing as an environmental protection measure, as well as a source of tax revenue.

The carbon pricing system in Europe is therefore complex, relying partly on a market mechanism, partly on taxation, and responding to different levels of commitment across countries. Therefore, whilst maintaining the existing ETS infrastructure, a price floor of €50/tCO_2 could be applied to permit purchases by operators, with revenues flowing into the EU's budget. For the non-ETS sectors, a surcharge of the same amount of €50/tCO_2 could be applied. This figure should be seen as a starting point, to be gradually increased in line with values established from scientific evidence.[7]

Based on estimates provided by Eurostat, in 2018, total CO_2 emissions were around 3.890 m. tonnes in the EU, and 2.978 m. tonnes in the Eurozone (Tab. 8.3). If an EU-wide price floor of €50/tCO_2 were to be applied to ETS emissions (around 45 % of the total), then the revenue from the sale of permits could range from a minimum of €43

[7] The report of the High-Level Commission on Carbon Prices led by Joseph Stiglitz and Nicholas Stern already stressed the need to move from a price of $40 to $80 in 2020 to $50 to $100 in 2030.

bn. (assuming 50 % of permits are sold and allocated to the budget) to a maximum of around €87 bn. (100 % of permits sold), for the EU, whilst for the Eurozone, we would have between €33 bn. and €67 bn., depending on whether 50 % or 100 % of the total permits are sold and allocated to the budget.

The remaining emissions, produced by sectors not covered by the ETS (mainly domestic consumption and transport), are estimated to amount to 2,140 m. tCO_2 for the EU and 1,341 m. tCO_2 for the Eurozone. Assuming a carbon pricing of 50 €/tCO_2, the revenue generated would be €107 bn. for the EU as a whole and €81,9 bn. for the Eurozone. This revenue could be used in part by the EU to finance compensatory measures at the national level, in order to alleviate forms of resistance, such as the *gilets jaunes* in 2018 in France. As noted by economist Pierre-Yves Geoffard, at the time of the protests, in the French case for a person living 25 km from his workplace and travelling an average of 1.000 km per month to get there, assuming that his car consumes 7 litres/100 km, a carbon tax of €0,14 per litre represents €10 per month (with a carbon tax of around €60/tCO_2).[8] For many poor households this is a significant expense. These regressive income effects could be neutralised by income support measures.

For the domestic sector, we could draw on the German case, where carbon pricing will be accompanied by a reduction in the surcharge on the electricity bill to finance renewable energy, or the energy cheque in France, which helps families in situations of energy poverty. These measures are forms of carbon dividend, which accompany the introduction of carbon pricing. A similar measure has been advocated by a group of American economists,[9] who suggest that carbon pricing revenues could be returned directly through rebates to all citizens, regardless of income. The main reason why Macron's proposal triggered the protests of the *gilets jaunes* in France is that he did not accompany the tax tightening measure with social compensatory measures to mitigate the regressive nature of the carbon tax.

Whilst recognising the usefulness of a carbon dividend, it is appropriate to provide for a differentiation in its distribution according to income,

---

8 The combustion of one litre of fuel (0,74 kg) generates about 2,34 kg of CO2.

9 Economists' statement on carbon dividends (https://clcouncil.org/economists-statement/).

to focus on the less wealthy. For instance, in the case of Italy, the revenue from the domestic and transport sectors (non-ETS) is around €12 bn. Two-thirds of this amount, €8 bn., could be redistributed as tax credit to all individuals with a total gross annual income of between €8.145 and €26.000. The bonus would result in an increase in the average individual's salary of about €800 per year, for those with a total income of no more than €24.000; if this limit were exceeded, the dividend would fall to zero on a total income level of €26.000.[10]

As companies are tempted to move production to countries with less stringent emission standards, Europe's efforts to become carbon neutral by 2050 could be undermined by the risk of carbon leakage. Therefore, the Commission is working on a carbon border adjustment mechanism, i.e. a tariff on imports commensurate with the amount of CO_2 emitted during the production of the imported goods. The introduction of carbon pricing on imports of certain goods from outside the EU would prevent carbon leakage. By treating domestic and foreign production on an equal footing, it would also avoid the need for free allocation of allowances.

According to Eurostat data based on a consumption perspective, in 2018, EU import-related CO_2 emissions were 980 kg per capita, or 437 m. tCO_2 in terms of total EU emissions. A carbon border adjustment of €50/tCO_2 on all imports would therefore generate potential revenue of €21,8 bn. that would flow directly to the EU budget, as it relates to customs policy, which is an exclusive competence of the EU.

8.6 Tax avoidance

The OECD has been working since 2013 to combat tax avoidance, the practices by which multinational companies exploit loopholes and asymmetries in international rules to shift profits to countries with more favourable tax regimes (BEPS – base erosion and profit shifting). The action is based on two pillars: the first concerns digital giants and proposes to tax them where they sell their services and not only where

---

10 Potential beneficiaries of the credit are all taxpayers with income from employment, assimilated employment and self-employment. It would be paid by the withholding agent in such a way as to ensure that the credit is received in the same pay period by all those entitled to it, while those without withholding agent can claim the credit in the relevant tax return.

Tab. 8.3: Author's simulation of a European carbon pricing on total CO_2 emissions in EU and Eurozone countries

	Emissions 2018 (million tonnes CO_2)	**Revenues from 50 €/tCO2 levy (€ bn.)**
Germany	888.720	44,44
France	462.800	23,14
Italy	439.260	21,96
Poland	415.860	20,79
Spain	352.210	17,61
Netherlands	200.460	10,02
Rep. Ceca	129.390	6,47
Belgium	123.640	6,18
Romania	116.530	5,83
Greece	96.110	4,81
Austria	81.500	4,08
Portugal	71.570	3,58
Ireland	64.240	3,21
Hungary	64.070	3,2
Finland	58.820	2,94
Bulgaria	58.600	2,93
Sweden	54.610	2,73
Denmark	51.300	2,57
Slovakia	43.530	2,18
Croatia	24.360	1,22
Lithuania	20.650	1,03
Estonia	20.180	1,01
Slovenia	17.600	0,88
Luxembourg	12.360	0,62
Latvia	12.200	0,61
Cyprus	9.860	0,49
Malta	2.660	0,13
Total EMU	**2.978.390**	**148,92**
Total EU	**3.893.100**	**194,66**

production takes place; the second includes global minimum taxation. As regards the second pillar, an important stimulus came from the Biden administration's 2021 proposal of a minimum global tax rate at 21 % on multinationals' foreign profits. However, Biden's proposal was later revised with the agreement reached in the OECD on a minimum corporation tax to ensure that large companies pay a minimum rate of 15 % on corporate income.

The US decision should be seen in the light of the overall package proposed, which includes on the one hand a public investment plan, the *American Jobs Plan*, which will mobilise $2 tn. (about 1 % of GDP per year), and on the other a tax reform programme, the *Made in America Tax Plan*. The aim is to modernise infrastructure, revitalise production and invest in research. Evidently future generation will be the beneficiaries of these investments; however, in order not to put all the burden of financing on them, and be sure that the corporate sector pays its fair share, the current regime on corporate income has to be reformed.

The EU is pushing for a taxation of digital activities as a way to tackle the disparity between digital, and non-digital companies. Under current rules, multinationals pay taxes where production takes place, rather than where consumers/users are located. This provision benefits digital companies, which can operate in any number of countries without the need for tangible structures. The minimum global tax would put all companies on an equal footing, regardless of technology, and oblige them to pay taxes uniformly. But pending a global agreement, the EU is also determined to act unilaterally. At the European Council on 25 March 2021, Member States reiterated that, while preferring a concerted solution, the EU should be ready to move forward, based on the Commission's proposal for a digital levy, to be introduced by 1 January 2023 at the latest.

The US decision to propose a minimum global tax is an important signal of President Biden's shift in US policy towards a stricter attitude towards corporate income taxation, from which the EU can benefit greatly. First, a global agreement on international fiscal rules will contribute to interrupting practices pursued by national governments of fiscal dumping, which is a typical European practice. Second, the revenues from a corporate tax could fulfil the need for additional financing to sustain public expenditure, both at the national and European level. Estimates of the effect of tax avoidance for the Euro area (Tab. 8.4) indicate

Tab. 8.4: Missing revenue from tax avoidance by multinationals (€ m.)

	Profit shifted	Revenue loss	Effective tax rate	Statutory tax rate
France	19.647	6.894	35,1%	33,3%
Germany	18.807	4.122	21,9%	29,8%
Italy	15.684	3.929	25,1%	24,0%
Belgium	11.644	2.637	22,7%	34,0%
Spain	10.604	2.512	23,7%	25,0%
Austria	4.202	1.356	32,3%	25,0%
Ireland	7.836	1.004	12,8%	12,5%
Portugal	2.676	640	23,9%	21,0%
Finland	2.095	347	16,6%	20,0%
Greece	1.646	176	10,7%	29,0%
Slovenia	736	78	10,7%	19,0%
Lithuania	179	26	14,8%	15,0%
Cyprus	-223	-10	4,5%	12,5%
Luxemburg	-52.908	-396	0,8%	27,1%
Netherlands	-41.468	-2.042	4,9%	25,0%
Slovakia	2.268	390	17,2%	21,0%
Total EMU*	**3.425**	**21.663**		
Sweden	3.267	750	23,0%	22,0%
Poland	4.486	701	15,6%	19,0%
Denmark	2.342	617	26,4%	22,0%
Rep. Ceca	2.626	492	18,8%	19,0%
Hungary	1.17	408	34,9%	9,0%
Romania	1.903	344	18,1%	16,0%
Croatia	503	63	12,6%	20,0%
Bulgaria	824	61	7,4%	10,0%
Total EU*	**-1.176**	**23.614**		
UK	-6.493	-684	10,5%	19,0%
Switzerland	-14.059	-801	5,7%	17,8%

Source: Cobham A., Garcia- Bernardo J.and Mansour M.B.(2020), *The Axis of Tax Avoidance*, Tax Justice Network.https:// www.tax just ice.net/ wp- cont ent/ uplo ads/ 2020/ 04/ The-axis- of- tax- avoida nce_ Tax- Just ice- Networ k_ Ap ril- 2020- 1.pdf (Accessed October 14, 2021).

*Estonia, Latvia and Malta excluded

an annual loss of revenues approximately of €21,6 bn. whilst for the EU it is €23,6 bn. (Cobham et al., 2020).[11]

8.7 Financial transactions

In the aftermath of the 2008 financial crisis, the Financial Transaction Tax (FTT) has often been invoked as a response to the severe imbalance that has developed in recent decades, between the growth of the real economy, and the growth of speculative finance. Thus, the aims of the FTT are to discourage transactions that affect the efficient allocation of resources by financial markets, and to ensure that the financial sector contributes its fair share to national tax revenues. Although there are considerable differences between countries within the EU, some countries such as Belgium, Finland, France, Ireland, Italy, and Poland, currently apply forms of FTT.

In 2011, the European Commission proposed the creation of a common EU-wide FTT, with the aim of harmonising taxation and thus avoiding a fragmentation of financial services within the single market. However, once it was established that unanimity could not be achieved in the Council, a group of FTT-friendly Member States (Austria, Belgium, Estonia, France, Germany, Greece, Italy, Portugal, Slovakia, Slovenia, and Spain) moved towards enhanced cooperation in 2013. The FTT proposal envisaged the application of a tax of 0,1 % on the transaction value of shares and bonds and 0,01 % on derivative contracts. By using not only the establishment principle (if at least one of the two parties involved in the transaction is based in a country that has adopted the tax, then the tax applies) but also the issuance principle (the place where the company issuing the security that is the subject of the transaction is based), the proposal would make it more difficult to evade tax by relocating activities and establishments outside the jurisdictions that adopt the FTT. Preliminary estimates of the 2013 proposal for enhanced cooperation in the eleven EU countries (which became ten after Estonia's withdrawal) indicate that the revenue from tax could be in the order of magnitude of €31 bn. each year.

---

[11] Cobham A., Garcia-Bernardo J. and Mansour M. B. (2020), *The Axis of Tax Avoidance*, Tax Justice Network, https://www.taxjustice.net/wp-content/uploads/2020/04/The-axis-of-tax-avoidance_Tax-Justice-Network_April-2020-1.pdf (Accessed October 14, 2021).

However, the project remains unfinished due to resistance from Member States. In 2019, France and Germany put forward a proposal to introduce an FTT based on the French model.[12] This would be a levy made upon the transfer of ownership of shares and similar instruments, (but not debt securities), admitted for trading on regulated markets. The levy would apply to listed companies established in an EU Member State with a market capitalisation exceeding €1 bn. on 1 December of the previous year, and as such would not affect smaller companies. Initial public offerings, market making, and intraday trading would also be exempt. According to the document, the tax rate would not be less than 0,2 %, with the revenue going into the European budget or the budget of the Eurozone yet to be created, and as part of a compensation mechanism the proceeds would be distributed between the states wishing to participate in the initiative. In this new version, the reduced scope of the tax would generate revenue estimated at a much lower level than in the Commission's original proposal, in the order of €3,5 bn., compared with €31 bn.

In the Tabs. 8.5 and 8.6 we provide estimates of the potential revenue from the introduction of a comprehensive, wide-ranging FTT that can be applied to all financial transactions without exemptions. On applying the tax rate of 0,1 % on share and bond trades and 0,01 % on derivative transactions to two different scenarios, one conservative and the other optimistic, as illustrated by the Austrian Institute for Economic Research,[13] the revenues would amount to around €29 billion each year in a conservative scenario (Tab. 8.5) and around €49 billion in an optimistic scenario (Tab. 8.6). Finally, it would be appropriate to apply both the establishment and issuance principles as suggested by the Commission, in order to make it more difficult to pursue tax avoidance practices.

12 Council of the European Union (2019), *Council Directive Implementing Enhanced Cooperation in the Area of Financial Transaction Tax*, https://data.consilium.europa.eu/doc/document/ST-10097-2019-INIT/en/pdf (Interinstitutional file from the German Delegation). (accessed October 14, 2021)

13 Pekanov A. and Schratzenstaller M. (2019), *A Global Financial Transaction Tax. Theory, Practice and Potential Revenues*, WIFO Working Papers No. 582, https://www.wifo.ac.at/jart/prj3/wifo/resources/person_dokument/person_dokument.jart?publikationsid=61805&mime_type=application/pdf (Accessed October 14, 2021)

Tab. 8.5: Simulation of an FTT of 0,1 % on shares and bonds and 0,01 % on derivatives (€ bn.), conservative scenario

	Equities	Exchange trade derivatives	OTC derivatives	Interest rate derivatives	Bonds	Total
Austria	273,6	75,72	45,08	0,36	569,74	964,50
Belgium	328,09	90,8	55,3	15,91	683,2	1.173,30
Finland	176,26	48,78	32,46	1,18	367,04	625,72
France	2.017,11	558,27	433,27	83,59	4.200,31	7.292,55
Germany	2.170,87	600,82	279,2	29,69	4.520,50	7.601,08
Greece	91,89	25,43	2,43	-	191,35	311,10
Ireland	153,09	42,37	5,27	-	318,8	519,53
Italy	922,73	255,38	42,6	6,44	1.921,45	3.148,60
Latvia	16,02	4,43	1,42	-	33,36	55,23
Lithuania	21,56	5,97	0,56	-	44,89	72,98
Luxemburg	212,15	58,72	88,3	0,15	441,77	801,09
Netherlands	784,9	217,23	204,14	20,98	1634,43	2.861,68
Portugal	106,1	29,37	5,78	0,09	220,94	362,28
Slovakia	53,22	14,73	5,84	-	110,82	184,61
Spain	727,49	201,34	78,22	1,82	1.514,88	2.523,75
Total EMU*	8.055,08	2.229,36	1.279,87	160,21	16.773,48	**28.498**
Bulgaria	33,81	9,36	4,24	-	70,41	117,82
Czec Republic	112,12	31,03	9,17	-	233,47	385,79
Denmark	649,31	179,71	241,88	6,88	1.352,08	2.429,86
Hungary	76,47	21,16	7,93	0,13	159,23	264,92
Poland	271,48	75,14	21,87	2,01	565,33	935,83
Romania	104,61	28,95	6,93	-	217,84	358,33
Sweden	440,63	121,95	100,61	20,59	917,55	1.601,33
Total EU**	9.743,51	2.696,66	1.672,50	189,82	20.289,39	**34.591,88**

Source: elaborations adapted from Pekanov A. and Schratzenstaller M. (2019).
Slovenia excluded.

Tab. 8.6: Simulation of an FTT of 0,1 % on shares and bonds and 0,01 % on derivatives (€ bn.), optimistic scenario

	Equities	Exchange trade derivatives	OTC derivatives	Interest rate derivatives	Bonds	Total
Austria	319,21	388,05	232,93	1,87	664,70	1.606,76
Belgium	382,77	465,32	285,70	82,19	797,06	2.013,04
Finland	205,64	249,99	167,71	6,08	428,22	1.057,64
France	2.353,29	2.860,83	2.238,56	431,86	4.900,37	12.784,91
Germany	2.532,68	3.078,91	1.442,56	153,41	5.273,91	12.481,47
Greece	107,21	130,33	12,58	-	223,24	473,36
Ireland	178,61	217,13	27,23	-	371,93	794,90
Italy	1.076,52	1.308,70	220,09	33,25	2.241,69	4.880,25
Latvia	18,69	22,72	7,33	-	38,91	87,65
Lithuania	25,15	30,58	2,89	-	52,37	110,99
Luxemburg	247,51	300,89	456,24	0,79	515,39	1.520,82
Netherlands	915,71	1.113,21	1.054,70	108,41	1.906,83	5.098,86
Portugal	123,79	150,48	29,84	0,48	257,76	562,35
Slovakia	62,09	75,48	30,17	-	129,29	297,03
Spain	848,73	1.031,78	404,13	9,41	1.767,36	4.061,41
Total EMU*	9.397,60	11.424,40	6.612,66	827,75	19.569,03	**47.831,44**
Bulgaria	39,45	47,96	21,90	-	82,15	191,46
Czec Republic	130,80	159,01	47,37	0,02	272,38	609,58
Denmark	757,53	920,90	1.249,73	35,53	1.577,43	4.541,12
Hungary	89,21	108,45	40,97	0,69	185,77	425,09
Poland	361,73	385,04	112,99	10,36	659,55	1.529,67
Romania	122,05	148,37	35,79	-	254,15	560,36
Sweden	514,07	624,94	519,80	106,37	1.070,47	2.835,65
Total EU**	11.412,44	13.819,07	8.641,21	980,70	23.670,93	**58.524,37**

Source: Elaborations adapted from Pekanov A. and Schratzenstaller M. (2019).

* Cyprus, Estonia, Malta and Slovenia excluded.

** Cyprus, Croatia, Estonia, Malta and Slovenia excluded.

Conclusions

Over the last thirteen years, the EU has experienced two of the most severe economic crises since the Great Depression after the Second World War. These crises have been different in nature, and have had different consequences in terms of the response the EU has been able to deploy, and the timing of change. In the financial crisis, the EU reacted slowly, not proportionate to the needs, and failed to overcome ideological differences between its Member States on economic policy solutions. In contrast, in the pandemic crisis, the EU was united in sustaining its economy, with different solutions aimed at the labour, business and government sectors.

What the two crises have in common is the crucial role investment has to play as an engine to stimulate the economy, not only in the short term, but also in the long term. In spite of their tragic nature, the crises have focused attention on the need to safeguard investments, with *ad hoc* measures used to channel excess savings on the market into sectors considered strategic for the EU as a whole. The issue of the investment gap, which emerged forcefully after the financial crisis, framing the question in quantitative terms, starting by pointing out that the framework of fiscal rules for Member States had a negative effect on public investment.

However, further reflection developed over the question of how much investment was needed, but crucially on which investments to support, and in which sectors. This new reflection was even more salient, given the fact that the financial crisis had led to the emergence of a core-periphery pattern with an inflow of capital to periphery countries, mainly into non-growth oriented sectors, such as real estate and current public spending.

The investment debate then developed, to become strongly linked to that of the long-term development agenda. With the launch of the EDG, the EU created links between different policies. The common goal of combating climate change is being addressed through a variety of measures – regulatory, fiscal, industrial – that effect different levels of government, from local to European. As we have tried to highlight in this book, this strategy of carbon neutral development at the EU domestic level needs to be strongly linked to two further elements. First of all, the EGD must not neglect the social dimension, which is fundamental to getting the political consensus needed to proceed with the ecological transition. The second pillar of the EGD concerns the involvement of the African continent, as a strategic partner to which the EU seems to be linked in the medium and long term. This is not for reasons of mere charitable solidarity, but of mutual necessity, and on the EGD model that we intend to pursue.

The principle expressed in the Schumann Declaration in 1950, that "Europe will not be built all at once, or according to a single plan. It will be built through concrete achievements that first create de facto solidarity" is still relevant today, but requires strong vision and comprehensive planning. The EGD should therefore be seen as a green industrial policy, where the two legs of climate policy (whose goal is decarbonisation) and industrial policy (whose goal from a modern perspective is social welfare) combine to result in an industrial policy where climate change mitigation becomes a binding constraint in achieving the goal of social welfare.

The leap forward in the process of European integration that the response to the pandemic has enabled, through the launch of the NGEU, among other things, is a fundamental element in accompanying an ecological transition through European instruments. It is the key to create a double link. First, between national investments of Member States and the EGD objectives and targets; second, between the EGD and new European own resources needed to finance these investments.

As regard the first point, nearly 90 % (€672,5 bn.) of NGEU is devoted to the RRF. This represents a tool to mitigate the economic and social impact of the coronavirus pandemic through new funding from the EU budget; however, the RRF could be more. It offers a great opportunity to reshape economic sectors, support communities and restore ecosystems, while at the same time creating jobs for resilient societies and contributing to a healthy and just economic recovery. Or at least it should be, given that each National Recovery and Resilience Plan (NRRP) – the document member states have to submit to the European Commission when applying for disbursement – has to include at least a minimum of 37 % of expenditure for climate investment and reforms, and a minimum of 20 % to foster the digital transition, a prerequisite to green transition. These link back to important EGD-related conditionality, so that what is at stake here is not a return to business as usual, but is about promoting the profound changes the EU needs to thrive.

According to the assessment of Member States NRRPs made by Dirth et al. (2021),[1] three common shortcomings emerge across the plans:

(1) a rigorous application of the *Do No Significant Harm principle* is lacking, and it is common to overlook the risks to biodiversity in particular;
(2) in addition to supporting industries affected by the pandemic, the recovery needs to create jobs in those regions that are most affected by the digital and green transition. This will be important to decrease social polarisation in the recovery process;
(3) a longer-term, overarching vision of the future must be strengthened and included in the process.

In particular, the NRRPs evidence missed opportunities in terms of translating solutions to social and environmental problems into new investments.

A source of concern related to the NGEU is often the risk that the amount of money made available to national governments will not be spent entirely. One serious problem with EU structural funds is the low capacity of local governments to spend money, due to inefficiencies in public administration. However, another crucial aspect not related to the success of the NGEU, but to that of the EGD, is the risk that funding will not channel to sectors and policy that rigorously *do not significant harm.*

Therefore, based on the reading of NRRPs presented by far, the risk is that an adaptative approach will affirm, where the focus is on a soft progressive change, where the economy and society could be made more resilient. Unfortunately, what the scientific community suggests is a more radical approach to change, where investment, taxes, and regulation may not be enough to succeed. A hard radical change may imply different ways we produce, consume, and behave, in practice "a cultural revolution which would fundamentally question capitalism and our vision of the world" (Pochet, 2021).[2] However, the two visions could

---

1 Dirth E., Barth J., Davies W., Gründahl M., Hafele J., Korinek L., Kiberd E. and Miller C., (2021), *A Future-Fit Recovery? A Sectoral Analysis of Practices for Promoting Systemic Change in the NRRPs Based on the Recovery Index for Transformative Change (RITC)*, Transformation Report #1 — 06/2021, Bonn: ZOE-Institute for future-fit economies.

2 Pochet P. (2021), *The Four 'I's of a New Socio-ecological Contract*, Social Europe, https://socialeurope.eu/the-four-is-of-a-new-socio-ecological-contract (Accessed October 15, 2021).

meet in an agenda that, on the one hand, pursues a progressive ecological transition where appropriate compensation measures are in place, and on the other draws on the costs of non-transition, rather than costs of transition, to promote a more radical societal change, that has to face the major limiting factor; time constraint. This scenario means speeding up the ecological transition and rapidly rethinking our growth model, with a return to public investment and services, public goods, and solidarity within and between states.

As regards the link between the EGD and new own resources, the creation of the NGEU represents the opportunity to move from a financing system essentially based on Member States' national contributions, towards a system fuelled by genuine European own resources, which accrue to the European budget.

The NGEU has introduced the issuance of European common debt as an instrument to finance disbursements to the EU's Member States. The European institutions, and thus also the Member States, have committed themselves to introducing new own resources to service the debt and interest payments over the next 30 years. While new own resources will therefore be needed for a very long time, it should be remembered that the NGEU is a temporary, crisis-related programme in force until 2026. The instruments introduced during the pandemic allow for some elements of common taxation, but they will first have to be consolidated in the institutional set-up of European economic governance and could lead to the establishment of a new fiscal capacity based on genuine European own resources. On the expenditure side, these resources can be accompanied by a redefinition of the role of the budget towards greater European public goods, oriented towards the ecological and digital transition, as well as a permanent stabilisation function specific to the Eurozone and to the EU as a whole. On the basis of the modelling in Chapter 8, the own resources identified (some of them already of the table of the Commission) could bring considerable additional revenue to European coffers, in the order of several tens of billions of euros. In particular, a carbon tax appears a promising source of revenues with the *plus* of being instrumental in mitigating climate change.

These two crucial issues highlight how important the NGEU is for the future of the EU. Of course, it is no panacea for all the long-standing problems of the EU, which have been mentioned in this book, and which certainly cannot be solved by a financial instrument. However, although it is still early to think in terms of a federal turn for the EU, were the NGEU to be successful – depending of course on whether and how countries will be able to spend money – more room for manoeuvre might be envisaged. This would be especially the case from a political point of view, at least in order to reach a permanent and additional spending capacity, and agreeing on a common definition of European public goods, that could allow the implementation of those investments related to a *Social* and *African* EGD.

Crises have always brought with them serious economic consequences. In Europe they have sometimes also been the occasion to bring important positive results in advancing the integration process. However, only certain catastrophic events are perceived as crises and set in motion a reaction involving instruments of various kinds – fiscal, monetary, normative – and cooperation between countries and institutions. Unfortunately, when it comes to longer-term phenomena with a relatively slower pace, such as climate change and other trends in our society, notably our ageing population and increasing inequality, the same speed is not observed. One of the (few) advantages of the pandemic is that it has revealed to us that solutions – political, economic, technological and social – exist and can be adopted relatively quickly. At least as far as investments are concerned, it can be said that in recent years the attitude of both academics and politicians has changed, recognising the importance they have in determining the success of the energy transition.

References

AfDB (2018a), *African Economic Outlook 2018.* African Development Bank, https://www.afdb.org/fileadmin/uploads/afdb/Documents/Publications/African_Economic_Outlook_2018_-_EN.pdf (Accessed October 14, 2021).

AfDB (2018b), *Annual Report 2018*, African Development Bank Group, https://www.afdb.org/fileadmin/uploads/afdb/Documents/Generic-Documents/AFDB_Annual_Report_2018_and_Appendices_ -English.pdf (Accessed October 14, 2021).

Afonso A. and St. Aubyn M. (2008), *Macroeconomic Rates of Return of Public and Private Investment, Crowding-in and Crowding-out Effects*, ECB Working Paper Series No. 864, Frankfurt am Main: European Central Bank.

Aiginger A. and Janger J. (2015), "Intangibles and Green Investments for Restarting Growth", in Austrian Federal Ministry of Science, Research and Economy (Eed.), *Investing in Europe's Future. Restarting the Growth Engine* (pp. 1166-146), Wien: Federal Ministry of Science, Research and Economy.

Aiginger K. and Siber S. (2006), "The Matrix Approach to Industrial Policy", *International Review of Applied Economics*, Vol. 20, No. 5, pp. 573-601. DOI: 10.1080/02692170601005507.

Alesina A. and Giavazzi F. (2006), *The Future of Europe: Reform or Decline*, Cambridge: MIT Press.

Altenburg T. and Assmann C. (eds.) (2017), *Green Industrial Policy, Concept, Country Experiences*, UN Environment; German Development Institute (DIE), https://www.un-page.org/files/public/green_industrial_policy_book_aw_web.pdf (Accessed October 14, 2021).

Alves Dias, P., Kanellopoulos, K., Medarac, H., Kapetaki, Z., Miranda Barbosa, E., Shortall, R., Czako, V., Telsnig, T., Vazquez Hernandez, C., Lacal Arantegui, R., Nijs, W., Gonzalez Aparicio, I., Trombetti, M., Mandras, G., Peteves, E. and Tzimas, E. (2018), *EU Coal Regions: Opportunities and Challenges Ahead, JRC Science for Policy Report*, Luxembourg: European Commission.

Angenendt S., Martin-Shields C. and Schraven B. (2017), *More Development, More Migration? The "Migration Hump" and Its Significance for Development Policy Co-operation with Sub-Saharan Africa*, SWP Comment 2017/C 40, https://www.swp-berlin.org/publications/products/comments/2017C40_adt_etal.pdf (Accessed October 14, 2021).

Anghel S., Immenkamp B., Lazarou E., Saulnier J.L.and Wilson A.B.(2020), *On the Path to "strategic autonomy": The EU in an Evolving Geopolitical Environment*, Bruxelles: European Parliamentary Research Service. DOI:10.2861/ 60568.

Armstrong K., Begg I. and Zeitlin J. (2008), "JCMS Symposium: EU Governance After Lisbon", *Journal of Common Market Studies*, Vol. 46, No. 2, pp. 413-50.

Austrian Federal Ministry of Science, Research and Economy (Ed.) (2015), *Investing in Europe's Future Restarting the Growth Engine*, Wien: Federal Ministry of Science, Research and Economy.

Baldwin R. et al., (2015), *Reeboting the Eurozone: Step I – Agreeing a Crisis Narrative*, CEPR Policy Insight n. 85, https://cepr.org/sites/default/files/policy_insights/PolicyInsight85.pdf (Accessed October 14, 2021).

Barana L. (2017), *The EU Trust Fund for Africa and the Perils of a Securitized Migration Policy*, IAI Commentaries 17, https://www.iai.it/en/pubblicazioni/eu-trust-fund-africa-and-perils-securitized-migration-policy (Accessed October 14, 2021).

Baranzini A., van den Bergh J. C. J. M., Carattini S., Howarth R. B., Padilla E. and Roca J. (2017), "Carbon Pricing in Climate Policy: Seven Reasons, Complementary Instruments, and Political Economy Considerations", *WIRE's Climate Change*, Vol. 8, No. 4. DOI: doi.org/10.1002/wcc.462.

Barbiero F. and Darvas Z. (2014), *In Sickness and Health: Protecting and Supporting Public Investment in Europe*, Bruegel Policy Contribution, Issue 2014/02, https://www.bruegel.org/wp-content/uploads/imported/publications/pc_2014_02.pdf (Accessed October 15, 2021).

Belladonna A. and Gili A. (2020), *How the European Green Deal Will Drive the Next Generation*, ISPI Commentary, 24 June, https://www.ispionline.it/it/pubblicazione/how-european-green-deal-will-drive-next-generation-eu-26494 (Accessed October 14, 2021).

Bénassy-Quéré, A., Brunnermeier M. K., Enderlein H., Farhi E., Fratzscher M., Fuest C., Gourinchas P.-O., Martin P., Pisani-Ferry J., Rey H., Schnabel I., Véron N., Weder di Mauro B. and Zettelmeyer J. (2018), *Reconciling*

Risk Sharing with Market Discipline: A Constructive Approach to Euro Area Reform, CEPR Policy Insight 91, https://cepr.org/sites/default/files/policy_insights/PolicyInsight91.pdf (Accessed October 14, 2021).

Berensmann K., Ordu A. and Senbet L. W. (2021), *Covid-19 Crisis: G20 and Debt Sustainability in Sub-Saharan Africa*, ISPI Commentary, https://www.ispionline.it/en/pubblicazione/covid-19-crisis-g20-and-debt-sustainability-sub-saharan-africa-29953 (Accessed October 14, 2021).

Bertelsmann Foundation (2013), *The European Added Value of EU Spending: Can the EU Help Its Member States to Save Money?*, Exploratory Study, Gütersloh: Bertelsmann Stiftung, https://www.zew.de/en/publikationen/the-european-added-value-of-eu-spending-can-the-eu-help-its-member-states-to-save-money/?cHash=97f2540cb3f5d496e7e3e10872bf0b98. (Accessed October 14, 2021).

Beyond GDP (2007), *Summary Notes from the Beyond GDP Conference Highlights from the Presentations and the Discussion. International Conference 19–20 November,* https://ec.europa.eu/environment/beyond_gdp/download/bgdp-summary-notes.pdf (Accessed October 15, 2021).

Blanchard O. J. and Giavazzi F. (2004), *Improving the SGP Through a Proper Accounting of Public Investment*, No 4220, CEPR Discussion Papers.

Blanchard O. and Giavazzi F. (2002), "Current Account Deficits in the Euro Area", *Brookings Papers on Economic Activity*, Vol. 2002, No. 2, pp. 147-186.

Blanchard O. J. and Leigh D. (2013), "Growth Forecast Errors and Fiscal Multipliers", *American Economic Review*, Vol. 103, No. 3, pp. 117-20.

Blanchard O. J., Amighini A. and Giavazzi F. (2010), *Macroeconomics. A European Perspective*, Harlow: Pearson Education Limited.

Bluhm R., Dreher A., Fuchs A., Parks B., Strange A. and Tierney M. (2018), *Connective Financing: Chinese Infrastructure Projects and the Diffusion of Economic Activity in Developing Countries*, Aid Data Working Paper No. 64, http://docs.aiddata.org/ad4/pdfs/WPS64_Connective_Financing_Chinese_Infrastructure_Projects_and_the_Diffusion_of_Economic_Activity_in_Developing_Countries.pdf (Accessed October 14, 2021).

Bongardt A. and Torres F. (2010), "The Competitiveness Rationale, Sustainable Growth and the Need for Enhanced Economic Coordination, in Europe 2020 – A Promising Strategy?", *Intereconomics*, Vol. 45, No. 3, pp. 136-170.

Bubbico R. L., Brutscher P. and Revoltella D. (2020), "Europe Needs More Public Investment", in Saraceno F. and Cerniglia F. (eds.), *A European Public Investment Outlook*, Cambridge: Openbook Publishers.

Buti M. and Mohl P. (2014), *Lacklustre Investment in the Eurozone: Is There a Puzzle?,* VOXeu.org CEPR, https://voxeu.org/article/raising-investment-eurozone (Accessed October 14, 2021).

Campiglio E., Dafermos Y., Monnin P. et al. (2018), "Climate Change Challenges for Central Banks and Financial Regulators", *Nature Climate Change*, Vol. 8, No. 6, pp. 462-468, https://doi.org/10.1038/s41558-018-0175-0.

Campiglio E., Godin A., Kemp-Benedict E. and Matikainen S. (2017), "The Tightening Links Between Financial Systems and the Low-Carbon Transition", in Arestis, P. and Sawyer, M. (eds.), *Economic Policies Since the Global Financial Crisis*, pp. 313-356, London: Palgrave Macmillan.

Carbon Brief (2016), *Explainer: 10 Ways 'negative emissions' Could Slow Climate Change*, 11 April, https://www.carbonbrief.org/explainer-10-ways-negative-emissions-could-slow-climate-change (Accessed October 15, 2021).

Caslin O. (2020), Josep Borrell, chef de la diplomatie européenne: "L'Afrique n'a pas besoin d'un concours de bonté", *JeuneAfrique*, May 6.

Celi G., Ginzburg A., Guarascio D. and Simonazzi A. (2018), *Crisis in the European Monetary Union. A Core-Periphery Perspective*, Abingdon: Routledge.

Christensen M., Weiers G., Conte A., Wolski M. and Salotti S. (2019), *The European Fund for Strategic Investments: The RHOMOLO-EIB 2019 Update*, https://ec.europa.eu/jrc/sites/default/files/jrc118260.pdf (Accessed October 15, 2021).

Claessens S., Mody A. and Vallée S. (2012), *Paths to Eurobonds*, IMF Working Paper n.172, Washington, D.C.: International Monetary Fund.

COACCH (2018), *The Economic Cost of Climate Change in Europe: Synthesis Report on State of Knowledge and Key Research Gaps. Policy Brief by the COACCH Project*, https://www.ecologic.eu/sites/files/publication/2018/2811-coacch-review-synthesis-updated-june-2018.pdf (Accessed October 14, 2021).

Cobham, A., Garcia-Bernardo, J. and Mansour, M. B. (2020), *The Axis of Tax Avoidance*, Tax Justice Network, https://www.taxjustice.net/wp-content/uploads/2020/04/The-axis-of-tax-avoidance_Tax-Justice-Network_April-2020-1.pdf (Accessed October 14, 2021).

Cœuré B. (2018), *Monetary Policy and Climate Change*, conference in Berlin, November 8, https://www.ecb.europa.eu/press/key/date/2018/html/ecb.sp181108.en.html (Accessed October 14, 2021).

Coffman D., Cardinale R., Meng J. and Mi Z. (2020), "Ecological Transition", in Saraceno F. and Cerniglia F. (eds.), *A European Public Investment Outlook*, Cambridge: Openbook Publishers.

Council of the European Union (2017), *The Rome Declaration. Declaration of the Leaders of 27 Member States and of the European Council, the European Parliament and the European Commission*, Statements and Remarks 149/17, https://www.consilium.europa.eu/en/press/press-releases/2017/03/25/rome-declaration/pdf (Accessed October 14, 2021).

Council of the European Union (2019), *Council Directive Implementing Enhanced Cooperation in the Area of Financial Transaction Tax*, https://data.consilium.europa.eu/doc/document/ST-10097-2019-INIT/en/pdf (Interinstitutional file from the German Delegation) (Accessed October 14, 2021).

Council of the European Union (2011), *Directive 2011/64/EU on the Structure and Rates of Excise Duty Applied to Manufactured Tobacco*, https://eur-lex.europa.eu/legal-content/EN/TXT/PDF/?uri=CELEX:32011L0064&from=en (Accessed October 14, 2021).

Creel J., Holzner M., Saraceno F., Watt A. and Wittwer J. (2020), *How to Spend It*, IMK Policy Brief No. 92, June, Düsseldorf: Hans-Böckler-Stiftung, Institut für Makroökonomie und Konjunkturforschung, https://www.econstor.eu/bitstream/10419/224266/1/p_imk_pb_92_2020.pdf (Accessed October 14, 2021).

Creel J., Laurent É. and Le Cacheux J. (2005), *Delegation in Inconsistency: The Lisbon Strategy Record as an Institutional Failure*, Documents de Travail de l'OFCE 2005-07, Paris : Observatoire Francais des Conjonctures Economiques (OFCE).

D'Alfonso A. (2021), *National Ratification of the Own Resources Decision*, EPRS Briefing, https://www.europarl.europa.eu/RegData/etudes/BRIE/2021/690520/EPRS_BRI(2021)690520_EN.pdf (Accessed October 14, 2021).

D'Aprile P., Engel H., van Gendt G., Helmcke S., Hieronimus S., Nauclér T., Pinner D., Walter D. and Witteveen M. (2020), *Net-zero Europe. Decarbonization Pathways and Socioeconomic Implications*, McKinsey & Company, https://www.mckinsey.com/business-functions/sustainability/our-insights/how-the-european-union-could-achieve-net-zero-emissions-at-net-zero-cost (Accessed October 14, 2021).

Dabrowski M. and Myachenkova Y. (2018), *Free Trade in Africa: An Important Goal But Not Easy to Achieve*, Bruegel Blog Post, https://www.bruegel.org/2018/04/free-trade-in-africa-an-important-goal-but-not-easy-to-achieve/ (Accessed October 14, 2021).

Dafermos Y., Nokolaidi M. and Galanis G. (2018), *Can Green Quantitative Easing (QE) Reduce Global Warming?*, FEPS Policy Brief, https://www.feps-europe.eu/attachments/publications/feps%20gperc%20policybrief greenqe.pdf (Accessed October 14, 2021).

Dauderstädt M. (2015), *How to Close the European Investment Gap,* Bruxellles: Friedrich Ebert Shiftung, https://brussels.fes.de/fileadmin/public/editorfiles/publications/562_European_investment-june_adpt.pdf (Accessed October 14, 2021).

Daveri F. (2002), "The New Economy in Europe 1992-2001", *Oxford Review of Economic Policy*, Vol. 18, No. 3, pp. 345-362.

De Grauwe P. (2019), *Green Money without Inflation,* Social Europe, https://socialeurope.eu/green-money-without-inflation (Accessed October 15, 2021).

De Grauwe P. (2018), *Economics of Monetary Union,* Oxford: Oxford University Press.

Delors J. (2012), *For a Revival of Europe*, Paris: Institute Jacques Delors Tribune, https://institutdelors.eu/wp-content/uploads/2018/01/socialisteuropeanalternative_j_delors_ne_april2012.pdf (Accessed October 15, 2021).

Depla J. and von Weizsäcke J. (2010), *The Blue Bond Proposal*, Bruegel Policy Brief, Issue 2010/03, https://www.bruegel.org/wp-content/uploads/imported/publications/1005-PB-Blue_Bonds.pdf (Accessed October 15, 2021).

Desertec Foundation (2013), *Principles, Criteria and Indicators for the Evaluation of Renewable Energy Power Plants, Version 1.0*, https://www.desertec.org/wp-content/uploads/2019/01/DESERTEC-Criteria.pdf (Accessed October 15, 2021).

Dirth E., Barth J., Davies W., Gründahl M., Hafele J., Korinek L., Kiberd E. and Miller C. (2021), *A Future-Fit Recovery? A Sectoral Analysis of Practices for Promoting Systemic Change in the NRRPs Based on the Recovery Index for Transformative Change (RITC),* Transformation Report #1 – 06/2021, Bonn: ZOE-Institute for future-fit economies.

EFB (2020), *Assessment of the Fiscal Stance Appropriate for the Euro Area in 2021,* Bruxelles: European Commission, https://ec.europa.eu/info/sites/default/files/2020_06_25_efb_assessment_of_euro_area_fiscal_stance_en.pdf (Accessed October 15, 2021).

EIB (2020), *Statistical Report 2019*, Luxenbourg: European Investment Bank, https://www.eib.org/attachments/general/reports/eib_statistical_report_2019_en.pdf (Accessed October 15, 2021).

EIB (2019), *Investment Report 2019/2020. Accelerating Europe's Transformation*, Luxembourg: European Investment Bank. DOI: 10.2867/68943.

EIB (2018), *Investment Report 2018/2019: Retooling Europe's Economy – Key Findings,* Luxembourg: European Investment Bank. DOI: 10.2867/592592.

Enderlein H. (2020, July 18), [So, if I understand current #EUCO discussions correctly, some of the main proposed cuts are in: - Health (EU4Health) - Research (Horizon) - Climate transitition (JTF) This is not frugal. This is stupid.] ; Retrieved from https://twitter.com/henrikenderlein/status/1285295837380304896 (Accessed December 2, 2021)

EPSC (2017), *The Makings of an African Century*, Strategic Note, Issue 23, https://www.prospectivayestrategia.cl/pdf/strategic_note_issue_23.pdf (Accessed October 15, 2021).

EPSC (2019), *Delivering on European Common Goods. Strengthening Member States' Capacity to Act in the 21st Century.* DOI: 10.2872/875838.

Esping-Andersen G., Gallie D., Hemerijck A. and Myles J. (2002). *Why We Need a New Welfare State.* Oxford: Oxford University Press.

European Commission (2021), *Strategic Dependencies and Capacities*, Staff Working Document, SWD (2021) 352 final. Bruxelles: European Commission, https://ec.europa.eu/info/sites/default/files/swd-strategic-dependencies-capacities_en.pdf (Accessed October 15, 2021).

European Commission (2020a), *A New Industrial Strategy for Europe,* https://eur-lex.europa.eu/legal-content/EN/TXT/PDF/?uri=CELEX:52020DC0102&from=EN (Accessed October 15, 2021).

European Commission (2020b), *An EU-wide Assessment of National Energy and Climate Plans,* Bruxelles: European Commission, https://eur-lex.europa.eu/legal-content/EN/TXT/PDF/?uri=CELEX:52020DC0564&from=EN (Accessed October 15, 2021).

European Commission (2020c), *Identifying Europe's recovery needs*, Staff Working Document, https://eur-lex.europa.eu/legal-content/EN/TXT/?uri=SWD:2020:98:FIN (Accessed October 15, 2021).

European Commission (2020d), *Science, Research and Innovation Performance of the EU 2020. A Fair, Green and Digital Europe*, Bruxelles: European Commission. DOI:10.2777/534046.

European Commission (2019a), *Comprehensive Study of Building Energy Renovation Activities and the Uptake of Nearly Zero-energy Buildings in the EU, Final Report*, https://op.europa.eu/en/publication-detail/-/publication/97d6a4ca-5847-11ea-8b81-01aa75ed71a1 (Accessed October 15, 2021).

European Commission (2019b), *Towards a More Efficient and Democratic Decision Making in EU Tax Policy,* Bruxelles: European Commission, https://ec.europa.eu/taxation_customs/sites/taxation/files/15_01_2019_communication_towards_ a_more_efficient_democratic_decision_making_eu_tax_policy_en.pdf (Accessed October 15, 2021).

European Commission (2019c), *United in Delivering the Energy Union and Climate Action - Setting the Foundations for a Successful Clean Energy Transition*, Bruxelles: European Commission, https://eur-lex.europa.eu/legal-content/EN/TXT/PDF/?uri=CELEX:52019DC0285&from=EN. (Accessed October 15, 2021).

European Commission (2019d), *Vade Mecum on the Stability & Growth Pact 2019 Edition*, European Economy Institutional Paper 101, April 2019, Luxembourg: Publications Office of the European Union, https://op.europa.eu/en/publication-detail/-/publication/780c3262-a83c-11e9-9d01-01aa75ed71a1 (Accessed October 15, 2021).

European Commission (2019e), *Annual Sustainable Growth Strategy 2020*, Bruxelles: European Commission, https://ec.europa.eu/info/sites/default/files/2020-european-semester-annual-sustainable-growth-strategy_en.pdf (Accessed October 14, 2021).

European Commission (2018a), *A Clean Planet for All. A European Strategic Long-term Vision for a Prosperous, Modern, Competitive and Climate Neutral Economy*, Bruxelles: European Commission, https://eur-lex.europa.eu/legal-content/EN/TXT/PDF/?uri=CELEX:52018DC0773 (Accessed October 15, 2021).

European Commission (2018b), *Communication on a New Africa – Europe Alliance for Sustainable Investment and Jobs: Taking Our Partnership for Investment and Jobs to the Next Level*, Bruxelles: European Commission, https://eur-lex.europa.eu/legal-content/EN/TXT/PDF/?uri=CELEX:52018DC0643&from=EN (Accessed October 15, 2021).

European Commission (2017a), *Investment in the EU Member States. An Analysis of Drivers and Barriers*, Institutional Paper No. 062, Luxembourg: Publications Office of the European Union, https://ec.europa.eu/info/sites/default/files/ip062_en.pdf (Accessed October 15, 2021).

European Commission (2017b), *Reflection Paper on the Future of EU Finances*, Bruxelles: European Commission, https://ec.europa.eu/commission/sites/beta-political/files/reflection-paper-eu-finances_en.pdf (Accessed October 14, 2021).

European Commission (2017c), Questions and answers about the European External Investment Plan, https://europa.eu/rapid/press-release_MEMO-17-3484_en (Accessed October 15 2021).

European Commission (2015), *Making the Best Use of the Flexibility within the Existing Rules of the Stability and Growth Pact*, Strasbourg: European Commission, https://eur-lex.europa.eu/legal-content/EN/TXT/PDF/?uri=CELEX:52015DC0012&from=EN (Accessed October 15, 2021).

European Commission (2012a), *The Quality of Public Expenditure in the EU*, Occasional Paper, n. 125, Bruxelles: European Commission. DOI: 10.2765/25458.

European Commission (2012b), *Blueprint for Deep and Genuine Economic and Monetary Union – the Launching a European Debat*e, Bruxelles: European Commission, https://eur-lex.europa.eu/LexUriServ/LexUriServ.do?uri=COM:2012:0777:FIN:EN:PDF (Accessed October 15, 2021).

European Commission (2011), *The Added Value of the EU Budget*, p. 2, Bruxelles: European Commission, https://ec.europa.eu/info/sites/info/files/about_the_european_commission/eu_budget/sec-2011-867_2011_en.pdf (Accessed October 15, 2021).

European Commission (2010), *Revisione del bilancio dell'Unione europea*, p. 5, https://eur-lex.europa.eu/LexUriServ/LexUriServ.do?uri=COM:2010:0700:FIN:IT:PDF (Accessed October 15, 2021).

European Commission (1994), *White Paper on Growth, Competitiveness, Employment. The Challenges and Ways Forward into the 21st Century*, Bruxelles: European Commission.

European Commission (1985), *White Paper from the Commission to the European Council. Completing the Internal Market*, Bruxelles: European Commission.

European Commission and EIB (2015), *Why Does the EU Need and Investment Plan?, Factsheet 1*, https://ec.europa.eu/info/sites/default/files/factsheet1-why_en.pdf (Accessed October 14, 2021).

European Court of Auditors (2019), *European Fund for Strategic Investments: Action Needed to Make EFSI a Full Success,* Special Report No. 03, Luxembourg: Publications Office of the European Union. DOI:10.2865/074156.

European Court of Auditors (2018), *Public Private Partnerships in the EU: Widespread Shortcomings and Limited Benefits*, Special Report N. 9, Luxembourg: Publications Office of the European Union. DOI:10.2865/154598.

European Court of Auditors (2017), *EU Action on Energy and Climate Change*, p. 58, Luxembourg: Publications Office of the European Union. DOI: 10.2865/38310.

European Union (2017), *Regulation of the European Parliament and of the Council Establishing the European Fund for Sustainable Development (EFSD), the EFSD Guarantee and the EFSD Guarantee Fund*, Bruxelles: European Commission, https://eur-lex.europa.eu/legal-content/EN/TXT/PDF/?uri=CELEX:32017R1601&from=EN (Accessed October 15, 2021).

Eurostat (2019a), *Smarter, Greener, More Inclusive? Indicators to Support the Europe 2020 Strategy*, Luxembourg: Publications Office of the European Union. DOI:10.2785/379691.

Eurostat (2019b), *The European Union and the African Union. A Statistical Portrait,* Luxembourg: Publications Office of the European Union, https://ec.europa.eu/eurostat/documents/3217494/9767596/KS-FQ-19-001-EN-N.pdf/376dc292-0d2d-4c66-9a36-5bc63c87466c?t=1556886137000 (Accessed October 15, 2021).

Fabbrini F. (2019), *A Fiscal Capacity for the Eurozone: Constitutional Perspectives, In-depth Analysis Requested by the AFCO Committee.* DOI: 10.2861/705606.

Fabry E. (2010), *European Solidarity: Where Do We Stand? Should We Foster It and How? Synthesis of the 2010 Edition of the European Think Tank Forum Palais Pedralbes – 30 September and 1 October 2010*, Paris: Institute

Jacques Delors, https://institutdelors.eu/wp-content/uploads/2018/01/cr-forum-think-tanks-barcelone-2010-en.pdf (Accessed October 15, 2021).

Fankhaeser S., Sehlleier F. and Stern N. (2008), "Climate Change, Innovation and Jobs", *Climate Policy*, Vol. 8, Issue 4, pp. 421-429.

Fantacci L. and Papetti A. (2013), *Il debito dell'Europa con sé stessa. Analisi e riforma della governance europea difronte alla crisi*, Costituzionalismo.it, 2/2013 (Accessed October 12, 2021).

Fiott D. and Theodosopoulos V. (2020), Sovereignty Over Supply? The EU's Ability to Manage Critical Dependences While Engaging with the World, *EU Institute for Security Studio* (ISS), Brief No. 21, https://www.iss.europa.eu/content/sovereignty-over-supply (Accessed October 15, 2021).

Fontana O. and Gasbarro L. (2021), *European Fiscal Capacity and New Own Resources: Proposals and Scenarios*, CSF Research Paper, http://www.csfederalismo.it/images/Research_paper/CSF-RP_Fiscal-Capacity-Own-Resources_O.Fontana-L.Gasbarro_June2021.pdf (Accessed October 15, 2021).

Fontana O. and Venturi B. (2018), *I beni pubblici europei nel bilancio dell'Unione*, Centro Studi sul Federalismo, Research Paper, http://www.csfederalismo.it/images/CSF-IAI_QFP/CSF-IAI_RP_OFontana-BVenturi_BeniPubblici_QFP_Aprile2018.pdf (Accessed October 15, 2021).

Fracasso A. (2018), "Solidarity and Responsibility in the Euro Area: Foes or Friends?", *The Economists' Voice*, De Gruyter, Vol. 15 Issue 1, pp. 1-4, December.

Fransen, L., del Bufalo G. and Reviglio E. (2018), *Boosting Investment in Social Infrastructure in Europe. Report of the High-Level Task Force on Investing in Social Infrastructure in Europe*, Luxembourg: Publications Office per the European Union. DOI: 10.2765/794497.

Fuest, C. and Pisani-Ferry, J. (2019), *A Primer on Developing European Public Goods. A Report to the Minister Bruno La Maire and Olaf Scholz*, 3 November, https://www.bruegel.org/wp-content/uploads/2019/11/European-public-goods-primer.pdf (Accessed October 15, 2021).

Galgóczi B. (2014), "The Long and Winding Road from Black to Green: Decades of Structural Change in the Ruhr Region", *International Journal of Labour Research*, Vol. 6, issue 2, pp. 217-240.

Garcia-Herrero A. and Xu J. (2019), *China's Investment in Africa: What the Data Really Says, and the Implications for Europe*, Bruegel Blog post, https://bruegel.org/2019/07/chinas-investment-in-africa-what-the-data-really-says-and-the-implications-for-europe/ (Accessed October 15, 2021).

Georgieva K. (2021), IMF Managing Director Kristalina Georgieva Welcomes the Executive Board's Backing for a New US$650 Billion SDR Allocation, Press Release 21/208, https://www.imf.org/en/News/Articles/2021/07/08/pr21208-imf-managing-director-kristalina-georgieva-executive-board-backing-new-us650b-sdr-allocation (Accessed October 15, 2021).

Global companies call for more action of November 2018, https://orsted.com/-/media/WWW/Docs/Corp/COM/News/Carbon-pricing-declaration-november-2018.pdf (Accessed October 15, 2021).

Gordon R. (2012), *Is U.S. Economic Growth Over? Faltering Innovation Confronts The Six Headwinds*, NBER Working Paper 18315, Cambridge: National Bureau of Economic Research, https://www.nber.org/system/files/working_papers/w18315/w18315.pdf (Accessed October 15, 2021).

Gourinchas P. O. (2020), Flattening the Pandemic and Recession Curves, in Baldwin R. and Weder di Mauro B. (eds.), *Mitigating the COVID Economic Crisis: Act Fast and Do Whatever It Takes*, London: CEPR Press VoxEU.org eBook, https://voxeu.org/content/mitigating-covid-economic-crisis-act-fast-and-do-whatever-it-takes (Accessed October 15, 2021).

Gräbner C., Heimberger P., Kapeller J. and Schütz B. (2020), "Is the Eurozone Disintegrating? Macroeconomic Divergence, Structural Polarisation, Trade and Fragility", *Cambridge Journal of Economics*, Vol. 44, Issue 3, pp. 647-669. DOI: 10.1093/cje/bez059.

Grevi G. (2019), *Strategic Autonomy for European Choices: The Key to Europe's Shaping Power*, Discussion Paper Europe in the World Programme, Bruxelles: European Policy Centre, https://www.epc.eu/content/PDF/2019/190719_Strategicautonomy_GG.pdf (Accessed October 15, 2021).

Gros D. (2015), "Investment as the Key to Recovery in the Euro Area?", in Austrian Federal Ministry of Science, Research and Economy (ed.), *Investing in Europe's Future. Restarting the Growth Engine*, Wien: Federal Ministry of Science, Research and Economy.

Große- Puppendahl S. and Bilal S. (2018), "What Is the European External Investment Plan Really About?", ECDPM Briefing Note n. 101, Bruxelles: ECDPM, (Accessed October 15 2021).

Guéret A., Malliet P., Saussay, A. and Timbeau, X. (2018), *An Explorative Evaluation of the Climate Debt,* OFCE Policy briefs 45, https://www.ofce.sciences-po.fr/pdf-articles/actu/OFCE-Policybrief45Eng.pdf (Accessed October 15, 2021).

Guigou J. L. and Beckouche P. (2017), *Afrique Méditerranée Europe: La Verticale de l'avenir*, Bruxelles: Nevicata.

Hamouchene H. (2020), *Desertec: What Went Wrong?,* EcoMENA, https://www.ecomena.org/desertec (Accessed October 15, 2021).

Helbling T., Hakura D. S. and Debrun X. (2004), "Fostering Structural Reforms in Industrial Countries", in *World Economic Outlook 2004,* Washington, D.C.: International Monetary Fund.

Hemerijck, A. (2014), "Social Investment 'stocks', 'flows' and 'buffers'", *Rivista delle Politiche Sociali*, Vol. 1, No. 1, pp. 9-26.

HLGOR (2016), *Future Financing of the EU: Final Report and Recommendations*, Bruxelles: European Union, https://ec.europa.eu/info/sites/default/files/about_the_european_commission/eu_budget/future-financing-hlgor-final-report_2016_en.pdf (Accessed October 14, 2021).

Holland S. and Varoufakis J. (2012), "A Modest Proposal for Resolving the Eurozone Crisis", *Intereconomics*, Vol. 47, No. 4, pp. 240-247.

IEA (2010), *Technology Roadmap – Concentrating Solar Power*, Paris: IEA, https://iea.blob.core.windows.net/assets/663fabad-397e-4518-802f-7f1c94bc2076/csp_roadmap.pdf (Accessed October 15, 2021).

ILO (2014), *Skills Mismatch in Europe. Statistics Brief,* Geneva: International Labour Office, https://www.ilo.org/wcmsp5/groups/public/---dgreports/---stat/documents/publication/wcms_315623.pdf (Accessed October 14 2021).

IMF (2015), *Making Public Investment More Efficient*, Staff report, Washington, D.C.: International Monetary Fund.

IMF (2014), "Is It Time for and Infrastructure Push? The Macroeconomic Effects of Public Investment", in *World Economic Outlook*, Washington, D.C.: International Monetary Fund. DOI: 10.5089/9781498331555.081.

Juncker J.C. (2015), "Preface", in Austrian Federal Ministry of Science, Research and Economy (ed.), *Investing in Europe's Future. Restarting the Growth Engine*, Wien: Federal Ministry of Science, Research and Economy.

Juncker J.C. and Tremonti G. (2010), "E-bonds Would end the Crisis", *Financial Times*, 5 December.

Kappeler A. and Valila T. (2007), *Composition of Public Investment and Fiscal Federalism: Panel Data Evidence From Europe*, Luxembourg: European Investment Bank, Economics Department.

Karingi S., Mevel S. and Valensisi G. (2015), "The EPAs and Africa's Regional Integration", *Bridges Africa*, Vol. 4, No. 6, pp. 14-16.

Koll W. (2015), "Investment in the European Union – Beyond the Juncker Plan", in Austrian Federal Ministry of Science, Research and Economy (ed.), *Investing in Europe's Future. Restarting the Growth Engine*, Wien: Federal Ministry of Science, Research and Economy.

Kok W. (2004), *Facing the Challenge: The Lisbon Strategy for Growth and Employment. Report from the High-Level Group*. Bruxelles: European Commission.

Koo R. (2014), *Balance Sheet Recession Is the Reason for 'secular stagnation'*, VoxEU CEPR, https://voxeu.org/article/balance-sheet-recession-reason-secular-stagnation (Accessed October 15, 2021).

Kregel J. (2018), "Growth and the Single Currency: The Fiscal Policy Paradox", in Savona, P. (ed.), *Una politeia per un'Europa diversa, più forte e più equa*, Presidenza del Consiglio Dipartimento per le Politiche Europee, http://www.eurojus.it/wp-content/uploads/2018/09/per-uneuropa-piu-forte-e-piu-equa-2-versione-finale-impaginato-1.pdf (Accessed October 14 2021).

Krenek A., Sommer M. and Schratzenstaller M. (2019), *Sustainability-Oriented Future EU Funding. A European Border Carbon Adjustment*, WIFO Working Papers, No. 587, https://www.wifo.ac.at/jart/prj3/wifo/resources/person_dokument/person_dokument.jart?publikationsid=61931&mime_type=application/pdf (Accessed October 15, 2021).

Krugman P. (2012), "Death of a Fairy Tale", *The New York Times*, 26 April.

Laurent É. (2021), *From Welfare to Farewell: The European Socio-ecological State Beyond Economic Growth*, ETUI Working Paper No. 4, https://www.etui.org/publications/welfare-farewell (Accessed October 15, 2021).

Laurent É. (2015), *Social-Ecology: Exploring the Missing Link in Sustainable Development*, Documents de Travail de l'OFCE 2015-07, Paris : Observatoire Francais des Conjonctures Economiques (OFCE).

Le Moigne M., Saraceno F. and Villemot S. (2016), *Probably Too Little, Certainly Too Late. An Assessement of the Juncker Investment Plan*, Document de travail de l'OFCE (10), Paris : Observatoire Francais des Conjonctures Economiques (OFCE).

Leoni T. (2016), "Social Investment as a Perspective on Welfare State Transformation in Europe", *Intereconomics,* Vol. 51, pp. 194-200.

Lisbon European Council (2000), Presidency Conclusions, 23-24 March, https://www.consilium.europa.eu/uedocs/cms_data/docs/pressdata/en/ec/00100-r1.en0.htm (Accessed October 12, 2021).

Losch M. (2015), "Introduction: The economic policy debate on investment", in Austrian Federal Ministry of Science, Research and Economy (ed.), *Investing in Europe's Future. Restarting the Growth Engine*, Wien: Federal Ministry of Science, Research and Economy.

Mabbet D. and Schelkle W. (2007), "Bringing Macroeconomics Back into the Political Economy of Reform: The Lisbon Agenda and the 'Fiscal Philosophy' of EMU", *Journal of Common Market Studies*, Vol. 45, No. 1, pp. 81-103.

Majocchi A. (2020), "A Green New Deal for Europe and Africa", in Majocchi A. (ed.), *A Green New Deal for Europe and Africa*, Bruxelles: Peter Lang.

Majocchi A. (2007), *Un'agenda per promuovere la crescita europea*, Working Paper No. 509, Pavia: Società italiana di Economia Pubblica.

Marhold H. (2015), "A European Common Good?", *L'Europe en formation*, n. 376, Summer.

Medinilla A. and Bossuyt J. (2019), *Africa-EU Relations and Post-Cotonou: African Collective Action or Further Fragmentation of Partnerships?*, ECDPM Briefing Note 110, https://ecdpm.org/wp-content/uploads/BN-110-Africa-EU-relations-post-CotonouAfrica-EU-relations-and-post-Cotonou-african-collective-action-fragmentation-partnerships-ECDPM-March-2019.pdf (Accessed October 15, 2021).

Mehling M., van Asselt H., Das K. and Droege S. (2019), *What a European 'carbon border tax' Might Look Like,* VoxEU CEPR, https://voxeu.org/article/what-european-carbon-border-tax-might-look (Accessed October 15, 2021).

Merkel: Germany must help other EU states get back on their feet, euractiv.com with Reuters, 13 May 2020, https://www.euractiv.com/section/economy-jobs/news/merkel-germany-must-help-other-eu-states-get-back-on-their-feet/ (Accessed October 15, 2021).

Merler S. (2020a), *EU Recovery Fund: A Franco-German Revolution, Algebris Policy Forum Blog,* https://www.algebris.com/it/policy-research-forum-it/eu-recovery-fund-una-rivoluzione-franco-tedesca/ (Accessed October 15, 2021).

Merler S. (2020b), *Next Generation, chi ci guadagna e chi ci perde*, Lavoce.info, https://www.lavoce.info/archives/68692/next-generation-chi-ci-guadagna-e-chi-ci-perde/ (Accessed October 15, 2021).

Musgrave R. A. (1959), *The Theory of Public Finance*, New York: McGraw-Hill.

Musgrave R. A. (1939), "The Nature of Budgetary Balance and the Case for Capital Budget", *American Economic Review*, No. 29, pp. 260-271.

Núñez Ferrer J. and Katarivas M. (2014), *What Are the Effects of the EU Budget: Driving Force or Drop in the Ocean?*, CEPS Special Report n. 86, Bruxelles: CEPS.

OECD (2013), *Supporting Investment in Knowledge Capital, Growth and Innovation*, Paris: OECD Publishing. DOI:10.1787/9789264193307.

Owen G. (2012), *Industrial Policy in Europe since the Second World War: What Has Been Learnt?*, ECIPE Occasional Paper n.1, Bruxelles: ECIPE.

Pack H. and Saggi K. (2006), "Is There a Case for Industrial Policy? A Critical Survey", *The World Bank Research Observer*, Vol. 21, Issue 2, Fall, pp. 267-297.

Padoa-Schioppa A. (2012), *Il trattato ESM. Osservazioni critiche*, CSF Discussion paper 06, http://www.csfederalismo.it/images/policy_paper/06_a_p_schioppa_it.pdf (Accessed October 15, 2021).

Padoa-Schioppa A. and Iozzo, A. (2020), *Globalizzazione e Unione europea: sfide e strategie – Profili istituzionali del Green Deal*, Centro Studi sul Federalismo, Policy Paper No. 42 http://www.csfederalismo.it/images/policy_paper/CSF_PP42_APS-Iozzo_Globalizzazione-Ue_Genn2020_def.pdf (Accessed October 15, 2021).

Padoa-Schioppa T. (2004), *The Euro and Its Central Bank: Getting United After the Union*, Cambridge: MIT Press.

Paramithiotti G. (1995), "Il libro Bianco di Delors per la crescita economica, la competitività e l'occupazione in Europa", *Il Politico*, Vol. 60, No. 2 (173), pp. 293-311.

Paramithiotti G. and Zatti A. (2015), *Il bilancio dell'Unione europea. Origini, principi ed elementi costitutivi*, Pavia: Pavia University Press.

Pekanov, A. and Schratzenstaller, M. (2019), *A Global Financial Transaction Tax. Theory, Practice and Potential Revenues*, WIFO Working Papers No. 582, https://www.wifo.ac.at/jart/prj3/wifo/resources/person_dokument/person_dokument.jart?publikationsid=61805&mime_type=application/pdf (Accessed October 15, 2021).

Pellegrin J., Giorgetti M. L., Jensen C. and Bolognini A. (2015), *EU Industrial Policy: Assessment of Recent Developments and Recommendations for Future Policy*, Bruxelles: European Parliament Policy Department A: Economic and Scientific Policy.

Performance of European countries against the SDGs. Part 1, https://eu-dashboards.sdgindex.org/chapters/part-1-performance-of-european-countries-against-the-sdgs (Accessed October 15, 2021).

Pettis M. (2013), *The Great Rebalancing: Trade, Conflict, and the Perilous Road Ahead for the World Economy*, Princeton: Princeton University Press.

Pianta M. (2014), *An Industrial Policy for Europe*, Working Paper Series in Economics, Mathematics and Statistics, No. 2014/1, Milan: Università degli Studi "Carlo Bo", http://www.econ.uniurb.it/RePEc/urb/wpaper/WP_14_01.pdf (Accessed October 15, 2021).

Pierluigi B. and Sondermann D. (2018), *Macroeconomic Imbalances in the Euro Area: Where Do We Stand?*, ECB Occasional paper series No. 211, Frankfurt am Main: European Central Bank, https://www.ecb.europa.eu/pub/pdf/scpops/ecb.op211.en.pdf (Accessed October 15, 2021).

Piodi F. (2010), *From the Schuman Declaration to the Birth of the ECSC: The Role of Jean Monnet*, Bruxelles: Cardoc Journals, n. 6, May. DOI: 10.2861/16402.

Pisani-Ferry J. (2019a), "When Facts Change Change the Pact", *Project Syndicate.*

Pisani-Ferry J. (2019b), *A Credible Decarbonization Agenda Can Help Strengthen Europe's Economy*, Real Time Economic Issues Watch, Peterson Institute for International Economic, https://www.piie.com/blogs/realtime-economic-issues-watch/credible-decarbonization-agenda-can-help-strengthen-europes (Accessed October 15, 2021).

Pisani-Ferry J. (2019c), *Europe Can Take a Bigger Role in Providing Public Goods*, Bruegel, https://www.bruegel.org/2019/12/europe-can-take-a-bigger-role-in-providing-public-goods/ (Accessed October 15, 2021).

Pochet P. (2021), *The Four 'I's of a New Socio-ecological Contract*, Social Europe, https://socialeurope.eu/the-four-is-of-a-new-socio-ecological-contract (Accessed October 15, 2021).

Pochet P. (2010), *What's Wrong with EU2020?*, Bruxelles: The European Trade Union Institute, https://www.etui.org/publications/policy-briefs/european-economic-employment-and-social-policy/what-s-wrong-with-eu2020. (Accessed October 12, 2021).

President of the European Council (2012), *Towards a Genuine Economic and Monetary Union*, https://www.consilium.europa.eu/media/23807/134190.pdf (Accessed October 15, 2021).

Procopio M. (2020), *The International Politics around Africa's Debt*, ISPI Dossier, https://www.ispionline.it/it/pubblicazione/international-politics-around-africas-debt-27020 (Accessed October 15, 2021).

Quadrio Curzio A. (2011), "On the Different Types of Eurobonds", *Economia Politica*, Issue 3, December. DOI: 10.1428/35912.

Randers J., Rockström J., Stoknes P., Golüke U., Collste D. and Cornell S. (2018), *Transformation Is Feasible – How to Achieve the Sustainable Development Goals within Planetary Boundaries – A Report to the Club of Rome, for Its 50 Years Anniversary*, report to the Club of Rome from Stockholm Resilience Centre and BI Norwegian Business School, https://www.stockholmresilience.org/download/18.51d83659166367a9a16353/1539675518425/Report_Achieving%20the%20Sustainable%20Development%20Goals_WEB.pdf (Accessed October 15, 2021).

Ritchie H. (2019), *How Do CO2 Emissions Compare When We Adjust for Trade?*, Our World in Data, https://ourworldindata.org/consumption-based-co2 (Accessed October 15, 2021).

Robinson (2009), "The European Investment Bank: The EU's Neglected Institution", *Journal of Common Market Studies*, Vol. 47, Issue 3, pp. 651-673.

Rodriguez R., Warmerdam J. and Triomphe C.-E. (2010), *The Lisbon Strategy 2000–2010. An Analysis and Evaluation of Methods Used and Results Achieved. Study for the European Parliament, Directorate General for Internal Policies*, Brussels: European Parliament.

Rodriguez-Palenzuela D., Dées S., Andersson M. et al. (2016), *Savings and Investment Behaviour in the Euro Area*, Occasional Paper Series 167, Frankfurt am Main: European Central Bank.

Rodrik D. (2004), *Industrial Policy for the Twenty-First Century*, KSG Faculty Research Working Paper Series RWP04-047.

Rodrik D. and Altenburg T. (2017), "Green Industrial Policy: Accelerating Structural Change towards Wealthy Green Economies", in Altenburg T. and Assmann C. (eds.), *Green Industrial Policy, Concept, Country Experiences*, UN Environment; German Development Institute (DIE), https://www.un-page.org/files/public/green_industrial_policy_book_aw_web.pdf (Accessed October 15, 2021).

Rubio E., Rinaldi D. and Pellerin-Carlin T. (2016), *Investment on Europe: Making the Best of the Juncker Plan*, Studies & Reports No. 109, Paris: Notre Europe Jacques Delors Institute.

Sachverständigenrat zur Begutachtung der gesamtwirtschaftlichen Entwicklung – SVR (2007), *Staatsverschuldung wirks am begrenzen, Expertise im Auftrag des Bundesministers für Wirtschaft und Technologie*, Wiesbaden: Sachverständigenrat zur Begutachtung der gesamtwirtschaftlichen Entwicklung.

Sandrey R. (2015), *The African Trading Relationship: New, Old and Good Friends*, Tralac ebook, https://www.tralac.org/publications/article/8223-africa-s-trade-relations-old-friends-good-friends-and-new-friends.html (Accessed October 15, 2021).

Sapir A. (2016), *The Eurozone Needs Less Heterogeneity*, VoxEU CEPR, https://voxeu.org/article/eurozone-needs-less-heterogeneity (Accessed October 15, 2021).

Sapir A. et al. (2004). *An Agenda for a Growing Europe*, Oxford: Oxford University Press.

Saraceno F. (2020), *La riconquista*, Roma: LUISS University Press.

Saraceno F. (2018), *La scienza inutile*, Roma: LUISS University Press.

Saraceno F. (2016), *When Keynes Goes to Brussels: A New Fiscal Rule for the EMU*, SciencesPo publications n. 32, https://ideas.repec.org/p/spo/wpmain/infohdl2441-19jos6046o8m6qe8fce98t1bmp.html (Accessed October 14, 2021).

Sartori N. and Colantoni L. (2019), "Empowering Africa", in Colantoni L., Montesano G. and Sartori N. (eds.), *Empowering Africa. Access to Power in the African Continent*, Bern: Peter Lang.

Scheller H. K. (2004), *The European Central Bank. History, Role and Functions*, Frankfurt am Main: European Central Bank.

Schmöller M. (2018), *Secular Stagnation: A False Alarm in the Euro Area?*, Bank of Finland Bulletin No. 4, https://www.bofbulletin.fi/en/2018/4/secular-stagnation-a-false-alarm-in-the-euro-area/ (Accessed October 15, 2021).

Schratzenstaller-Altzinger M. (2017), *The Next Multiannual Financial Framework (MFF), Its Structure and the Own Resources, European Parliament In-depth Analysis*. Bruxellles: European Union, https://www.europarl.europa.eu/RegData/etudes/IDAN/2017/603800/IPOL_IDA%282017%29603800_EN.pdf (Accessed October 14, 2021).

Spalaore E. (2013), "What Is European Integration Really About? A Political Guide for Economists", *Journal of Economic Perspectives*, Vol. 27, No. 3, Summer 2013, pp. 125-44. DOI: 10.1257/jep. 27.3.125.

Sparks D. L. and Barnett S. T. (2010), "The Informal Sector in Sub-Saharan Africa: Out of the Shadows to Foster Sustainable Employment and Equity?", *International Business & Economics Research Journal* (IBER), Vol. 9, No. 5, https://doi.org/10.19030/iber.v9i5.563.

Stockhammer E. and Sotiropoulos D. (2014), "Rebalancing the Euro Area: The Costs of Internal Devaluation", *Review of Political Economy*, Vol. 26, No. 2, pp. 210-233. DOI: 10.1080/09538259.2014.881011.

Summers, L. H. (2014), *Reflections on the 'New Secular Stagnation Hypothesis'*, VoxEU CEPR, https://voxeu.org/article/larry-summers-secular-stagnation (Accessed October 14, 2021).

Susskind D., Manyika J., Saldanha J., Burrow S., Rebelo S. and Bremmer I. (2020), "How Will the World Be Different After Covid-19?", *Finance & Development*, June, Vol. 57, No. 2, pp. 26-29, https://www.imf.org/external/pubs/ft/fandd/2020/06/how-will-the-world-be-different-after-COVID-19.htm (Accessed October 15, 2021).

Szczepański M. (2016), *Public Investment to Support Long Term Economic Growth*, EPSF Briefing, Bruxelles: European Parliamentary Research Service.

Tabellini G. (2002), *The Assignment of Tasks in an Evolving European Union*, CEPS Policy Brief No. 10, https://www.ceps.eu/download/publication/?id=4609&pdf=111.pdf (Accessed October 15, 2021).

Teulings C. and Baldwin R. (2014), *Secular Stagnation: Facts, Causes, and Cures*, London: CEPR; VoxEU.org Book.

Tooze A. and Schularick M. (2020), "The Shock of Coronavirus Could Split Europe – Unless Nations Share the Burden", *The Guardian,* 25 March.

Tralac (2019), *The African Continental Free Trade Area, a Tralac guide – 5th Edition*, https://www.tralac.org/documents/resources/booklets/2878-afcfta-a-tralac-guide-5th-edition-june-2019/file.html (Accessed October 15, 2021).

Trichet J. C. (2010), "Stimulate No More – It Is Now Time for All to Tighten", *The Financial times*, 22 July.

Truger A. (2016), *The Golden Rule of Public Investment – a Necessary and Sufficient Reform of the EU Fiscal Framework?* Hans-Böckler-Schiftung

Working Paper No. 168, https://www.boeckler.de/pdf/p_imk_wp_168_2016.pdf (Accessed October 15, 2021).

Truger A. (2015), "Austerity, Cyclical Adjustment and the Remaining Leeway for Expansionary Fiscal Policies within the Current European Fiscal Framework", *Journal for a Progressive Economy*, 6 July, pp. 32-37.

UNCTAD (2016), *World Investments Report 2016*, https://unctad.org/system/files/official-document/wir2016_en.pdf (Accessed October 15, 2021).

Vaneecloo C. (2006), "Fiscal Federalism Perspective(s) and the European Union. Introductory Framework", in C. Vaneecloo, A. Badriotti e Fornasini M. (eds.), *Fiscal Federalism in the European Union and Its Countries. A Confrontation between Theories and Facts*, Bruxelles: P.I.E. Peter Lang.

Warwick K. (2013), *Beyond Industrial Policy: Emerging Issues and New Trends*, OECD Science, Technology and Industry Policy Papers, No. 2, Paris: OECD Publishing. DOI: 10.1787/5k4869clw0xp-en.

Wildauer R., Leitch S. and Kapeller J. (2020), *How to Boost the European Green Deal's Scale and Ambition*, Greenwich Papers in Political Economy, Greenwich: University of Greenwich, https://www.jku.at/fileadmin/gruppen/108/ICAE_Working_Papers/wp111.pdf (Accessed October 15, 2021).

Wolf M. (2019), "How the Euro Helped Germany Avoid Becoming Japan", *The Financial Times*, 29 October.

Wolff G. (2015), "The Juncker Plan – No Risk, No Return", in Austrian Federal Ministry of Science, Research and Economy (ed.), *Investing in Europe's Future. Restarting the Growth Engine*, Wien: Federal Ministry of Science, Research and Economy.

Zuleeg F. (2009), *The Rationale for EU Action: What Are European Public Goods?*, Prepared for the BEPA Workshop on The political economy of EU public finances: designing governance for change, 5 February.

Sitography

https://ec.europa.eu/info/strategy/eu-budget/spending/topic/eu-funding-programmes-2014-2020_en (Accessed October 15, 2021).

https://ec.europa.eu/europeaid/regions/africa/continental-cooperation/pan-african-programme_en (Accessed October 15, 2021).

https://www.oecd.org/gov/budgeting/oecd-principles-for-public-governance-of-public-private-partnerships.htm (Accessed October 8, 2021).

https://www.unfpa.org/demographic-dividend (Accessed October 15, 2021).

Manifesto for the Democratization of Europe at http://tdem.eu/ (Accessed 15 October, 2021).

Ministry of Commerce People's Republic of China at http://english.mofcom.gov.cn/article/statistic/lanmubb/AsiaAfrica (Accessed 15 October, 2021).

The Schuman Declaration at https://europa.eu/european-union/about-eu/symbols/europe-day/schuman-declaration_en (Accessed October 15, 2021).

https://www.numbeo.com/cost-of-living/country_price_rankings?itemId=17&displayCurrency=EUR (Accessed 15 October, 2021).

Economists' statement on carbon dividends at https://clcouncil.org/economists-statement (Accessed 15 October, 2021).

Federalism

The book series Federalism, run by the Centro Studi sul Federalismo (CSF) aims to disseminate knowledge in the field of studies on federalism, as well as to feed the academic and public debate and support the activity of decision-makers, confronted with demands for autonomy by local governments, along with forms of regional and world integration needed to govern global processes.

The book series is divided into two sub-series: *Studies and Classics*. The former mostly contains the research outcome and the proceedings of conferences and seminars promoted by the CSF while the latter consists in reprints of the federalist classic works and English translations of Italian federalists' works.

The CSF is a think tank that carries out activities of interdisciplinary research, documentation, information regarding domestic and supranational federalism, developments in the area of regional and continental integration – first and foremost the European Union – and problems related to the world order and the process of democratisation of the international system. The CSF has been founded under the auspices of the Compagnia di San Paolo and the Universities of Turin, Pavia and Milan and has the Turin Polytechnic as co-founder.

Centro Studi sul Federalismo
Piazza Vincenzo Arbarello 8
10122 Torino – Italy
Tel. + 39 011.6705024 Fax + 39 011.6705081
E-mail: info@csfederalismo.it
Website: www.csfederalismo.it

Series Editor: Lucio Levi , Former Professor of Political Science and Comparative Politics at the Turin University, Editor of The Federalist Debate and Scientific Director of the International Democracy Watch

Editorial Board

Series titles

No.1 – Giovanni Finizio and Ernesto Gallo (eds.), *Democracy at the United Nations. UN Reform in the Age of Globalisation*, 2013.

No.2 – Roberto Castaldi (ed.), *Immanuel Kant and Alexander Hamilton, the Founders of Federalism. A Political Theory for Our Time*, 2013.

No.3 – Claudio Giulio Anta (ed.), *Lord Lothian: The Paths of Federalism. Writings and Speeches*, 2014.

No.4 – Filippo Maria Giordano and Stefano dell'Acqua (eds.), *"Die Welt war meine Gemeinde". Willem A. Visser 't Hoof – A Theologian for Europe between Ecumenism and Federalism*, 2014.

No.5 – Giampiero Bordino (ed.), *A New Right for Democracy and Development in Europe. The European Citizens' Initiative (ECI)*, 2015.

No.6 – Filippo Maria Giordano, *Unity through Diversity. An Insight into Federalism and Ecumenism within Italian Protestantism*, 2016.

No.7 – Lucio Levi, Giampiero Bordino and Antonio Mosconi (eds.), *Federalism. A Political Theory for Our Time*, 2016.

No.8 – Lorenzo Vai, Pier Domenico Tortola and Nicoletta Pirozzi (eds.), *Governing Europe. How to Make the EU More Efficient and Democratic*, 2017.

No.9 – Korwa G. Adar, Giovanni Finizio and Angela Meyer (eds.), *Building Regionalism from Below. The Role of Parliaments and Civil Society in Regional Integration in Africa*, 2018.

No.10 – Alberto Majocchi, *European budget and sustainable growth. The Role of a Carbon Tax*, 2018.

No. 11 – Elena Flor, *SDR: from Bretton Woods to a world currency*, 2019.

No. 12 – Lucio Levi (ed.), *Albert Einstein from Pacifism to the Idea of World Government*, 2020.

No. 13 – Alberto Majocchi (ed.), *Africa and Europe: a Shared Future*, 2020.

No. 14 – Olimpia Fontana, *Investing in Europe: Old Problems and New Opportunities*, 2022.

www.peterlang.com

www.ingramcontent.com/pod-product-compliance
Ingram Content Group UK Ltd.
Pitfield, Milton Keynes, MK11 3LW, UK
UKHW020153290926
15471UKWH00005B/844

9 782875 744203